About the Editors

Aziz Choudry is assistant professor in the Department of Integrated Studies in Education at McGill University, Canada. He is co-author of *Fight Back: Workplace Justice for Immigrants* (Fernwood, 2009), and co-editor of *Learning from the Ground Up: Global Perspectives on Social Movements and Knowledge Production* (Palgrave Macmillan, 2010) and *Organize! Building from the Local for Global Justice* (PM Press/Between the Lines, 2012). With over 25 years of experience as a social, environmental and political activist, educator and researcher, he currently sits on the boards of the Immigrant Workers Centre, Montreal and the Global Justice Ecology Project. He is also a co-initiator and part of the editorial team of www.bilaterals.org, a website supporting resistance against bilateral free trade and investment agreements.

Dip Kapoor is professor of international education in the Department of Educational Policy Studies at the University of Alberta, Canada. He is Research Associate and Founding Member of the Centre for Research and Development Solidarity (CRDS), an Adivasi (original dweller)-Dalit rural peoples' organization in Orissa, India. His relationship with the Adivasi-Dalit Ekta Abhijan (ADEA) land and forest movement in Orissa goes back to the early 1990s. Recent co-edited collections include: *Education, PAR, and Social Change*; *Education, Decolonization and Development*; *Indigenous Knowledge and Learning in Asia/Pacific and Africa*; *Learning from the Ground Up: Global Perspectives on Social Movements and Knowledge Production* and *Globalization, Culture and Education in South Asia: Critical Excursions*.

NGOization

Complicity, Contradictions and Prospects

Edited by Aziz Choudry and Dip Kapoor

Zed Books
London & New York

NGOization: Complicity, Contradictions and Prospects was first published in 2013 by Zed Books Ltd, 7 Cynthia Street, London N1 9JF, UK and Room 400, 175 Fifth Avenue, New York, NY 10010, USA

www.zedbooks.co.uk

Editorial Copyright © Aziz Choudry and Dip Kapoor 2013
Copyright in this collection © Zed Books 2013

The right of Aziz Choudry and Dip Kapoor to be identified as the editors of this work have been asserted by them in accordance with the Copyright, Designs and Patents Act, 1988

Typeset in Plantin by Palimpsest Book Production Ltd, Falkirk, Stirlingshire
Index: Rohan Bolton
Cover design: www.reactor15.com
Printed and bound by TJ International Ltd, Padstow, Cornwall

Distributed in the USA exclusively by Palgrave Macmillan, a division of St Martin's Press, LLC, 175 Fifth Avenue, New York, NY 10010, USA

A catalogue record for this book is available from the British Library
Library of Congress Cataloging in Publication Data available

ISBN 978 1 78032 258 2 hb
ISBN 978 1 78032 257 5 pb

Contents

Acknowledgments

The impetus for this collection emerges from our own involvement with social movements and non-governmental organizations (NGOs), conversations, dilemmas and questions shared with colleagues, friends and comrades, including each other. While the concerns and tensions which propel this book are not new, we hope that, collectively, we bring some new perspectives to help think through the complexities of social, political and ecological action in ways that are relevant to present and future movements of resistance, as well as to critical scholars, students, NGO practitioners and a wider public.

First, we extend our heartfelt gratitude to all of the contributors to this book for their insights and willingness to see this project through to its completion. Many thanks to Sangeeta Kamat for her preface.

Secondly, our thanks go to Tamsine O'Riordan, our editor at Zed Books, Ken Barlow and Kika Sroka-Miller for their commitment to this book. We are grateful to our editorial assistant, Rima Athar, for her excellent work in copy-editing and formatting the manuscript. We also thank the team at Palimpsest Book Production for their professionalism in the final layout stages.

Aziz is deeply indebted to the many activists, organizers, colleagues and friends with whom he has worked, and the hours and days of discussions on the role of NGOs and the impacts of NGOization on social movements for many years. In particular, he is grateful for the unfailing support and comradeship of Radha D'Souza, Leigh Cookson, Sunera Thobani, Chris Rahim, David Bleakney, Devlin Kuyek, Renée Vellvé, Eric Shragge, David Austin, Steve Jordan and Wali Haider.

Preface

Sangeeta Kamat

The future of neoliberalism is uncertain today, and with it the institutional form of the NGO (non-governmental organization) that has existed as a compulsory feature of neoliberalization for the past four decades. To say neoliberalism is 'dominant but dead' (Smith, 2008) is to recognize that the crisis-ridden nature of neoliberalism is evident today on a global scale, but in the absence of a convincing alternative, it remains the dominant model of economic and social ruling. The links between neoliberalism and the growth of NGOs are documented by scholars from diverse disciplines, studying vastly different geographical contexts across multiple institutional scales that span the local to the global. An argument distinctive to critical scholarship on NGOs is that there is a synergy in the spread of neoliberalism in the late twentieth century and the rise of the NGO sector, and that NGOs have a vital part in articulating the dramatic transformations in state and economy brought about by neoliberalism. It is not that one is the cause and the other the effect, or that one is necessarily contingent on the other, but rather NGOs are what Arundhati Roy has called 'indicator species', in that 'the greater the devastation caused by neoliberalism, the greater the outbreak of NGOs' (2004). This correlation, which cannot be denied but needs to be explained and theorized to the fullest extent, has generated an influential body of work on what is variously represented as the 'NGOization of democracy' or the 'NGOization of grassroots politics' (Kamat, 2004), or what the authors in this volume reference as the 'professionalization of dissent'.

As this collection of research on NGOs and NGOization in diverse contexts illustrates, neoliberal policies and NGOs appear to be ubiquitous. The chapters in this collection represent the spread of NGOs in places as diverse as South Africa, Kyrgyzstan, India, Canada, Serbia and the Philippines, among equally diverse communities including Indigenous Peoples, fishing communities, feminists, farmers and the urban poor.

What is common among these research sites, each possessing remarkably different histories that have been richly delineated, is that NGOs are the favored institutional form through which every social problem is to be addressed, be it domestic violence, ecological devastation, food security or the aftermath of war. The present volume is a collection of case studies about NGOization that are exceptional for their 'thick descriptions' of the contestations within NGOs and the solidary between NGOs and people's movements and issues that show up in unlikely places in unexpected moments. While the case studies unequivocally establish that NGOization stalls and obstructs processes of authentic democratization, the studies also caution us against easy equivalences between NGOs and NGOization.

As one reads across these varied contexts, the book's project of interrogating the precise character of NGOization in specific places – of appreciating the differences in political trajectories and social relations that embed and define the limits of NGOization in each context, and the struggles and contestations made palpable by the authors' analytic oeuvre – appears in sharp relief to the generalities about NGOs as handmaidens of imperialism or bearers of cosmopolitan democracy. The importance of this project, which seeks to produce a politics of 'militant particularisms' (Williams, 1989) and mobilize resources for creative engagement rather than cynicism and despair, is not to be underestimated.

A radical transformative politics requires that 'militant particularisms' – that is, particular struggles in particular places – are 'properly brought together' to advance the general interest (Williams, 1989, cited in Harvey, 1996, p. 32). The decisive challenge here is 'properly brought together' – of how to properly articulate struggles and issues that appear specific with universal aspirations for a socially just and humane world order. The case studies in this volume provide insights into the contexts in which NGOs are catalysts in articulating a radical politics linked with people's struggles, while also elaborating situations in which NGO work actively precludes the articulation of specific struggles with radical politics. If one were to elicit the conditions of possibility for NGOs to act one way or the other, the case studies point to two major factors. First, the weight of geopolitical imperatives is repeatedly invoked as playing a decisive role in NGO promotion and the creation of an NGO comprador class. Second, the nature of the state influences the self-fashioning of NGOs either in the direction of NGOization or towards building alliances with social movement organizations and people's struggles.

Geopolitics as an important factor in NGOization is most evident in the post-socialist countries (Kyrgyzstan and Serbia in this case), where the rush to showcase the success of capitalist democracy by western powers and national elites leads to a veritable explosion of NGOs that struggle to become adept with the requirements of international aid agencies and are unable to respond to the true suffering of the people in whose name they serve. In these, as in other case studies (notably Orissa, Tamil Nadu, Serbia and the Indigenous Peoples' movements in North America), the political convictions of the activists and the histories and memories of organizing they share, each probably co-constitutive of the other, lead them to resist processes of NGOization and in some instances to reject NGOs as a politically viable organizational form.

The second recurring theme is the extent to which the broader context and history of the state suggests the measure of maneuverability that NGOs have. A simple scale that identifies states in terms of sustained periods of political mobilization and radicalization, and a vibrant array of party and non-party political organizations, may show that the processes of NGOization are limited and highly uneven in such states and that NGOs are more likely to seek relations of solidarity with people's struggles in such contexts. It is also likely that NGOs in these national contexts acquire the repertoire for working in the interstices of international donor agencies, the state and social movements. In turn, the neoliberal state invokes the norm of national security to suppress such alliances as anti-national. The case studies on South Africa, Orissa, Tamil Nadu and the Philippines in particular elucidate this aspect of the fraught but mobile relation between NGOs and the state.

Most importantly, the authors draw our attention to the essential problems that people everywhere are faced with today – of how to be viable, effective and expansive in a context where 'special interest' is professionalized and where aid-dependent NGOs shape political discourse and define the limits of democracy. There are no easy answers for how social movements may be nurtured and supported in times of increased state repression and neoliberalization, nor are there 'rules for radical NGOs' to aid and abet social movements in their struggles for social justice. On the contrary, as the case study on Orissa highlights, the state and multinational corporations are aggressive in their efforts to destroy democratic movements, employing the same crude tactics of bribery, deception, intimidation and outright lying that were common to the usurer in the colonial period. In other words, state and capital seek to fully exploit the ambivalent and accommodating position of NGOs to crush peoples' movements. On the other hand, the strategic relationships that social movements at times seek with NGOs work as a safety measure against the repression by political and corporate elites that has intensified under neoliberalism.

Although NGOs that become politically engaged or vocal may likely draw the wrath of the state and international donors, Choudry and Kapoor make a compelling case for not treating NGOs as rigid, with singular unchanging histories and identities, and instead to study their variability in terms of their engagement with politics on the ground. The thesis of this book is an exemplary instance of Gramsci's theorization of state and civil society as co-extensive with one another, wherein NGOs belong neither to state nor civil society but are contested sites in the struggle between the interests of capital and people's aspirations for a just and humane world. If we view NGOs as not outside of or external to state, market or society, but as representing – as does each of these realms – one more institutional form through which class relations are being contested and reworked, then indeed NGOization must be considered as an always unfinished and unstable project, contingent on the oppositional politics of subaltern movements and the presence of a social democratic state. To borrow Bourdieu's remark about the state, NGOs too carry the 'trace of social struggles of the past' (1998, p. 2).

From Europe to Latin America, North America and the pan-Arab world, the slow and painful death of neoliberalism is visible, as protests and new experiments in democracy are on the rise, bringing into force historic alliances of social movements, political parties and NGOs. We know as well that in response to every crisis of capitalism, neoliberal forms of regulation have been revived in ways that are increasingly perverse and anti-people. NGOs will become ever more contested sites as the stakes get higher in the conflict between popular movements and neoliberal governments. This collection is both a cautionary tale and one of hope that can instruct movement activists and NGO professionals on navigating the contradictions of NGOs to become effective allies in the struggle for a post-neoliberal world.

References

Bourdieu, P. (1998). 'The Left Hand and the Right Hand of the State'. In P. Bourdieu (Ed.) *Acts of Resistance* (pp. 1–10). Cambridge: Polity.

Harvey, D. (1996). *Justice, Nature and the Geography of Difference*. Oxford: Blackwell Publishers.

Kamat, S. (2004). 'The NGO-ization of Grassroots Politics'. In P. Leistyna (Ed.) *Cultural Studies and Practical Politics* (pp. 142–156). Boston: Blackwell Publishers.

Roy, A. (2004). 'Help That Hinders'. *Le Monde Diplomatique* (English Edition). Available from: http://mondediplo.com/2004/11/16roy.

Smith, N. (2008). 'Neoliberalism: Dominant But Dead'. *FOCAAL: Journal of Global and Historical Anthropology* 51:1, 155–7.

Williams, R. (1989). *Resources of Hope*. London: Verso.

Introduction

NGOization: Complicity, Contradictions and Prospects

Aziz Choudry and Dip Kapoor

The term 'NGOization' is commonly used among many social movements, activist networks and academics to refer to the institutionalization, professionalization, depoliticization and demobilization of movements for social and environmental change (Armstrong & Prashad, 2005; Burrowes, Cousins, Rojas, & Ude, 2007; Kamat, 2004; A. Smith, 2007a). Partial accounts of non-governmental organizations (NGOs) pay inadequate attention to questions of power, dependence and/or complicity with state, market and multilateral/international institutions made evident in analyses which consider the political economy of NGOs in an era characterized by a globalizing capitalist colonization of territories, nature, peoples and cultures. Building on previous work (Choudry & Kapoor, 2010), this book revisits and augments critiques of NGOization and the professionalization and depoliticization of social action by drawing on knowledge produced in contemporary social struggles and everyday practice pertaining to NGO–social movement relations. The contributors explore whether or not NGOs open up political space or represent specific forms of regulation and containment in the interest of a contemporary capitalist (re)colonization. They ask how the related phenomena of the rise of NGOs and NGOization have impacted struggles for social and environmental justice in various contexts of engagement. What political, economic, social and cultural interests do these trends serve? Alternatively, how have NGOs challenged or reinforced 'the inhuman conditions of global, colonial capitalism' (Williams, 2010, p. 100)?

While acknowledging the variety in NGO forms, ideological positioning and contexts, this book argues that in order to effectively work for social justice, we must learn from grounded critical analyses of NGOization, and grapple with the warp and weft of the contradictions and tensions inherent in different models of social change in order to reconceptualize resistance against capitalism and colonialism. Drawing from perspectives of activists and critically engaged academics, we argue that NGOs – and the process of NGOization – frequently undermine local and international movements for social change and environmental justice and/or oppositional anti-colonial and anti-capitalist politics, in complicity with state and private-sector interests. The collection highlights tensions, contradictions, ambiguities and possibilities emerging from a number of contexts. We think through prospects for social change, arising from organizational/movement forms and actors' relationships to larger political and economic processes which are in tension with the dominant tendencies of NGOization. By unpacking 'NGOization and its discontents', the collection outlines some of the prospects and possibilities for social action and moves beyond dominant 'civil society' frames of politics and action. This includes attending to the variety in NGO and other organizational/movement types and formations in varied contexts of resistance and mobilization.

A non-typology and short recent history of NGOs

Fisher (1997) argues that there is a danger of over-essentializing NGOs and a need to unpack micropolitics, complexities and interconnections between local sites and larger contexts. Networks of movements and NGOs are often complex and difficult to fit into compartmentalized analyses or typologies, although many have tried to do so. Dominant strands of social movement scholarship have been criticized for their levels of abstraction, limited sets of variables, lack of political economy analysis, ethnocentrism and irrelevance to social movements themselves. Catherine Eschle (2001) warns that

> movements that do not share the perspective of the particular group taken as an exemplar by the theorist are simply defined out of existence. . . . Oppression and conflict within civil society and between social movement actors cannot simply be wished away or ignored, and neglect of this issue represents a central failing of post-Marxist versions of civil society (p. 74).

NGOs operate in so many contexts and roles that it is difficult to generalize about them. Some have origins in missionary and/or faith-based charitable and philanthropic work (De Waal, 1997; Gallin, 2000; Manji & O'Coill, 2002). While the term 'NGO' usually implies a non-profit organization, some are little more than businesses and/or operate with a hierarchical, corporate management structure (Jordan & Maloney, 1997; Petras & Veltmeyer, 2001; Reinsborough, 2004). Others are volunteer-driven and claim community constituencies and a democratic structure. Some emerge from, and remain accountable to, broader social struggles. Others, as Gallin (2000) notes, 'have a self-appointed and co-opted leadership, are not accountable to any constituency other than public opinion and their funders, do not provide public financial information, and have no clear monitoring and evaluation procedures' (p. 27). Many NGOs are themselves sites of considerable internal struggle over politics, positioning, program priorities – and power.

Several factors account for the growth of aid and development NGOs, and their relationships with governments and the private sector. Fowler (2000) sees the rightwards shift in Northern politics during the Reagan-Thatcher era as key to 'the start of the rise in official finance to, and number of NGOs that continues today'. This was due to the move away from government to the market as the engine of growth and progress, and 'meant more responsibility to citizens and their organizations' (p. 2). Although such funds used to flow primarily from Northern governments or financial institutions to Southern governments, NGOs have increasingly become channels for, and direct recipients of, this 'development assistance' (Biel, 2000; Petras & Veltmeyer, 2001; Wallace, 2003). NGOs have often grown to fill gaps in the provision of services and public goods which the public sector used to, or was never able to, provide. In many countries, NGOs provide employment for former civil servants, as public sectors are downsized under structural adjustment or other free market reform programs imposed by donors. The policies and statements of intergovernmental organizations, such as the United Nations, World Bank and the Asian Development Bank, also set parameters for which NGOs are officially recognized through dialogue or other forms of engagement.

Discussing human rights advocacy NGOs, Richard Falk (1999) argues that:

[t]he main human rights NGOs were very much outgrowths of Western liberal internationalism and looked mainly outward to identify abuses in Communist and Third World countries. In part, this reflected civilizational, as well as partisan and ideologized, orientations. It was expressed by a very selective emphasis by human rights organizations on the abuse of dissenters and political opposition or on the denial of Western-style political liberties . . . In other words, human rights progress, while definitely subversive of statist pretensions in certain key respects, still remained generally compatible with the maintenance of existing geopolitical structures of authority and wealth in the world and, as such, exerted only a marginal influence (p. 98).

Priorities for official development assistance shifted gears after the end of the Cold War. Increasingly, governments, intergovernmental organizations and international financial institutions promoted the policy and practice of 'strengthening civil society' along with 'good governance' (Petras & Veltmeyer, 2001, 2005; Veltmeyer, 2007). These are intrinsic pillars of neoliberal policy, as Kamat (2004) and Petras and Veltmeyer (2005) argue. Northern government and private sector funding agencies resourced NGOs as part of an economic and foreign policy strategy to 'democratize' countries through 'civil society' (Mojab, 2009; Petras & Veltmeyer, 2001, 2005; Veltmeyer, 2007) in a unipolar world. With the invasion and occupation of Afghanistan and Iraq, as well as the broader focus on geopolitical and security concerns in economic and foreign policy since the attacks of 11 September 2001, came renewed, explicit linkages gathering state actors, the private sector and NGOs in the name of development, humanitarianism, peace and security (Al-Ali & Pratt, 2009; Bebbington, Hickey, & Mitlin, 2008; Mojab, 2009). This is what others have referenced as the militarization of aid or humanitarian imperialism, as development and security agendas cohere in the interests of global capitalist governance (Bricmont, 2006; Duffield, 2001). This entailed support for only a limited, restructured state, free market economic reforms, and an increased role for NGOs and private sector organizations in providing social services and local development initiatives. For Kamat (2004) and Petras and Veltmeyer (2005), the professionalization and depoliticization of community-based NGOs work well for neoliberal regimes. Indeed, for Petras and Veltmeyer, it serves to keep 'the existing power structure (vis-à-vis the distribution of society's resources) intact while promoting a degree (and a local form) of change and development' (p. 20). Instead, these organizations merely seek to ameliorate some of the social or environmental impacts through community development and participation-based development projects (see Fernando, 2011, on NGOs in Bangladesh and Sri Lanka). With the rise of NGOs and the enlargement of NGO political space, forms of hegemonic NGO politics emerged, wherein the terms of social change amount to limited gains as opportunities might permit *within* existing structures (Choudry & Shragge, 2012). For Kamat (2004), rather than 'deepening the gains made on the basis of popular democratic struggles, NGOs are being re-inscribed in the current policy discourse in ways that strengthen liberalism and undermine democracy' (p. 171).

Analysis of NGOs and NGOization should examine ways in which funding and other material support can orient organizations to prioritize institutional survival and maintenance at the expense of mobilization, and account for how NGO/movement actions may be shaped by material incentives. This has implications for the professionalization of social change (Reinsborough, 2004; A. Smith, 2007b) and the spread of forms of marketization, territorialism and competition among NGOs and social movements for mobilization against neoliberalism. Petras and Veltmeyer (2001) see the vast majority of NGOs as serving to displace, destroy or neutralize social movements fighting for economic and social injustice throughout the Third World. Rajagopal (2003) and Williams (2010) suggest that NGO-led processes of human rights intervention are often inherently imperialist and colonial, as opposed to struggles which address the processes of imperialism and colonialism (Choudry, 2009; Kapoor, 2012) as explicit targets for political action. This is made evident in their tolerance for and complicity with development/market violence in contexts of displacement and dispossession (for instance, see chapters by Africa, Choudry, Kapoor, and Swamy in this volume). The dominant notion of 'civil society' emphasizes rights of individuals to pursue their self-interest rather than collective rights and upholds the interests of states and capital. It also facilitates what Kamat (2004) calls the privatization of the notion of public interest. Within the context of neoliberal transformation, development and advocacy NGOs in particular come to contribute to managing and structuring dissent, channeling this into organizational structures and processes that do not threaten underlying power relations. Further, these organizations act to absorb cuts in services and a reduced role for the state under neoliberal restructuring and/or as a safety valve or lid on more militant opposition against such policies (Choudry & Shragge, 2012).

Wood (1995), Greenfield (2001), Petras and Veltmeyer (2001) and McNally (2002) suggest (as we do in this collection) that NGOs tend to operate in ways which accept capitalism rather than seeking to transform the system *altogether*.

> At the very moment when a critical understanding of the capitalist system is most urgently needed, large sections of the intellectual left, instead of developing, enriching and refining the required conceptual instruments, show every sign of discarding them altogether. [. . .] Intellectuals on the left, then, have been trying to define new ways, other than contestation, of relating to capitalism. The typical mode, at best, is to seek out the interstices of capitalism, to make space within it for alternative 'discourses', activities and identities (Wood, 1998, pp. 1–2).

Such discourses and 'alternatives' may sound invitingly progressive at face value, but are frequently disconnected from struggles that confront the state and capital (Petras, 2002) and the knowledge produced therein. Instead, most NGOs have focused on lobbying and trying to influence elites rather than movement-building. In doing so, they have often become more driven by notions of polite reformism and self-interest in the maintenance of their organization and funding relationships – and ultimately serve dominant political and economic interests (McNally, 2002; Rojas, 2007; A. Smith, 2007a). In some cases, these organizations have become corporate entities in their own right (Blood, 2005), part of what Rojas (2007) and A. Smith (2007b) describe as 'the non-profit industrial complex' (A. Smith, 2007b, p. 3), modeled after capitalist structures. While some NGOs maintain a focus almost solely on the international arena, and some look for new opportunities for political leverage at a supranational or transnational level, for many NGOs and social movements the state remains both a target and terrain of struggle (Goodman, 2002; Keck & Sikkink, 1998). Some NGOs cooperate closely with domestic governments at an international level, while others are diametrically opposed to such collaboration. Organizations that frame their demands in liberal social democratic traditions tend to demand a humanized form of capitalism and a retooled state, although some view incremental gains and reforms as necessary steps in a longer term transformation of society and social and economic relations.

Goodman (2002) raises important questions about the legitimacy of international NGOs, predominantly based in the global North, to become vehicles for 'people power' (p. xvii) in this international space, and also questions their political leverage and institutional capacity to perform this task. He sees NGOs that operate at this level as broadly reformist, seeking greater institutional accountability and the formulation of goals that address popular priorities rather than elite interests. But this mode of operating is itself elitist and only open to a privileged few with access (albeit limited and contested) to either critique or advise agents of capitalist globalization, and who are willing to operate within the parameters set by those institutions. The ability for these actors to pursue such a mode of action is frequently linked to their relationships with state governments in Northern countries and the fact that their ideologies and political platforms do not reject the fundamental principles of these institutions.

Some NGOs have roots in popular progressive social movements, but have become disconnected from them and institutionalized (Burrowes, Cousins, Rojas & Ude, 2007; Petras & Veltmeyer, 2005). Kamat (2004) highlights a shift among community-based NGOs in a number of Third World contexts 'from broad-based political education and organization of the poor to providing social and economic inputs based on a technical assessment of capacities and needs of the community' (p. 168). This resonates with critical perspectives on trends in community organizing in the global North. For Piven and Cloward (1977), for example, writing on poor people's movements in the USA, '[o]rganizations endure, in short, by abandoning their oppositional politics' (p. xi). They hold that the preoccupation with financial survival, building and maintaining these organizations diverts energy and resources away from organizing and escalating popular protest movements, and indeed often blunting or curbing them. Arguably, we can see that trend at the local, national and international level, where many NGOs lose their capacity (assuming that they ever had one) to remain critical or to support popular education and mobilization programs. Yet Rucht (1999) notes that the 'shift from radical challenger groups to pragmatically oriented pressure organizations' can lead to a 're-radicalization at the fringes' (p. 220). Thus, while changed structures and self-interest in organizational survival may often lead to changed, deradicalized ideologies, this process of institutionalization can drive others to seek different, more contestational forms of politics and models for their movements. It is in this dynamic that we see one source of building intellectual spaces and action that goes beyond dominant forms of 'civil society' intervention and NGOization.

Some NGOs were set up by, and have managed to remain attached and accountable to, people's movements for specific purposes (Burrowes, Cousins, Rojas & Ude, 2007; Petras & Veltmeyer, 2001, 2005; Rojas, 2007). However, these tend to be exceptions. The IBON Foundation in the Philippines is one such example relevant to this book (see Africa, in this volume). IBON was born during the Marcos dictatorship, established by people's movements and radical currents within churches as an autonomous research and databank organization. IBON works closely with a multi-sectoral people's movement providing research and education materials for use in campaigns and longer-term struggles. Its close connections with mass-based social movements, such as the militant Kilusang Mayo Uno (KMU) trade union center and the Kilusang Magbubukid ng Pilipinas (KMP) peasant farmers' movement, as well as other sectoral, national democratic movements on the left have helped to maintain its accountability to people's struggles in the Philippines. Such organizations are often hybrid activist/social movement organizations which work at building social movements and community mobilization and are also constituted in a way that allows them to seek support from philanthropic foundations, or state funding and tax-exempt status where these exist (Burrowes, Cousins, Rojas & Ude, 2007; A. Smith, 2007b). For example, Burrowes, Cousins, Rojas and Ude (2007) note that South Africa's LPM (Landless People's Movement) and Brazil's MST (Movimento dos Trabalhadore Rurais Sem Terra – landless rural workers' movement) have had strategic relationships with NGOs, many of which 'were started at the request of the movements, usually to provide specific skills or resources' but 'ultimately . . . are not essential. If those NGOs collapsed tomorrow, the movements would remain intact' (p. 231). Meanwhile, some Third World NGOs – often funded by Northern NGOs, private foundations and government development assistance programs – have been vehicles for relatively privileged intellectuals to research, or to conduct professionalized lobbying of, governments or international institutions, but have later reached out to social movements as their legitimacy and lack of a grassroots base has been challenged, for example, in the context of the growth of the global justice movement.

An additional concern relating to the process of NGOization is the way in which some NGOs – especially aid and development agencies with funding relationships with partner organizations in the Third World, as well as some established research and advocacy NGOs in both North and South – position themselves as the gatekeepers between social movements and other organizations. That is, they act as intermediaries, and yet their roles and interests in doing so and the power inherent in acting in this way are frequently opaque and rarely subject to critical examination (Burrowes, Cousins, Rojas & Ude, 2007; Choudry & Shragge, 2012). Townsend and Townsend (2004) note that gatekeeper NGOs 'command the discourse, can write the funding proposals . . . and are "in the information loop"' (p. 281), often creating a sense of powerlessness for those on the outside. Northern NGOs and social movement activists are often unaware of, or seemingly unconcerned about whether Southern organizations and their representatives have a genuine grassroots base or, rather, whether they represent a professional class of NGO representatives with access to international networks. Kamat (2004) argues that this process of professionalization is driven by the neoliberal policy context in which NGOs operate. Organizations must demonstrate managerial and technical capabilities to administer, monitor and account for project funding. Mass-based organizations of movements which represent their demands themselves through various forms of political mobilization have often been overshadowed or displaced by organizations which claim to represent the poor and marginalized, but in fact have no mass base or popular mandate (Faraclas, 2001; Hewson, 2005; McNally, 2002; Petras & Veltmeyer, 2001, 2003, 2005; Veltmeyer, 2007).

Grappling with NGOization

In thinking through and responding to the dynamics and tendencies we have described, it is important to draw upon conceptual resources from older struggles (e.g. Fanon, 1968), to pay attention to local contexts, and highlight the importance of a critical examination of historical processes. Notwithstanding our goal to move past simple NGO/social movement dichotomies, we suggest that the phenomenon of the NGOization of social action unfolds and manifests in different contexts and struggles, and yet that common concerns about its implications for political space and action persist. As Shahrzad Mojab (2009) suggests, 'It is difficult to make sense of NGOs if we do not look at the historical context of the idea and practice of NGOs' (p. 111). A number of critiques of NGOization have been advanced by feminist, Marxist, critical race and anti-colonial scholars among others, considering different national and regional contexts. Sonia Alvarez's (1999, 2009) reflections on the 'Latin American feminist NGO boom' are often cited. Islah Jad (2004, 2007) has written on the NGOization, co-optation and undermining of the women's movement and other parts of Palestinian 'civil society'. She suggests that in the Palestinian context, 'profession-alization produces upward, rather than downward accountability, exclusion rather than inclusion' (2007, p. 625). Sangeeta Kamat's (2002, 2004) work examines the impacts of NGOization and the growth of NGOs on political space and development in India and internationally. INCITE! Women of Color Against Violence's (2007) analysis of the 'non-profit industrial complex' addresses both the USA and Latin America. Mojab's (2009) research on women's NGOs in Iraqi Kurdistan looks at the foreign funding of women's NGOs in creating a new political/ economic elite, which depoliticizes the women's movement and further marginalizes the poor, in a so-called 'post-war' context. Dru Oja Jay and Nik Barry-Shaw's (2012) recent book is a welcome critical exam-ination of the role of Canadian international development NGOs. Perhaps, as Fisher (1997) suggests, '[t]he trick is to differentiate among various forms of organizing while avoiding reified and reductionist uses of the concept NGO' (p. 449). Analysis, and in turn strategy and decision-making in activist struggles impacted by the dominance of NGOs, is happening in many different communities, international and transnational movement networks. The tensions and struggles sometimes seem like hydra heads, or forest fires which may die down only to flare up again in different situations, at different times.

While focusing on specific contexts, this collection is tied together by an analysis that attempts to move beyond simplified dichotomies and typologies. Indeed, we pose the question: can we move beyond the dichotomy between NGOs and social movements whose organizational form makes them likely to be regarded as conformist/reformist and radical respectively? We are describing a dominant trend in the context of socio-economic transformation, rather than subscribing to an over-simplified dichotomy between conformity/co-optation and transformation/radical politics. Yet while NGOs and mass social movements sometimes seemingly put aside their differences to forge coalitions, alliances and networks on shared concerns or against common opponents, tensions and divergent views and values often remain. In some cases there is outright hostility and suspicion towards NGOs from progressive mass movements, especially towards those which receive government and/or foreign funding. We recognize that some NGOs act in opposition, mobilize, and are committed to supporting and building broad social and political movements, but we contend that these constitute the minority and are often marginalized. As mentioned earlier, these organizations and the networks they inhabit are themselves the sites of significant internal struggles over political position and practice (see Sinwell, in this volume).

As editors of this book, our interest in these issues emerges from our own engagements in struggles for social change. Choudry's experience with NGOs, social movements, activist groups and community organizations in Aotearoa/New Zealand, North America, the broader Asia-Pacific region and global levels informs his interest in multi-scalar organizational/movement forms, critical traditions of organizing and the question of NGOization. He has long been active as an organizer, educator and researcher in a wide range of anti-colonial, anti-imperialist, global justice, ecological, food sovereignty, labor, and immigration justice networks, among others.

Kapoor's participatory action research (2009) and popular education and organizing work with Adivasi and Dalit (or Scheduled Tribe and Castes in Indian state parlance) community-based organizations, small/village-based NGOs and Adivasi-Dalit social movements in Orissa, India, goes back to the early 1990s and includes his current association with the Adivasi-Dalit Centre for Research and Development Solidarity (CRDS) as voluntary Research Associate and founding member. His experiences in this context inform his academic and practical interest in NGO relations (Kapoor, 2005) and NGO-social movement relations in particular, in contexts of rural displacement and dispossession.

Many of the contributions in this book critically analyze NGO complicity with capital and colonial processes and explore the contradictions implicit in NGO activities and other contemporary sites of social action. In doing this, the authors examine the material, political, economic and/or cultural forces behind NGOization in specific contexts such as connectivities between development and advocacy NGOs, neoliberalism, humanitarianism, privatization of social contracts, and the reproduction of capitalism/colonialism. Does NGO intervention, advocacy and lobbying amplify the voices of people at the grassroots, reframe or appropriate them or drown them out? How does the institutionalization and bureaucratization of organizational forms advance or inhibit movements for social change? Alvarez (2009) observes: 'Which actors, discourses, practices and organizational forms prevail or are most politically visible at any given time in a given socio-political context therefore necessarily varies. There is, in short, no twenty-first century Iron Law of NGOization' (p. 182). Is she correct? The range of perspectives of this book's authors suggest that the term 'NGOization', and the urgency of particular concerns about this phenomenon, may indeed differ across contexts. Yet while the forms and expressions of NGOization at different times and places may lead some actors to emphasize specific characteristics, we suggest that it is conceptually useful to group these concerns into the two interrelated strands of critique which follow.

NGOs as agents of capitalist colonization of material space

A crucial question that directs the forms and arenas for contestation is the perspective of an organization or movement on capitalism, and specifically, the form of capitalism being advanced through neoliberal globalization. Goodman (2002) offers three models of social movements under globalization. These are: (1) elite cosmopolitanism of those international NGOs seeking to impose checks on or reform intergovernmental agencies, which he dubs 'globalist adaption'; (2) 'localist confrontation' where struggles for forms of autonomy take place at a local or national level, usually disconnected from the global arena; and (3) 'transnational resistance'. This last model refers to the way in which some movements have remained focussed on local mobilization and on state power, 'especially as neoliberal integration has defined new and more authoritarian roles for the national state' (p. xxi). The latter movements have also built transnational alliances and exploited transnational political leverage. However, the models that have been used to understand these spheres frequently fail to take account of the diverse histories, forms and politics of actors, the nature of organizations, and concrete conditions on the ground.

Furthermore, the process of co-optation of some NGOs cannot be divorced from the reverse side of the coin for those who refuse to operate within the parameters set from above, which may include increased repression, surveillance and the criminalization of dissent. McNally (2002) notes that

> many NGO and labour leaderships have sought to prove their respectability by denouncing those who engage in less polite forms of protest . . . The reality of the international Left today is a global parting of the ways, particularly in the South, where increasingly militant protests and rebellions against neoliberalism pursue a radically different strategy from the reform-minded lobbying efforts of mainstream NGOs and labour leaders (p. 198).

Organizations and movements critical of the terms 'civil society' and 'global civil society' point to the way in which these phrases are being promoted by the very institutions and governments which are the targets for opposition movements (McNally 2002; Petras & Veltmeyer, 2001; Veltmeyer, 2007). They see that the terms fit comfortably within, and indeed are taken up by, neoliberal discourse and public relations strategies of governments and international financial and economic institutions. In 1996, the World Trade Organization (WTO) adopted guidelines for relations with NGOs (WTO, 1996). The World Bank electronically publishes a monthly 'civil society engagement newsletter' (World Bank, 2008). The processes of external and internal regulation, funding criteria, accreditation and recognition from governments, United Nations (UN) agencies or other international institutions discipline organizations to operate within parameters and frameworks set by these actors. In turn, many NGOs are charged with being self-referential in the sense that they develop priorities and strategies internally without reference to peoples and social movements they claim to advocate on behalf of, or communities in which they operate.

As noted, a common critique of many NGOs contends that they favor strategies that preserve the capitalist system and the interests of large corporations while attempting to alleviate specific problems. This critique focuses on funding as a factor in their support for market mechanisms and technological fixes over economic and social reforms, and explores the impact of well-funded NGOs on the nascent growth of emerging grassroots organizations and movements. In this collection, as suggested in chapters by Choudry, Kapoor, and Swamy, NGOization also refers to processes of material complicity with capital. Choudry draws from examples in the Asia-Pacific and Latin America to discuss the ways in which major environmental NGOs are complicit with colonial and capitalist designs, and Indigenous resistance to their actions. Kapoor's chapter examines how NGOs actively engage in attempts to demobilize, immobilize and derail Adivasi-Dalit anti-mining/ anti-colonial activism in Orissa, India, addressing these incursions into Scheduled Areas where the explicit movement objective is to maintain forests, land and water-bodies, by putting a stop to mining activities. NGOs utilize micro-credit interventions (often funded by mining corporations), for instance, to subvert and divide movement constituencies. Similar to analyses pertaining to 'disaster capitalism' (Klein, 2007), Swamy demonstrates how post-tsunami reconstruction is deployed by NGOs to reconfigure space in the interests of the project of capital while disregarding the politics and ways of coastal fisher communities in Tamil Nadu. Responses, by Adivasi and fisher communities, respectively, to such incursions are also highlighted as affected social groups continue their action in the face of tremendous odds.

The professionalization of dissent and knowledge colonization for capital

The trend of professionalization over the past 30 years has led to a concentration of power as a result of internal position and training. This has three related characteristics. The first is the centrality of paid staff. Although formally accountable to boards of directors, staff direct day-to-day operations, and longer-term agendas and activities. The second is that, increasingly, staff are not movement activists who have found paid work in the organization, but people who have received professional training in many new university programs that train people in management of NGOs and community organizations. This training is largely technical and draws from traditional management literatures including organizational development, and strategic planning. The underlying assumptions of these programs are drawn from the corporate world and assumed to make non-profits more efficient and accountable. Yet this prepares professional staffers with a model of managerialism that emphasizes organizational governance over radical politics and support for mobilization and social movements. Finally, professional staffers tend to represent their organizations in public as spokespeople, at negotiating tables, and in partnership structures, whereas they could instead support mobilization on the ground, and help movement activists to develop leadership skills and represent their movements as they see fit.

Professionalization brings with it important broader political and social consequences. Reinsborough (2004) writes of a 'terrifyingly widespread conceit among professional 'campaigners' that social change is a highly specialized profession best left to experienced strategists, negotiators and policy wonks. NGOism is the conceit that paid staff will be enough to save the world' (p. 194). The professionalization of dissent, the valorization of certain kinds of knowledge, the devaluing of other forms which emerge from within social struggles, and dubious claims to representation frequently go hand in hand in these milieus. Dorothy Smith (1987) writes that professionalization 'uses knowledge to restructure collective non-capitalist forms of organization into hierarchical strata, detaching them from the movements they originate in and connecting them to the relations of ruling' (pp. 216–7). Thus, NGOs often create and become enmeshed and invested in maintaining webs of power and bureaucracy, which divert energy and focus away from building oppositional movements for social change. Sinwell's chapter in this volume notes that even in a South Africa apparently 'liberated' from apartheid, and with long histories of people's struggles through mass social movements, NGOs, which were once largely oppositional (to the state) during the anti-apartheid struggle, have had to redefine their role and now act primarily as service delivery agents for the ruling African National Congress (ANC). He charts the way in which the reformist character of South African NGOs may have led to the containment of militant and potentially counter-hegemonic struggles in communities and explores alternative forms of opposition which seek to build a counter-hegemonic force against free market capitalism. In another chapter, Africa discusses similar tensions over Philippine NGOs' complicity with imperialism and state power in service delivery and governance and more contestational popular struggles which work for systemic change.

Moreover, we see a deeply colonial and (re)colonizing aspect in this process. The professionalization of knowledge for NGOs is largely drawn from Western sources and assumptions. Maori scholar Linda Smith (1999) critiques many imperialist and colonial assumptions, which underpin Western knowledge and research. She asks whose knowledge matters, where it comes from and who controls it. Where, then, do the rules for NGO practices originate? Are Western models of NGOs forged during the years of structural adjustment the best solution to bring about social change, and what are the implications for local knowledge and traditions of reliance on them? The chapters by Kim & Campbell, Venne, Vukov, and Swamy, build on these insights. While emphasizing the importance of context-specific approaches to understanding NGOs and social movements, we contend that a dominant tendency of NGOs is to fragment and compartmentalize the world into 'issues', and 'projects', in ways which entail an unwillingness to name or confront capitalism or historical and contemporary manifestations of colonialism. The positions and practices of these NGOs, which replicate, rather than challenge dominant national practices, serve to undermine and contain more critical forms of knowledge production and action in relation to confronting global capitalism and colonialism (see chapters by Kim & Campbell, Choudry, and Kneen).

Smith (1999) argues that the West has imposed legal frameworks, textual orientation, views about science, rules for practice, and selection of speakers and experts, which derive from liberal scholarship. Prevailing approaches to formal NGO development tend to require a legal framework for organization rather than informal or traditional forms. A textual orientation insists that practice is not real unless it can be documented in writing; oral traditions then lose their legitimacy. Science, expressed as social science research is the means for evaluation, and increasingly organizations are required to use tools and criteria from the business world to plan, with quantitative methods used to evaluate success in practice (Dar & Cooke, 2008). The expert has become the person of training, speaking for those served by service organizations. Greater training, obsession with technicism and professionalism has resulted in the devaluing and displacement of people who speak and act on their own behalf. This tends to lead to formal rules for practice with common forms of governance and similar expectations for formal accountability upwards to funders. Local knowledge and power is often cast aside or lost in the process. Such professionalization has implications for dividing NGOs and community organizations from social movements that are by definition less structured, have non-professional leadership, and are based on experiential/ struggle knowledge/traditions and radical ideologies (INCITE! Women of Color Against Violence, 2007; Choudry, 2009; Choudry & Shragge, 2012). Most chapters in this collection, especially those by Africa, Vukov, and Sinwell, address these concerns.

Another pressure which forces managerialist organizational governance structures and practices onto local organizations comes through donor funding from NGOs (mainly based in the North, and often themselves heavily reliant on state support) or governments, often expressed as sub-contracting relationships, or foundations/trusts (see Sinwell, and Kim & Campbell in this collection). Funding criteria and reporting guidelines place a heavy burden of expectations on organizations which may not have the capacity to do the administrative work associated with this, nor fit neatly into criteria, guidelines and goals set by funders. Organizations are then in a dilemma, forced to stand on principles and strive for self-reliance or at least identify those relatively rare funders who do not impose such conditions. They may be compelled to transform their organization by adopting particular forms of professional practices, functions and priorities. Project-by-project funding can also constrain or undermine the building of a broader framework of analysis and focus for mobilization (Kamat, 2004; Petras & Veltmeyer, 2001, 2005). In this book, Kim & Campbell's chapter on Kyrgyzstan notes how routine practices of 'good governance' required of local NGOs in managing externally funded projects and in accounting for that funding are integral and taken for granted elements of global neoliberal capitalism, thus subverting the interests of women who are supposedly being empowered through NGO projects.

We are concerned with the limits that these trends – and others identified by the contributors in this volume – place on the nature of political space available for more sharply critical or reflexive views inside NGO networks and official community organizations, and in wider society. Frequently, organizers' insights and theorizing from within the context of concrete social struggles are not seen as being as worthy, informed and valid as academic viewpoints, or the perspectives of professional lobbyists and campaigners (Bevington & Dixon, 2005; Kelley, 2002; Reinsborough, 2004). Moreover, there is an underlying assumption that NGOs can convince officials and politicians with rational persuasion, drawing upon the work of people seen as credible researchers, rather than through building counter-power from below. In his chapter on food movement politics in this volume, for example, Kneen asks whether it should be a priority to build a political movement from the bottom up, or to pursue a more elitist course whereby an NGO addresses the state rather than the public?

Prospects: Looking ahead

A major contribution of this collection is the explicit grounding of these chapters in an analysis that builds on social movement critiques of state, capital and civil society. While cautioning against overextension of analyses and forms of social action and counter-power which have arisen in response to the phenomena associated with NGOization, we believe that lessons learnt in each chapter can inform wider social struggles and ways forward. In conclusion, we re-emphasize the importance of both micro- and macro-political and economic analysis, an understanding of the dialectical relationship between organizational form, geo-historical, socio-political, and economic contexts, the politics of knowledge production and forms of social action, and histories, trajectories, and repertoires of social movements in different contexts.

This book attends to connections between national and global shifts in capitalism and colonial relations, as well as critical traditions of organizing for social change. Hence NGOs and NGOization are discussed in terms of how these actors and processes play out on the ground and relate to specific contexts and geo-historical processes. We show how social movements/local traditions of social action and broader political struggles respond to these challenges and the impacts of NGOs on political space and society (particularly Sinwell, Africa, Kapoor and Swamy in this collection). We also demonstrate how these are linked with global/intergovernmental processes or institutions that have encouraged new spaces and roles for certain kinds of NGOs to operate in multi-scalar ways (see Venne, Choudry, Swamy, and Kim & Campbell chapters). Our volume therefore links how all of these trends relate to the challenges for building and strengthening social movements that will confront capitalist/colonial relations at national and international levels.

Hegemonic NGO practices and the dynamic of NGOization are being challenged by knowledge and mobilization strategies arising from past and present anti-imperialist and anti-colonial struggles (see chapters by Africa, Choudry, Kapoor, and Venne in this volume). While in some contexts there appear to be stark, polarized differences in organizational forms and political positions, between NGOs and social movements and/or community mobilizations (as in Kapoor's chapter), this collection also highlights the tensions, contradictions and ambiguities which can help to problematize overly binaristic, generalized characterizations of 'co-opted NGOs' vs. 'radical social movements'. But by bringing together and drawing upon contributions from a range of contexts and struggles it also re-examines common concerns and phenomena arising from NGOization.

Linda Smith (1999) notes the way in which international Indigenous Peoples' networks with an anti-colonial analysis of 'development' can offer alternatives to the dominant model: 'The sharing of resources and information may assist groups and communities to collaborate with each other and to protect each other. The development of international protocols and strategic alliances can provide a more sustained critique of the practices of states and corporations' (p. 105). Burgmann and Ure (2004) suggest that in the struggle for opponents of neoliberalism to theorize a convincing alternative, the contributions of Indigenous Peoples' struggles for self-determination are very useful. They assert that

the practical critique of neoliberalism embodied in indigenous people's resistance to their incorporation into the global market is one informed by an often acute recognition of not only the global dimensions of such resistance but also an acknowledgment of anti-imperialist struggles stretching back over many hundreds of years (p. 57).

This has also 'enabled non-indigenous groups and movements to root their critique in an anti-capitalist perspective that emanates from non-Western sources' (p. 57). Venne's chapter here however warns that that some Indigenous Peoples' NGOs have assisted state governments in undermining the Declaration on the Rights of Indigenous Peoples and other initiatives of Indigenous Peoples for self-determination. D'Souza (2010) contends that one of the most urgent tasks for today is the reconceptualization of decolonization. We concur. As Randall Williams (2010), argues 'nothing seems . . . *less* outdated than the work of Fanon and the by-now classic decolonizing ideal of justice he advanced' (p. 106).

References

Al-Ali, N. & Pratt, N. (2009). *What Kind of Liberation? Women and the Occupation of Iraq*. Berkeley: University of California Press.

Alvarez, S.E. (1999). 'Advocating feminism: The Latin American Feminist NGO "Boom"'. *International Feminist Journal of Politics, 1*(2), 181–209.

Alvarez, S.E. (2009). 'Beyond NGO-ization? Reflections from Latin America'. *Development 52*(2), 175–184.

Armstrong, E. & Prashad, V. (2005). 'Exiles from a Future Land: Moving Beyond Coalitional Politics'. *Antipode, 37*(1), January, 181–185.

Barry-Shaw, N. & Jay, D.O. (2012). *Paved with Good Intentions: Canada's Development NGOs from Idealism to Imperialism*. Black Point, NS: Fernwood.

Bebbington, A.J., Hickey, S., & Mitlin, D.C. (Eds.). (2008) *Can NGOs Make a Difference? The Challenge of Development Alternatives*. London and New York: Zed Books.

Bevington, D. & Dixon, C. (2005). 'Movement-Relevant Theory: Rethinking Social Movement Scholarship and Activism'. *Social Movement Studies 4* (3), 185–208.

Biel, R. (2000). *The New Imperialism: Crisis and Contradictions in North/South Relations*. London and New York: Zed Books.

Blood, R. (2005). 'Should NGOs be viewed as "political corporations"?' *Journal of Communication Management, 9*(2), 120–133.

Bricmont, J. (2006). *Humanitarian Imperialism: Using Human Rights to Sell War*. New York: Monthly Review Press.

Burgmann, V. & Ure, A. (2004). 'Resistance to neoliberalism in Australia and Oceania'. In Polet, F, and CETRI. *Globalizing Resistance: The State of Struggle* (pp. 52–67). London: Pluto.

Burrowes, N., Cousins, M., Rojas, P.X., & Ude, I. (2007) 'On Our Own Terms: Ten Years of Radical Community Building with Sista II Sista' In: INCITE! Women of Color Against Violence. (Eds.). *The Revolution Will Not be Funded: Beyond the Non-Profit Industrial Complex* (pp. 215–234). Boston, MA.: South End Press.

Choudry, A. (2009). 'Challenging Colonial Amnesia in Social Justice Activism'. In Kapoor, D. (Ed.) *Education, Decolonization and Development: Perspectives from Asia, Africa and the Americas*. Rotterdam: Sense.

Choudry, A. & Kapoor, D. (Eds.) (2010). *Learning from the Ground Up: Global Perspectives on Social Movements and Knowledge Production*. New York: Palgrave Macmillan.

Choudry, A. & Shragge, E. (2012). 'Disciplining Dissent: NGOs and Community Organizations'. In L. Montesinos Coleman & K. Tucker (Eds.) *Situating Global Resistance: Between Discipline and Dissent* (pp.109–123). London: Routledge.

Dar, S. & Cooke, B. (Eds.) (2008). *The New Development Management: Critiquing the Dual Modernization*. London and New York: Zed Books.

De Waal, A. (1997). *Famine Crimes: Politics and the Disaster Relief Industry in Africa*. Bloomington: Indiana University Press.

D'Souza, R. (2010). 'Three Actors, Two Geographies, One Philosophy: The Straightjacket of Social Movements'. In S.C. Motta & A. Nilsen (Eds.) *Social Movements and the Postcolonial Dispossession, Development and Resistance in the Global South* (pp. 227–249). New York: Palgrave Macmillan.

Duffield, M. (2001). *Global Governance and the New Wars: The Merging of Development and Security*. London: Zed Books.

Eschle, C. (2001). 'Globalizing Civil Society? Social Movement and the Challenge of Global Politics from Below'. In P. Hamel, H. Lustiger-Thaler, J. Nederveen Pieterse, & S. Roseneil (Eds.) *Globalization and Social Movements* (pp. 61–85). Basingstoke: Palgrave.

Falk, R. (1999). *Predatory Globalization: A Critique*. Cambridge: Polity Press.

Fanon, F. (1968). *The Wretched of the Earth*. New York: Grove Press.

Faraclas, N. (2001). 'Melanesia, the Banks, and the BINGOs: Real Alternatives are Everywhere (Except in the Consultants' Briefcases)'. In V. Bennholdt-Thomsen, N. Faraclas, & C. von Werlhof (Eds.) *There is an Alternative: Subsistence and Worldwide Resistance to Corporate Globalization* (pp. 67–76). London: Zed Books.

Ferguson, J. (1994). *The Anti-Politics Machine: 'Development', Depoliticization, and Bureaucratic Power in Lesotho*. Minneapolis: University of Minnesota Press.

Fernando, J.L. (2011). *The Political Economy of NGOs: State Formation in Sri Lanka and Bangladesh*. London: Pluto.

Fisher, W.F. (1997). 'Doing Good? The Politics and Antipolitics of NGO Practices'. *Annual Review of Anthropology*, 26, 439–64.

Fowler, A.F. (2000). 'Introduction – Beyond Partnership: Getting Real About NGO Relationships in the Aid System'. In A.F. Fowler (Ed.) *Questioning Partnership: The Reality of Aid and NGO Relations – Special issue of Institute of Development Studies Bulletin, 31* (3), 1–13.

Gallin, D. (2000, June). 'Trade Unions and NGOs: A Necessary Partnership for Social Development'. *Civil Society and Social Movements Programme Paper* (1). United Nations Research Institute for Social Development.

Goodman, J. (2002). 'Introduction'. In J. Goodman (Ed.). *Protest and Globalization: Prospects for Transnational Solidarity* (pp. viii–xxv). Sydney: Pluto.

Greenfield, G. (2001). 'The Success of Being Dangerous: Resisting Free Trade and Investment Regimes'. *Studies in Political Economy*, 64, 83–90.

Hewson, P. (2005). '"It's the Politics, Stupid". How Neoliberal Politicians, NGOs and Rock Stars Hijacked the Global Justice Movement at Gleneagles . . . and How We Let Them'. In D. Harvie, K. Milburn, B. Trott, & D. Watts (Eds.) *Shut them down! The G8, Gleneagles 2005 and the Movement of Movements* (pp. 135–149). Leeds: Dissent! and New York: Autonomedia.

IBON Research Department. (2003). 'Campaigning Against Oil TNCs in the Philippines'. In A. Choudry (Ed.) *Effective Strategies in Confronting Transnational Corporations* (pp. 89–111). Manila: Asia-Pacific Research Network.

INCITE! 'Women of Color Against Violence' (Ed.) (2007). *The Revolution Will Not be Funded: Beyond the Non-Profit Industrial Complex*. Cambridge, MA: South End Press.

Jad, I. (2004). 'The NGO-isation of Arab Women's Movements'. *IDS Bulletin*, 35: 34–42.

Jad, I. (2007). 'NGOs: Between Buzzwords and Social Movements'. *Development in Practice, 17,* 622–629.

Jordan, G. & Maloney, W.A. (1997). *The Protest Business? Mobilizing Campaign Groups.* Manchester and New York: Manchester University Press.

Kamat, S. (2002). *Development Hegemony: NGOs and the State in India.* Oxford: Oxford University Press.

Kamat, S. (2004). 'The Privatization of Public Interest: Theorizing NGO Discourse in a Neoliberal Era'. *Review of International Political Economy, 11* (1) (February), 155–176.

Kapoor, D. (2005). 'NGO Partnerships and the Taming of the Grassroots in Rural India'. *Development in Practice, 15*(2), pp. 210–215.

Kapoor, D. (2009). 'Participatory Action Research (par) and People's Participatory Action Research (PAR): Research, Politicization and Subaltern Social Movements (SSMs) in India'. In D. Kapoor & S. Jordan (Eds.) *Education, Participatory Action Research and Social Change: International Perspectives* (pp. 29–44). New York: Palgrave Macmillan.

Kapoor, D. (2012). 'Human Rights as Parabox and Equivocation in Contexts Adivasi (original dweller) Dispossession in India'. *Journal of Asian and African Studies, 47*(4), 404–420.

Keck, M.E. & Sikkink, K. (1998). *Activists Beyond Borders: Advocacy Networks in International Politics.* Ithaca, NY: Cornell University Press.

Kelley, R.D.G. (2002). *Freedom Dreams: The Black Radical Imagination.* Boston: Beacon Press.

Klein, N. (2007). *The Shock Doctrine: The Rise of Disaster Capitalism.* New York: Metropolitan Books.

Manji, F. & O'Coill, C. (2002). 'The Missionary Position: NGOs and Development in Africa'. *International Affairs, 78*(3), 567–83.

McNally, D. (2002). *Another World is Possible: Globalization and Anti-Capitalism.* Winnipeg: Arbeiter Ring.

Mojab, S. (2009). 'Imperialism, "Post-War Reconstruction" and Kurdish Women's NGOs'. In N. Al-Ali & N. Pratt (Eds.) *Women and War in the Middle East: Transnational Perspectives* (pp. 99–128). London: Zed Books.

Petras, J. (2002). 'Porto Alegre 2002: A Tale of Two Forums'. *Monthly Review, 53,* 56–61.

Petras, J. & Veltmeyer, H. (2001). *Globalization Unmasked: Imperialism in the 21st Century.* New Delhi: Madhyam Books.

Petras, J. & Veltmeyer, H. (2003). *System in Crisis: The Dynamics of Free Market Capitalism.* Black Point, N.S.: Fernwood.

Petras, J. & Veltmeyer, H. (2005). *Social Movements and State Power: Argentina, Brazil, Bolivia, Ecuador.* London: Pluto Press.

Piven, F.F. & Cloward, R.A. (1977). *Poor People's Movements: Why They Succeed, How They Fail.* New York: Pantheon.

Rajagopal, B. (2003). *International Law from Below: Development, Social Movements and Third World Resistance.* Cambridge: Cambridge University Press.

Reinsborough, P. (2004). 'Post-Issue Activism – Decolonizing the Revolutionary Imagination: *Values Crisis, the Politics of Reality and Why There's Going to be a Common Sense Revolution in this Generation'.* In D. Solnit (Ed.) *Globalize Liberation:*

How to Uproot the System and Build a Better World (pp. 161–211). San Francisco: City Lights.

Rojas, P.X. (2007). 'Are the Cops in Our Heads and Hearts?' In INCITE! Women of Color Against Violence (Ed.) *The Revolution Will Not be Funded: Beyond the Non-Profit Industrial Complex* (pp. 197–214). Boston, MA: South End Press.

Rucht, D. (1999). 'The Transnationalization of Social Movements: Trends, Causes, Problems'. In D. della Porta, H. Kriesi, & D. Rucht (Eds.) *Social Movements in a Globalizing World* (pp. 206–222). Houndmills, Basingstoke: Macmillan Press and New York: St Martin's Press.

Smith, A. (2007a). 'The NGOization of the Palestine Liberation Movement: Interviews with Hatem Bazian, Noura Erekat, Atef Said and Zeina Zaateri'. In INCITE! Women of Color Against Violence (Eds.) *The Revolution Will Not be Funded: Beyond the Non-Profit Industrial Complex* (pp. 165–182). Boston, MA: South End Press.

Smith, A. (2007b). 'Introduction: The Revolution Will Not be Funded'. In INCITE! Women of Color Against Violence (Ed.) *The Revolution Will Not be Funded: Beyond the Non-Profit Industrial Complex* (pp. 1–18). Boston, MA: South End Press.

Smith, D.E. (1987). *The Everyday World as Problematic: A Feminist Sociology.* Toronto: University of Toronto Press.

Smith, L.T. (1999). *Decolonizing Methodologies: Research and Indigenous Peoples.* Dunedin: University of Otago Press and London: Zed Books.

Townsend, J.G. & Townsend, A.R. (2004). 'Accountability, Motivation and Practice: NGOs North and South'. *Social and Cultural Geography, 5*(2), 271–284.

Veltmeyer, H. (2007). *Illusions and Opportunities: Civil Society in the Quest for Social Change.* Halifax: Fernwood, and London: Zed Books.

Wallace, T. (2003). 'NGO Dilemmas: Trojan Horses for Global Neoliberalism?' In L. Panitch & C. Leys (Eds.). *Socialist Register 2004: The New Imperial Challenge* (pp. 202–219). London: Merlin.

Williams, R. (2010). *The Divided World: Human Rights and its Violence.* Minneapolis: University of Minnesota Press.

Wood, E.M. (1995). *Democracy Against Capitalism: Renewing Historical Materialism.* New York: Cambridge University Press.

Wood, E.M. (1998). 'Labor, Class and State in Global Capitalism'. In E.M. Wood, P. Meiksins, & M. Yates (Eds.) *Rising From the Ashes? Labor in the Age of 'Global' Capitalism* (pp. 3–16). New York: Monthly Review Press.

1

Saving Biodiversity, for Whom and for What? Conservation NGOs, Complicity, Colonialism and Conquest in an Era of Capitalist Globalization

Aziz Choudry

> Colonization is an age old process of theft and control facilitated by doctrines of conquest such as the Manifest Destiny and Terra Nullius, that claim the land as empty (except for the millions of aboriginals living there), and non-productive (in its natural state). As the self-proclaimed 'discoverers' of crops, medicinal plants, genetic resources, and traditional knowledge, these bioprospectors become the new 'owners'. Intellectual property rights are being used to turn nature and life processes into 'private property'. As private property, it is alienable; that is, it can be owned, bought and sold as a commodity. The result is a legitimized process for thievery, which we call 'biocolonialism' (Harry, 2001, n.p.).

Introduction

In many contexts, particularly (but not only) in the global South, longstanding resistance to global free market capitalism in its different forms has spanned several decades (Choudry, 2003, 2010; Flusty, 2004; McNally, 2002; Motta & Nilsen, 2011). From the more critical currents of the coalitions and networks of non-governmental organizations (NGOs), social movements and activist groups which came to be known as the 'global justice' or 'anti-globalization' movement – including Indigenous Peoples in both Southern and Northern contexts (Jackson, 2007), as well as the prescient anti-colonial thinking of Fanon (1968) – come reminders that today's 'globalization' is another stage in much older processes of colonialism and capitalism. While numerous scholars and political commentators celebrated the ascendancy of NGOs and the rise of 'global civil society', more radical critiques charged that the environmental, aid and development, and advocacy NGOs which dominated this milieu and their campaigns were attempting to humanize capitalist exploitation. Some take the critique further, arguing that through their refusal to confront ongoing colonial practices, these NGOs are themselves behaving as colonizers.

This chapter argues that rather than challenging dominant state or corporate practices and capitalist power relations, environmental NGOs often serve elite economic and political interests and are themselves deeply colonial in their practice and discourse. I situate my analysis of environmental NGO practices in an anti-colonial and anti-capitalist framework of understanding. Here I identify and question hegemonic environmental NGO practices, perspectives and normative frameworks in the context of new threats posed by the imposition of intellectual property rights (IPR) regimes, and the increasing power and reach of transnational capital into new frontiers for profit. Inclusion of intellectual property rights provisions in international free trade and investment agreements, and the rise in bioprospecting – what Executive Director of the Indigenous Peoples Council on Biocolonialism, Debra Harry (Northern Paiute) terms 'biocolonialism' – is an important factor, a major focus, and significant area of tension between some Indigenous Peoples and major environmental NGOs. To illustrate this, I discuss two examples of conflict between NGOs and struggles for self-determination by Indigenous Peoples in their territories: the Royal Forest and Bird Protection Society of New Zealand (Forest and Bird) and United States (US)-headquartered Conservation International. As Giovanna Di Chiro (1998) contends, challenges to mainstream environmentalism often argue that an effective movement 'must integrate, not dichotomize, the histories and relationships of people and their natural environments' (p. 138).

Many critical scholars and activists (Beder, 1997; Burton, 2001; Lubbers, 2002; Rowell, 1996; Tokar, 1997) have emphasized the role of major international environmental NGOs in facilitating the greenwashing of corporations with controversial records of violations of environmental and human rights violations through funding, joint initiatives and various 'partnerships' and collaborations which project environmental concern of some kind. Several contributors in this book illustrate how NGOs are often deeply integrated into neoliberal capitalist relations at national and international levels, attempt to dominate the political space and undermine grassroots movements, and abandon or pull back from demands for genuine and deep transformation of the capitalist system and its power relations. Alongside the extension of colonialism into the control of nature and the appropriation of Indigenous Peoples' knowledge by corporations for private profit, environmental NGOs through their acts and omissions often act in complicity with state and business interests encroaching on the lands of Indigenous communities. Reflecting on dominant forms of environmentalism, Di Chiro (1998) points out 'the colonial discourse of Euro-American forms of "nature talk"':

> Although 'nature talk' separates humans from nature and posits them as superior to nature, it specifies that some humans are in fact part of nature. In other words, particular Euro-American romantic constructions of nature have been and continue to be problematic and even genocidal for people who have been characterized as being more like nature and thus less than human (p.132).

Elsewhere I suggest that dominant forms of NGO practice tend to fragment and compartmentalize struggles for social and environmental justice (Choudry, 2010). In turn, compartmentalized approaches to addressing capitalist globalization that do not confront the systemic nature of capitalism can only be of limited effectiveness. For many NGO campaigns, this compartmentalization typically occurs around reducing systems to issues (e.g., agriculture, services, 'the environment', 'human rights', and so on), regional or country-specific priorities, sectors (women, workers, farmers, Indigenous Peoples, etc.) and institutions and agreements (World Trade Organization (WTO), Free Trade Area of the Americas (FTAA), etc.) without a broader underlying framework of analysis necessarily informing action against global capitalism. This produces a fragmented analysis. This chapter concludes with a discussion of challenges to move past this model: potential ways forward that arise from anti-colonial understandings and struggles.

Intellectual property rights and the genetic goldrush

The imposition and implementation of IPR regimes has been a major concern since the expansion of international trade and economic negotiations during the Uruguay Round of the General Agreement on Tariffs and Trade (GATT – which established the WTO). This has been particularly true with increased commercial interest in new avenues for profit extraction from biodiversity and traditional knowledge. The concept of intellectual property rights itself has been strongly challenged, especially by Indigenous Peoples. It is based on a scientific reductionism which arose within Western capitalist society and which reduces all phenomena to their component parts. Maori researcher Aroha Mead (1997) says: '[E]ach level of reduction presents an increased scientific opportunity' (p. 70). She explains that intellectual property laws 'do not regard existent Indigenous knowledge as being an intellectual property and deserving of protection, rather they consider such knowledge as "common" and define human intervention based on what non-Indigenous peoples "add" to what has existed for generations' (p. 70).

The notion of intellectual property arose from interlocking Western capitalist doctrines of commerce, science, and the law, which were used to justify and expand colonization. The idea that knowledge can be created, owned, bought, or sold by a single inventor conflicts with many Indigenous and non-capitalist views that knowledge is inextricably linked to culture, spirituality, identity, and place, and is created communally over time (Argumedo & Pimbert, 2006; Jackson, 1997, 2007). Intellectual property rights commodify and privatize knowledge for exclusive exploitation and private profit. Meanwhile, consolidation of the biotech industry has continued, creating mega-corporations with global reach and control. Owning a life-form patent has a far greater reach than owning an individual sheep or tree. For US researchers Hope Shand and Martin Teitel (1997), this distinction 'can be likened to the difference between owning a lake and owning the chemical formula for water. A patent holder for water's chemical formula would have the legal right not only to decide who could have access to a particular lake, but to water anywhere, and to the use of the chemical formula for any purpose'. The WTO's Agreement on the Trade-Related aspects of Intellectual Property Rights (TRIPS) and even more radical IPR provisions in bilateral and regional free trade agreements are all tools to expand, intensify, and lock in a regime of monopoly control over life itself.

Not seeing the forest for the trees: Silences and blinkers in environmental NGO discourse

In settler-colonial states like Aotearoa/New Zealand, particularly for many New Zealand NGOs, the dominant frame for most environmental, 'global justice', or 'anti-globalization' campaigns typically proposes a program of reforms and strengthening environmental regulation and social democratic governance as alternative solutions to the dominant model of development. However, underpinning this formula are assumptions about supposedly universal and shared national values that must be reclaimed to (re)build a fairer, greener society. There is little reflexivity on the part of such NGOs about the knowledge on which they base their concepts of social justice and their own roles in reproducing colonial power relations. Largely missing from this dominant frame is any genuine acknowledgment of the colonial underpinnings of the state and society, the ongoing denial of Indigenous Peoples' rights to self-determination, and the highly racialized construction of New Zealand citizenship and the state. For NGOs that address local issues, Maori have been frequently reduced to a token sidebar in policy statements and declarations, a tragic case study, or rendered invisible, marginal, irrelevant, or too problematic for inclusion in narratives and communications/campaigns designed to appeal to liberal (mainly non-Maori) audiences.

Maori concerns about the WTO TRIPS regime and threats to traditional knowledge have been widely expressed since the early days of the Uruguay Round of the GATT. With increasing pressures to harmonize intellectual property laws and growing commercial interest in Indigenous knowledge, Maori knowledge and native flora and fauna have been targeted by transnational corporations as new sources of profit. One treaty claim, heard before the Waitangi Tribunal[1] and known as WAI 262 – lodged over native flora, fauna, traditional knowledge, and intellectual property – had great international significance as an assertion of sovereignty and a direct challenge to companies that are commodifying and privatizing knowledge and biodiversity, facilitated by states which are revamping their patent laws and plant variety protection legislation for the benefits of industry. Globally, as Maori academic Linda Smith (1999) puts it, in this 'new wave of exploration, discovery, exploitation and appropriation'[,] '[r]esearchers enter communities armed with goodwill in their front pockets and patents in their back pockets . . . No matter how appalling their behaviours, how insensitive and offensive their personal actions may be, their acts and intentions are always justified as being for the "good of mankind"' (p. 24).

In this claim, Maori argued that traditional knowledge could not be squeezed into a colonial/Western legal intellectual property framework that denies spiritual, cultural, metaphysical aspects of traditional knowledge including its collective nature (Jackson, 1994; Smith, 1999). Several non-Maori environmental NGOs publicly opposed the WAI 262 claim, notably the Royal Forest and Bird Protection Society, viewing themselves and the government as the rightful guardians of Aotearoa/New Zealand's biodiversity. Founded in 1923, Forest and Bird is Aotearoa/New Zealand's largest conservation organization and claims to give nature 'a voice'.[2] For Maori lawyer Moana Jackson (1997) this NGO's positioning and discourse was deeply colonial:

> Conservationists have tended to adopt a narrow self-interested approach which in a revisiting of colonisation essentially claims that *iwi** have neither the right nor the ability to protect our resources. They seem to adopt the naïve view that the Crown should protect things for all New Zealanders, even though that is contrary to the Treaty, and even though the Crown is still attempting to sell off our assets to the highest multinational bidder (p. 2).

Maori mobilization in defense of traditional knowledge and resistance to the imposition of intellectual property regimes offers further possibilities to popularize a politics of decolonization/anti-colonial resistance interwoven with a clear rejection of free market capitalism. Maori expertise and advocacy on the threats of intellectual property regimes has also been mobilized internationally in coalitions of other Indigenous Peoples (see Venne in this volume).

Throughout the 1990s, in its campaign and media work against TRIPs and intellectual property provisions in other free trade and investment agreements, the small activist group GATT Watchdog, for which I was an organizer and educator, linked international struggles and concerns against these agreements with Maori struggles

---

* Often translated as 'nation' or 'tribe' – the largest social unit in Maori society.

for self-determination. Together with this, it openly confronted these environmental NGOs about their trust in a neoliberal, colonial state that had privatized, commodified, and commercialized as much of the country as it could, while Indigenous Peoples continued to protect what remained of their territories' biodiversity. At the time of the Forest and Bird statement, GATT Watchdog (1997) released the following response:

> Those who, like [Forest and Bird], take issue with much of the WAI 262 claim and advocate for property rights over Indigenous flora and fauna to be vested with the Crown not only choose to ignore violations of Indigenous rights in this country, but also recent history, where successive governments have sold off state-owned assets left, right and centre, and turned New Zealand into an open investment playground at the expense of local people. Effectively, [Forest and Bird's] opposition to this claim amounts to support for the likely eventuality that many of these property rights will be handed over or sold to foreign, probably transnational investors.

Such confrontations are necessary to contest racism and colonialism in dominant NGO discourses and practice and provided support for the analysis of Maori claimants, connecting Maori sovereignty and environmental justice to the increased unease and outrage felt by a growing number of New Zealanders towards economic globalization and domestic market reforms. Moreover, Maori – and other Indigenous Peoples' – mobilization around traditional knowledge and resistance to the imposition of intellectual property regimes offers further pedagogical possibilities to popularize a decolonization position that is interwoven with rejection of capitalism (Choudry, 2007). However, there are also obstacles to overcome when trying to build broader support for such a position. State, private sector, and international institutional claims to legally recognize Indigenous Peoples' status, or to consult and form 'partnerships' with them, must be critically examined to ascertain whether these are meaningful moves to address colonial injustice, or merely new forms of assimilation and cooptation into neoliberal/colonial frameworks (see Venne in this volume).

Tensions between Indigenous Peoples and environmentalist and human rights NGO networks can arise when NGOs do not see how integrationist approaches to development or conservation measures can violate Indigenous Peoples' rights. Other tensions stem from an emphasis by some NGOs to prioritize support for individual rather than collective rights. In the case of coalitions supporting the Lubicon Cree, in Canada, Long (1997) pointed out how the interests of different NGOs and activist groups in the issue of the forestry transnational corporation Daishowa's planned logging on unceded Lubicon territory could lead to a future clash. This would be between those who frame the struggle as being fundamentally about the right of Lubicon to self-determination and land rights and those adopting an environmentalist frame that emphasizes the protection and preservation of wildlife and the natural environment. Power dynamics in environmental coalitions often subordinate Indigenous Peoples' perspectives. Long contends that 'failure to take the diversity of coalition and movement supporters into account can lead to a distorted, even mythical view of coalitions as seen by the movements belonging to them. Since even the smallest coalitions give expression to a diversity of beliefs, perspectives, and interests that are themselves open to challenge and change, counter-hegemonic coalitions, and the larger social movements around them are inherently fragile phenomena' (p. 166). Indigenous Peoples' struggles for self-determination not only have to deal with colonial states and global capital, but often find themselves caught in an industry of making and marketing NGO advocacy campaigns where their contexts and histories are erased, contested, revised, or repackaged and where coalition power dynamics and hierarchies of knowledge subordinate the positions and experience of Indigenous Peoples in a reproduction of the status quo.

Conservation International: Leading brand of green imperialism?

Colonial occupation itself was a matter of seizing, delimiting, and asserting control over a physical geographical area – of writing on the ground a new set of social and spatial relations. The writing of new spatial relations (territorialization) was, ultimately, tantamount to the production of boundaries and hierarchies, zones and enclaves; the subversion of existing property arrangements; the classification of people according to different categories; resource extraction; and, finally, the manufacturing of a large reservoir of cultural imaginaries. These imaginaries gave meaning to the enactment of differential rights to differing categories of people for different purposes within the same space; in brief, the exercise of sovereignty. Space was therefore the raw material of sovereignty and the violence it carried with it. Sovereignty meant occupation, and occupation meant relegating the colonized into a third zone between subjecthood and objecthood (Mbembe, 2003, pp. 25–26).

While the Forest and Bird example highlights a domestic environmental NGO's complicity with a colonial state (New Zealand) and an uncritical stance toward global free market capitalism as a threat to the environment, the remainder of this chapter contends with a global organization with operations in over thirty countries on four continents. Conservation International (CI) occupies the highest rung of the environmental NGO ladder, along with The Nature Conservancy and the World Wide Fund for Nature (WWF) – 'Big Green' as these players are often referred to. CI's mission statement reads: 'Building upon a strong foundation of science, partnership and field demonstration, CI empowers societies to responsibly and sustainably care for nature, our global biodiversity, for the well-being of humanity'.[3] In recent years, CI has faced critical scrutiny at international and local levels, including as grounded opposition and critiques from those in the communities in which it operates and others monitoring 'conservation' (Carlsen, 2004; Choudry, 2003; Dowie, 2009; Radio Mundo Real, 2011a, 2011b). The complex global web of partnerships, collaborations, initiatives, and projects which CI weaves is expansive; its major corporate partners include BP, Cargill, CEMEX, Chevron, Exxon Mobil, JPMorgan Chase & Co., McDonalds, Mitsubishi, Northrop Grumman, Sony, Starbucks, United Airlines, Walmart, and Walt Disney.

Conservation International offers a concrete example of a 'non-governmental' vehicle for transnational corporations seeking to project a green image of themselves, at a time when they are confronted with global resistance and opposition to their activities. A June 2003 report by the Chiapas, Mexico-based El Centro para el Análisis Político y la Investigación Social (Center for Political Analysis and Social Investigation, or CAPISE) dubbed Conservation International a Trojan horse of the US government and transnational corporations (CAPISE, 2003; Bellinghausen, 2003). Many activists in Latin America (and beyond) view the organization as a new *conquistador* which displaces people, occupies lands, appropriates traditional knowledge, and contributes to conflict and militarization in the name of conservation.

CI has been a proponent – and beneficiary – of controversial debt-for-nature swaps whereby commitments to preserve and 'sustainably manage' ecologically significant lands have been traded for writing off a small part of a government's debt. CI's Guerin-McManus (2000) described this as the 'greening of international finance'. But others see these deals as an ingenious way to facilitate both easier access to bioprospectors for industry, as well as easier extraction of yet more resources from the South – from Indigenous Peoples in particular. Moreover, CI fails to challenge the social and environmental injustices created or worsened by a model of 'development' that burdens the majority of the world's peoples with unsupportable debts. Dowie (2009) has documented how many Indigenous Peoples have been displaced in the interests of 'conservation' through the establishment of conservation areas, sometimes set up at the behest of big environmental organizations.

In its first year, 1987, CI bought a small portion of Bolivia's debt in exchange for the Bolivian government agreeing to support the expansion of the Beni Biological Reserve, which contains some of the world's largest reserves of mahogany and tropical cedar. Critics charged that logging actually increased in the 'multiple use and conservation' buffer zone around the reserve. CI offered training and technical assistance on 'sustainable use' of the forest. The Chimane and Moxeno Indigenous Peoples were not consulted: their lands were divided up by sustainable development 'experts' and they were denied the chance to manage them communally (Tokar, 1997).

Despite a supposed mission shift in 2008, away from an almost singular emphasis on biodiversity conservation, bioprospecting remains central to CI's work. Its interest in 'hotspots' of endangered biodiversity has particular implications for many Indigenous Peoples who have endured and resisted waves of colonial dispossession, genocide and ecocide, including the appropriation of traditional knowledge and the flora and fauna that they have protected for many generations. Pharmaceutical companies seek to access Indigenous communities' knowledge in order to find valuable plants and their traditional ways of healing. This provides a far higher potential to develop pharmaceutical products than from random screening.

In the genetic gold rush, 'researchers' and companies, now backed by local and global patent regimes which grant the 'inventor' exclusive monopoly rights over new 'inventions', can deny the very communities which have developed natural cures or technologies the right to use them. CI's role is to provide relatively cheap scientific expertise for corporations well aware of the labor-intensive nature of searching out new potential products based on natural remedies or applications. A seemingly well-intentioned 'non-profit' organization like CI can act as an intermediary to gather knowledge and agreement from local communities, and can do much of the legwork in collecting and testing samples.

This friendly face of biocolonialism offers the modern-day equivalent of beads and trinkets to these communities. Exploitative and unethical 'benefit-sharing' agreements are drawn up, with a few market-based community economic development programs for the locals on the side: some ecotourism here, some fair trade coffee production there. CI's track record suggests a motivation to conserve biodiversity for bioprospecting by its private sector partners rather than concern for the rights of the peoples who have lived with – and protected – these ecosystems for so long.

In Panama, CI has collaborated with US-based International Cooperative Biodiversity Group (ICBG)[4], Monsanto and Novartis on what was claimed to be 'ecologically guided bioprospecting', seeking pharmaceutical and agricultural products from plants, fungi and insects (Kursar et al., 1999). The ICBG was also linked to CI's involvement in bioprospecting in Surinam, along with US pharmaceutical giant Bristol Myers Squibb, the Missouri Botanical Garden, BGVS (the Surinam Drug Company), and Dow AgroSciences. CI and the Missouri Botanical Garden collected plant samples. CI worked to win the trust of Indigenous communities and healers and negotiate a 'benefit-sharing' agreement. The Indigenous communities were offered a paltry percentage (believed to be around 2–3 percent) of any royalties, and it is unlikely that the communities fully understood the implications before they consented (van Vark, 1999; RAFI Communique, 1997). Without adequate and appropriate protection for the traditional knowledge of the communities, CI has helped clear the way for private companies to slap industrial patents on anything that looks promising.

By 2000, ICBG had reported that over 50 active compounds had been isolated from the Surinam samples (Kingston, 2001). In Mexico, CI's involvement in the Selva Lacandona, Chiapas, is deeply disturbing. Through a 1991 debt-for-nature swap, CI bought the right to set up a genetic research station in the Monte Azules Integral Biosphere reserve in the Selva (rainforest). The Mexican government has been engaged in a repressive military campaign against Indigenous Peoples in Chiapas, especially those which support the Zapatistas. They have been forcibly evicting Indigenous communities in Montes Azules, accusing them of destroying the rainforest (Bellinghausen, 2002). The Selva has been home to many Zapatista bases, as well as being an area rich in timber, biodiversity, oil, petroleum, and mineral resources. The presence of the Zapatistas and autonomous Indigenous communities in the region presents an obstacle to those like the Mexican government and transnational – especially US – corporations that want to exploit these resources.

CAPISE (2003) noted that CI's program of flyovers – part of their USAID-supported 'environmental monitoring' program – targeted areas occupied by Zapatista communities in planes bearing USAID (United States Agency for International Development) markings. In Chiapas, CI has been using state-of-the art geographical information systems technology, including high-resolution satellite imaging. CAPISE charged that the images from this operation were made available to USAID and could be used to identify the location of natural resources to commercial interests. CI has also given images to communities supported by the Mexican government as part of its campaign against the pro-Zapatista communities, which they claim are destroying the forest.

In the name of environmental protection, CI has contributed to the pitting of Indigenous communities against each other, raising fears of conflict in an area that is already heavily militarized by Mexico's army. In March 2003, the US NGO Global Exchange convened an emergency delegation to the area. According to one delegate, US activist Orin Langelle, contrary to CI claims, the destruction was most pronounced around military encampments, while the Indigenous villagers accused of destroying the forest had outlawed slash-and-burn techniques and were practicing sustainable organic agriculture (personal communication with author, 24 September 2003).

The giant Mexican agribusiness/biotechnology corporation, Grupo

Pulsar, has worked closely with CI in Mexico, donating USD 10 million to Conservation International-Mexico between 1996 and 2000. Pulsar's alleged concern for ecology and biodiversity does not extend to its main activities such as promotion of monoculture in Chiapas, including the planned planting of 300,000 hectares of eucalyptus trees. Chiapas-based Centro de Investigationes Economicas y Politicas de Accion Comunitaria (CIEPAC, 1999) argued that

> the Pulsar Group's 'donation' could more likely be a remuneration (but free of taxes, since it was a donation) for services lent by CI in bioprospecting within the Selva Lacandona. Pulsar has the technology, the resources and the business knowledge to know that there are large rewards awaiting the 'discovery' of some medicinal property extracted from samples from the Lacandona. CI 'facilitates' the Pulsar Group's entrance, it helps orient its technicians in the prospecting, while at the same time pacifying local populations with programmes that promote the expansion of monocrops around the Selva, while projecting a conservation façade to the world.

More recently, in the context of international approaches to climate change, the Mexican government has adopted a market-based vision of forests as mere carbon reservoirs. It has enthusiastically embraced the controversial market-based REDD (Reduced Emissions from Deforestation and Forest Degradation) mechanism. As noted by sociologist Gustavo Castro Soto (2011), director of Otros Mundos/Amigos de la Tierra México, the state of Chiapas

> . . . has thrown itself head-first into the race for climate change business, placing its forests, jungles and monoculture plantations at the service of the carbon market. Once again, in the climate change business, government subsidies for private companies are materialized with the participation of corporate transnational conservationist NGOs at the service of environmental profiteering. For instance, in 2009, the government of Chiapas began work on the Climate Change Action Program for the State of Chiapas (PACCCH), financed by the British Embassy, with Conservation International as a key actor in its implementation.

In December 2010, an agreement was signed between the Chiapas governor and Selva Lacandon communities who, says Castro Soto, will be used by the government 'to confront other organizations and Indigenous and peasant communities while facilitating their eviction, even with violence'. The governor is quoted as telling the communities involved in the agreement, 'You are going to be committed to protecting the reserves, to making sure no one goes in them, making sure no one cuts down the trees, making sure no one goes in there to hunt, you are going to protect them for the whole planet, for all of Chiapas, for all of Mexico, for all of humanity'. Yet right outside the area designated for the sale of carbon credits, the government will continue to promote the expansion of agro-industry, tourism development, industrial plantations of oil palm, and other activities that lead to deforestation (World Rainforest Movement, 2011).

In Chiapas, there are 1.3 million hectares of land considered natural reserves, of which almost 50 percent are in the Lacandon jungle. According to Castro Soto, the CI-planned pilot projects of 2011 in Chiapas come under the framework of a November 2010 agreement signed between former California Governor Schwarzenegger, Chiapas Governor Juan Sabines Guerrero and Brazilian Acre Governor Arnobio Marques de Almeida Junior. This agreement established the basis for initiating a carbon credit market incorporating REDD and other forest carbon schemes into the regulatory frameworks of the US and other countries (World Rainforest Movement, 2011; Bellinghausen, 2012).

Years earlier, in Guyana, Indigenous Peoples had accused CI of gross disrespect in signing a November 2002 memorandum of understanding with the Guyanese government to establish a protected area in the south of the country, impacting on the Wapishana and Wai Wai peoples. A statement from the Amerindian Peoples Association outlined various concerns, including CI's failure to consult with Indigenous Peoples, as well as how unresolved title claims to traditional lands that are now part of the new protected area were undermined by this new status imposed upon the communities (World Rainforest Movement, 2002).

CI has used its considerable financial resources, political influence and language of conservation to access, administer and buy biodiverse areas throughout the world and put them at the disposal of transnational corporations. CI's Center for Applied Biodiversity Science (CABS) claims to bring together leading experts in science and technology to collect and interpret data about biodiversity, develop strategic plans for conservation, and forge partnerships in all sectors that promote conservation goals. CABS runs what are typically three- to five week long Rapid Assessment Programs (RAPs) to 'rapidly provide biological information needed to catalyze the conservation of critically endangered habitats worldwide'. Through these and other programs, CI has been assembling biodiversity databases for different regions. RAP's slogan is 'So many species . . . so little time'. No doubt this sentiment is shared by the pharmaceutical and agro-chemical corporations that enjoy CI's support.

Controversy also shrouds CI's operations in Ecuador. In August 2011, Ecuador's Foreign Affairs Ministry and the Technical International Cooperation of Ecuador ruled that CI must leave Ecuador as a result of its refusal to fulfill two human rights protection resolutions (dated 2001 and 2010) from the Defensoria del Pueblo (Ecuador's Ombudsman), and because CI's state authorization to work in Ecuador expired in 2006 and had not been renewed. This followed two 2001 Defensoria del Pueblo rulings that CI should honor its obligations to Ecuadorian biologist Alfredo Luna by compensating him for the serious work-related injuries that he suffered several years before. CI, however, ignored these resolutions and, at the time of writing, remains in Ecuador (CONAIE, 2011). CI failed to adequately compensate Luna after he was severely disabled in an August 1993 plane crash in the Cordillera del Cóndor while working as part of a CI research team. Denied justice, Luna is a vocal critic of CI's activities and impacts in Ecuador. He has stated that the resource mapping, which CI conducted in its research mission on plant and animal species in the Cordillera del Cóndor and other parts of the region in the contested Amazon border between Ecuador and Peru, was sponsored by and used for the interests of mining companies and biopiracy (Radio Mundo Real, 2011b. See also: http://alfredolunavsconservacioninternacional.wordpress.com).

This raises questions as to whether, and how widely, major environmental NGOs like CI are employed by transnational corporations to make resource assessments in wilderness sensitive areas under the pretext of conservation. It also raises questions about whether this method is used as a way to bypass resource assessments that would require more legal mechanisms. Tamayo (2011) noted that oil company Texaco (now Chevron – one of CI's private sector partners) created a huge environmental disaster in Ecuador's Amazon region when it discharged massive amounts of contaminated water into lakes and rivers, poisoning many people and causing serious environmental damage. For this reason, Chevron has been prosecuted by a group of residents and Indigenous Peoples who demand a clean-up, compensation and reparation for the damages caused.

CI claims that it sets its priorities as follows: '[u]sing cutting-edge methods, we pinpoint specific regions overflowing with biological value where people, plants, and animals are desperately in need of conservation action. We focus on places where each dollar we spend will do the most good' (CI website, no date). Yet given the significant involvement of mining, oil, and gas corporations in CI's program, it is sobering to note that many of its 'biodiversity hotspots' and project operations are on or adjacent to major sites of oil, gas and mineral exploration and extraction. Conservation International also enjoys a close relationship with USAID – which actively promotes US corporate interests abroad (including biotechnology, pharmaceutical and agri-business sectors) in the guise of development assistance. Further, CI's website boasts that the US defense giant Northrop Grumman Corporation (NGC – maker of the Stealth bomber) 'is working with CI to develop and review its sustainability strategy and policies. NGC has also provided CI and its Tropical Ecology Assessment and Monitoring Network (TEAM) with remote sensing data as part of an effort to monitor long term biodiversity trends. NGC is also a member of CI's Business & Sustainability Council, a community of companies committed to leveraging their business experience and resources to protect nature for the benefit of humanity' (http://www.conservation. org/how/partnership/corporate/Pages/northrop–grumman.aspx).

Conclusion

Italian activist Antonio Onorati, in an interview with GRAIN (2012), discusses how many NGOs are 'self-referential', developing their strategies and priorities in isolation from social movements. In the case of Forest and Bird, the refusal to support Maori demands for self-determination and acknowledge their central role in maintaining the survival of Indigenous flora and fauna into the twenty-first century indicates a capitalist and colonial worldview which clearly delinks people from nature and compartmentalizes 'nature' as something which excludes humans. At the same time, one might argue that what Teju Cole (2012) calls the 'white savior industrial complex' characterizes the portrayal of the places in which CI operates. In this case it is perhaps doubly industrial, given the close involvement of transnational corporations and their executives in the organization. Conservation International is uncritical about the impact of economic injustice on the environment and biodiversity. Indeed, it proposes market solutions to address environmental destruction that has been caused or exacerbated by free market capitalism. It advances the view that the best way to conserve biodiversity is to privatize it. Bill Weinberg (2003) sees this worldview leading to tropical forests becoming 'corporate-administered genetic colonies'. While frequently opining that slash-and-burn agriculture and over-population threaten biodiversity, Conservation International willingly collaborates with, works for, and fails to condemn, some of the world's most ecologically destructive corporations and institutions devastating the planet.

Indeed there is an irony in CI's celebrity association with Harrison Ford, who is vice chair of its board of directors. The organization promotes itself as an environmental Indiana Jones, that consummate American hero/adventurer, which is up against '[i]mages of people of color in the mainstream environmental literature [which] not infrequently depict throngs of overbreeding, slashing-and-burning, border overflowing and ecologically incorrect Third Worlders or illegal immigrants' (Di Chiro, 1998, p. 132). As Di Chiro concludes: 'Such images encode these groups as anti-nature or out of touch with the natural world' (p. 132).

In addition to an analysis of globalization that understands it in terms of capitalist relations, an anti-colonial lens, drawing attention to past and present features of colonization and decolonization struggles, is a crucial conceptual resource for explicating and historicizing this phenomenon. It is essential to the understanding of contemporary asymmetries of power that exist between imperial powers (states and private capital) and Third World nations and within them. This lens is vital for analysis of the dynamics of contemporary capitalism and state power in colonial-settler states such as Aotearoa/New Zealand – and the roles that their governments, private sector, and NGOs play internationally. The diverse histories and dynamics of colonization and the rich conceptual resources that can be drawn from over five centuries of resistance to colonialism around the world are often overlooked in professionalized NGO approaches to the environment and social justice. As noted by D'Souza (2006), it is vital to retrieve, reappropriate and redevelop the idea of self-determination as a conceptual tool of social transformation in an era in which it has been overwritten or excluded from many scholarly analyses of imperialism and in the language of NGOs. Responses to biopiracy and the colonial intrusions of environmental NGOs in unceded Indigenous territories must go beyond mere state regulatory approaches, and be based on Indigenous Peoples' rights to self-determination – including the upholding of traditional systems, principles and practices of ecology and the right to regulate access to their territories and all that lies within them.

Notes

1   The Waitangi Tribunal is a commission of inquiry established under the Treaty of Waitangi Act 1975, charged with investigating and making recommendations on claims brought by Maori regarding actions or omissions of the Crown, since 1840, that breach promises made in the Treaty of Waitangi. It only has the authority to make recommendations to the New Zealand Government. See: http://www.waitangi-tribunal.govt.nz/. A Tribunal decision on the WAI 262 case was issued on 2 July 2011. For an overview and critique of the process from the perspective of a Maori lawyer involved with the claim, see: http://wai262.weebly.com/moana-jackson.html
2   See http://www.forestandbird.org.nz/.
3   CI statements on its mission and programs are taken from its website. See http://www.conservation.org.
4   The ICBG is a US-government backed program involving the National Institutes of Health, the National Science Foundation, the Foreign Agriculture Service of the US Department of Agriculture and the US Agency for International Development (USAID). See http://www.icbg.org.

References

Argumedo, A. & Pimbert, M. (2006). *Protecting Indigenous Knowledge Against Biopiracy in the Andes*. London: International Institute for Environment and Development (IIED). Available from: http://pubs.iied.org/14531IIED.html.

Beder, S. (1997). *Global Spin: The Corporate Assault on Environmentalism*. White River Junction, VT: Chelsea Green.

Bellinghausen, H. (2002, March 24). 'EU, organismos mundiales y trasnacionales quieren limpiar de indígenas *Montes Azules*'. *La Jornada*. Available from: http://www.jornada.unam.mx/2002/03/25/009n1pol.php?origen=politica.html.

Bellinghausen, H. (2003, June 8). 'Conservación Internacional, caballo de Troya de Gobierno y Trasnacionales de EU: Capise'. *La Jornada*. Available from: http://www.jornada.unam.mx/2003/06/08/016n1pol.php?origen=politica. php&fly=1.

Bellinghausen, H. (2012, 23 May). 'Cuestiona Investigación Programmea REDD porque se ha Destruido Identidad Indígena'. *La Jornada*. Available from: http://www.jornada.unam.mx/2012/05/23/politica/021n1pol.

Burton, B. (2001). 'When Corporations Want to Cuddle'. In G. Evans, J. Goodman, and N. Lansbury, N. (Eds.), *Moving Mountains: Communities Confront Mining and Globalization* (pp. 133–148). Otford, Sydney: Otford Press.

Carlsen, L. (2004). 'Conservation or Privatization? Biodiversity, the Global Market and the Mesoamerican Bio-Corridor'. In G. Otero (Ed.) *Mexico in Transition: Neoliberal Globalism, the State and Civil Society* (pp. 52–71). London and New York: Zed Books.

CAPISE (El Centro para el Análisis Político y la Investigación Social) (2003). 'Conservation International: The Trojan Horse'. Available from: http://enlinea. capise.org.mx/files/troan_horse.pdf.

Castro Soto, G. (2011, January 10). 'EnREDDar a Chiapas'. *El Escaramujo 1*. Available from: http://www.otrosmundoschiapas.org/index.php/component/content/article/118-el-escaramujo/897-el-escaramujo-enreddar-a-chiapas.html.

Choudry, A. (2003, October). 'Privatizing Nature, Plundering Biodiversity'. *Seedling*, 17–21.

Choudry, A. (2007). 'Transnational Coalition Politics and the De-Colonization of Pedagogies of Mobilization: Learning from Indigenous Movement Articulations Against Neo-Liberalism'. *International Education, 37*(1), 97–112.

Choudry, A. (2010). 'Global Justice? Contesting NGOization: Knowledge Politics and Containment in Anti-Globalization Networks'. In A. Choudry & D. Kapoor (Eds.) *Learning From the Ground Up: Global Perspectives on Knowledge Production in Social Movements* (pp. 17–34). New York: Palgrave Macmillan.

CIEPAC. (1999, September 18). 'Genetically Modified Organisms: Implications for Mexico and Chiapas'. *Chiapas al Dia*, No. 175. Available from: http://www. ciepac.org/bulletins/ingles/Ing175.html.

Cole, T. (2012, March 21). 'The White Savior Industrial Complex'. *The Atlantic*. Available from: http://www.theatlantic.com/international/archive/2012/03/the-white-savior-industrial-complex/254843/.

CONAIE (2011, January 18) 'Conservation International No Respeta a los Derechos Humanos en el Ecuador' – 'Conservation International does not Respect Human Rights in Ecuador'. *Confederación de Nacionalidades Indígenas del Ecuador (CONAIE)*. Available from: http://www.conaie.org/component/content/article/338-conservation-international-no-respecta-a-los-derechos-humanos-en-el-ecuador-?start=1.

Conant, J. (2011, April 7). 'A Broken Bridge to the Jungle: The California-Chiapas Climate Agreement Opens Old Wounds'. *Global Justice Ecology Project*. Available from: http://globaljusticeecology.org/publications.php?ID=546.

Conservation International website http://conservation.org

Di Chiro, G. (1998). 'Nature as Community: The Convergence of Environment and Social Justice'. In M. Goldman (Ed.), *Privatizing Nature: Political Struggles for the Global Commons* (pp. 120–143). New York: Pluto Press.

Dowie, M. (2009). *Conservation Refugees: The Hundred-Year Conflict Between Global Conservation and Native Peoples*. Cambridge, MA: MIT Press.

D'Souza, R. (2006). *Interstate Disputes Over Krishna Waters: Law, Science and Imperialism*. New Delhi: Orient Longman.

Fanon, F. (1968). *The Wretched of the Earth*. New York: Grove Press.

Flusty, S. (2004). *De-coca-colonization: Making the Globe from the Inside Out*. New York: Routledge.

GATT Watchdog (1997, September 15) 'Call for non-Maori to back Waitangi Tribunal Claim' (Media Release). Archived at: http://archives.econ.utah.edu/archives/aut-op-sy/1997m09/msg00070.html

GRAIN (2012). *The Great Food Robbery: How Corporations Control Food, Grab Land and Destroy the Climate*. Cape Town, Dakar, Nairobi and Oxford: Pambazuka Press.

Guerin-McManus, M. (2000). 'The Greening of International Finance: 10 Years of Debt-For Nature Swaps'. Unpublished paper on file with the author.

Harry, D. (2001). *Biopiracy and Globalization: Indigenous Peoples Face a New Wave of Colonialism*. Comments at the International Forum on Globalization Teach-in on Technology and Globalization, Humber College New York City, 24–25 February 2001. Available from: http://www.ipcb.org/publications/other_art/globalization.html.

Jackson, M. (1994, May). 'GATT and Rangatiratanga: Tripping the Lie Fantastic'. *Overview*, 50, 1–2.

Jackson, M. (1997, November). 'Flora, Fauna, and the Mysteries of GATT, APEC, and MAI.' *The Big Picture*. GATT Watchdog, *12*, 1–2.

Jackson, M. (2007). 'Globalisation and the Colonising State of Mind'. In M. Bargh (Ed.) *Resistance: An Indigenous Response to Neoliberalism* (pp. 167–182). Wellington: Huia.

Kingston, D. (2001). 'Biodiversity Conservation and Drug Discovery in Suriname. Explorations in Nature's Combinatorial Library'. *Pure Applied Chemistry*, *73*(3), 595–599.

Kursar, T.A., Capson, T. L., Coley, P. D., Corley, D.G., Gupta, M. B., Harrison, L.A., Ortega-Barria, E., & Windsor, D.M. (1999). 'Ecologically Guided Bioprospecting in Panama.' *Pharmaceutical Biology*, *37*, 114–126.

Long, D.A. (1997). 'The Precarious Pursuit of Justice: Counterhegemony in the Lubicon First National Coalition'. In Carroll, W.K. (ed.). *Organizing Dissent: Contemporary Social Movements in Theory and Practice* (pp. 151–170). Toronto: Garamond.

Lubbers, E. (Ed.) (2002). *Battling Big Business: Countering Greenwash, Infiltration and Other Forms of Corporate Bullying*. Monroe, Maine: Common Courage.

Mead, A.T.P. (1997). 'Cultural and Intellectual Property Rights of Indigenous Peoples of the Pacific'. In Government of the Republic of Fiji/Pacific Concerns Resource Center. *Report of the Inaugural Indigenous Peoples of the Pacific workshop on the UN Draft Declaration on the rights of Indigenous Peoples. Suva, Fiji, 2–6 September 1996* (pp. 65–79). Suva: Pio B Tikoisuva.

Mbembe, A. (2003). 'Necropolitics'. *Public Culture*, *15*(1), 11–40.

Motta, S. & Nilsen, A. (Eds.). (2011). *Social Movements in the Global South: Dispossession, Development and Resistance*. Basingstoke: Palgrave Macmillan.

RAFI. (1997, September/October). 'RAFI, Biopiracy Update: The Inequitable

Sharing of Benefits'. *RAFI (Rural Advancement Foundation International) Communique.*

Radio Mundo Real. (2011a, September 19). 'It was about time: NGO "Conservation International expelled from Ecuador"'. *Radio Mundo Real.* Available from: http://www.radiomundoreal.fm/It-Was-About-Time?lang=es.

Radio Mundo Real. (2011b, July 17). Ciencia embaucada. (Interview with Alfredo Luna). Available from: http://vimeo.com/26530561.

Rowell, A. (1996). *Green backlash: Global Subversion of the Environment Movement.* London: Routledge.

Shand, H. & Teitel, M. (1997, June). *The Ownership of Life: When Patents and Values Clash.* Institute for Agricultural Trade and Policy (IATP), http://www.iatp.org/files/Ownership_of_Life_When_Patents_and_Values_Clash.tml

Smith, L.T. (1999). *Decolonizing Methodologies: Research and Indigenous Peoples.* Dunedin: University of Otago Press and London: Zed Books.

Tamayo, E. (2011, September 27). 'Goodbye, Conservation International'. *Agencia Latinoamericana del Información (ALAI).* Available from: http://alainet.org/active/49720&lang=es.

Tokar, B, (1997). *Earth For Sale: Reclaiming Ecology in the Age of Corporate Greenwash.* Boston: South End Press.

Van Vark, M. (1997, August 28). 'Tribal cures for modern ailments'. *BBC News.* Available from: http://news.bbc.co.uk/2/hi/americas/431829.stm

Weinberg, B. (2003, August 21). 'Biodiversity Inc: Mexico Tries a New Tactic Against Chiapas Rebels – Conservation'. *In These Times.* Available from: http://www.inthesetimes.com/article/613/.

World Rainforest Movement (2002, December). 'Guyana: Conservation International Accused of "Gross Disrespect" to Indigenous Peoples'. *World Rainforest Movement Bulletin, No. 65.* Available from: http://www.wrm.org.uy/bulletin/65/viewpoint.html.

World Rainforest Movement (2011, April). 'Mexico:REDD+ in Chiapas finances disease, death and intercommunity conflicts'. *World Rainforest Bulletin,* No. 165. Available from: htt://www.wrm.org.uy/bulletin/165/viewpoint.html

2

Social Action and NGOization in Contexts of Development Dispossession in Rural India: Explorations into the Un-civility of Civil Society

Dip Kapoor

> People's movements of the traditional communities (*parompariko goshthi*) fighting for the protection of their natural resource base need to be more cautious about the role NGOs play. We all know that the government is pushing for not only mineral-based industries but also for creating SEZs (Special Economic Zones) for thermal and hydro-electric power and primarily in Dalit-Adivasi-fisher people's areas. With this in mind, the business and state/political interests have already put up their own NGO fronts to work on this directive to fool the people through charity and free services until displacement goals are met and they disappear. (KJ, Kalinganagar movement activist, Focus group notes, April 2009)
>
> We all know that our problems today are because of colonialism (*samrajyobad*) and capitalism (*punjibad*) and these MNCs (multinational corporations), NGOs, DFID (Department for International Development, UK) and the government are its forces (L, Niyamgiri Bachao Andolan (NBA) movement activist, Interview notes, February 2011).

Introduction

World Systems theorists have long recognized that the history of capitalism begins with the transformation of land rights, a complex process of commodification attached to the establishment of bourgeois property rights in land and its usage (Wallerstein, 2012). Included among the features of this process is 'the increasing privatization of the earth's surface through dispossession and displacement of peasants and indigenous populations' and the 'destruction of non-market access to food and self-sustenance and creation of a mobile global proletariat that is massively concentrated in the urban centres of the world economy' (often living under a regime of forced under-consumption). 'A current global land grab unprecedented since colonial times is underway as speculative investors . . . are acquiring millions of hectares of land in the global South' (Araghi, 2010; Araghi & Karides, 2012, pp.1–3). Often involving the eviction of local producers and forced expropriations even under the rubric of confronting the global food and energy crisis (GRAIN, 2012; McMichael, 2012), between 2001 and 2011 some 227 million hectares of land (an area the size of Western Europe) had been sold or leased to international investors (Oxfam, 2011).

The introduction of neoliberalism and the New Economic Policy of 1991 has heralded a similar process of accumulation by dispossession (Harvey, 2003) in India whereby land enclosures (for agro-industry, mining or industrial development) that dispossess Adivasis (Scheduled Tribes), Dalits (Scheduled Castes), and peasants help to turn land into property and capital (Levien, 2012; Walker, 2008) for transnational and domestic capitalists and feudal/landed elites (Padel & Das, 2010; Patnaik & Moyo, 2011). This process has been gathering momentum recently in the state of Orissa (the context of this chapter) and the mineral rich central-eastern region of India (Chattisgarh, Jharkhand and West Bengal). Under the 2006 National Mining Policy, the corporatized-state has leased one billion tons of bauxite (of an estimated 1.6 billion) to transnational and Indian corporations through Memorandums of Understanding (MoUs) (IPTEHR, 2006). Subsequently, while Adivasis constitute eight percent of the Indian population (or 80 million or more people belonging to some 612 Scheduled tribes), they account for forty percent of development-displaced persons (DDPs). In the state of Orissa where Adivasis make up twenty-two percent of the population, they account for forty-two percent of DDPs (Fernandes, 2006). According to some estimates, dams, mining, industries, and parks displaced 21.3 million people between 1951 and 1990 (prior to the neoliberal turn in the Indian economy and the establishment of Special Economic Zones (SEZs) that have accelerated this process) of which 40 percent were Adivasi and 20 percent were

Dalits (Nag, 2001). The government of India acknowledged a figure of 15.5 million displaced persons when it finally drafted a national rehabilitation policy in 1994, of which 75 percent are/or were still awaiting 'rehabilitation' (Bharati, 1999, p. 20).

These processes of displacement and dispossession or what some observers reference as 'development violence' (Kothari & Harcourt, 2004; Rajagopal, 2003) have been met with a proliferation of social movements/activism in the rural regions (Alvarez & Billorey, 1987; Baviskar, 1995; Ghai & Vivian, 1992; Ghosh, 2006; McMichael, 2010; Menon & Nigam, 2007; Oliver-Smith, 2010; Padel & Das, 2010; Rajagopal, 2003). For instance, a USD 12 billion project by POSCO Ltd. of South Korea (of which Citibank is a major shareholder) in Orissa is currently being held up by betel farmers and the POSCO Pratirodh Manch. Similar movements against mining/industrial displacement and dispossession (involving several transnational or Indian corporations including Tata, Vedanta/Sterlite (UK), Jindals, POSCO, Norsk Hydro (Norway), Alcan (Canada), Ambanis/Reliance etc., and various state agencies) in the rural regions of the state include relatively better-publicized movements in Lanjigarh, Kalinganagar, Kashipur, Earasama/Dhinkia and Keonjhar (Padel & Das, 2010), and several others (see Table 2.1 at the end of this chapter).

Non-governmental organizations (NGOs) as 'agents of development' are active in and around zones of mining and industrial development displacement and dispossession, some of whom claim to be supportive of, if not actively representing these movements in national and international forums, while others maintain a peripheral presence addressing social service needs of DDPs. Given that there are some 8000 NGOs operating in the state of Orissa alone (Padel & Das, 2010), they are clearly significant actors in the region and have yet to be seriously scrutinized in terms of their various engagements or disengagements with anti-mining and anti-industrial displacement social action/movements (see Table 2.1) in the state or in other parts of the country for that matter (Baviskar, 1995; Kamat, 2002; Menon & Nigam, 2007; Oliver-Smith, 2010). Based on a funded participatory action research project (2006-2010) (Kapoor, 2009), this chapter elaborates on an emergent thematic analysis of data generated from several focus group sessions and interviews with Lok Adhikar Manch (LAM) (Table 2.1) movement activists belonging to 15 anti-mining and anti-industrial development displacement and dispossession movements in the state pertaining to NGO-movement relations and the meaning and forms of NGOization (Alvarez, Dagnino & Escobar, 1998; Kamat, 2002) in this relationship.

Movement activists referred to small and large, national and international and Corporate/Government Organized NGOs (CONGOs/GONGOs) and voluntary/private NGOs at various points, sometimes making it difficult to avoid generalizations (i.e. activists referred to all of them at once as 'NGOs'. For example, Vedanta/Sterlite's social foundation and service wing was referenced as an NGO along with Action Aid UK) around emergent critical insights. The analysis that is entertained in this chapter needs to be understood as the perspective(s) of anti-mining and anti-industrial development displacement movements with distinctly anti-colonial and anti-capitalist politics. Not all movements would necessarily assess NGO engagements in like manner. While such movement-situated critiques resonate and occasionally intersect with theoretical critiques proposed by versions of Marxist and structuralist analyses (DeMars, 2005; Fernando, 2011; Kamat, 2002, 2004; Petras, 1997; Petras & Veltmeyer, 2001; Shivji, 2007) and Third Worldist anti-colonial vivisections (Barua, 2009; Goonatilake, 2006; Manji & O'Coill, 2002; Nandy, 1998; Quijano, 2000; Rajagopal, 2003), the propositions and analysis here originate from a movement activist experiential milieu (Bevington & Dixon, 2005) in a rural context scarred by a violent and unforgiving politics for subordinate classes, castes and ethnicities.

The anatomy of NGOization and the un-civility of civil society in rural contexts of development dispossession

Movement activist analysis of the politics of NGO-movement relations provides ample justification for what is advanced as a conscious, deliberate and systematic attempt by certain NGOs to undermine movements and their anti-displacement and anti-colonial politics – a process that was discussed in terms of *political obscurantism* and active attempts by NGOs to *demobilize and immobilize movements* opposed to the project, i.e., NGOs are predominantly viewed and assessed as *contributory agents* of state-corporate capital penetration and as being complicit in processes of rural displacement and dispossession as junior partners.

Political obscurantism: Red herrings, shape-shifters and the mystification of popular anti-mining/anti-industrial movement politics Through their presence in movement constituencies, NGOs provide the corporatized-developmental-state with a red-herring propaganda option as the state blames self-seeking NGOs (read as 'foreign interests') for instigating a false protest or conflict, i.e., one that is not in keeping with the *real* understanding of Adivasi and Dalit rural constituencies with respect to mining and development displacement. This enables the state-corporate nexus to divert attention away from, and to contribute towards, misrecognition and obscuring of popular movement politics unequivocally aimed against mining, industrial, and agro-forestry capitalist development dispossession ('we will not move for the mine' positions) by proposing that there is no *real* movement. Rather, they argue, there is only minor NGO-instigated misguided disaffection (political drama) masquerading as popular protest and resistance. According to a Kalinganagar movement activist, for instance, overt protests by Adivasi-Dalit-OBC (Other Backward Castes) movement constituencies against corporate industrial development in Kalinganagar by Tata and Jindal 'are explained away by certain politicians as the mischief of instigating NGOs, in order to make it seem that people are really not against such development and are willing to accept displacement for progress' (PM, Kalinganagar movement activist – Bisthapan Virodhi Manch, Interview notes, April, 2010). Or as in the case of the NBA in Niyamgiri,

NGO presence in Niyamgiri/Lanjigarh allows the government [the 2005 report of the Central Empowerment Committee of the Union government's Ministry of Social Justice and Empowerment is cited in relation to same] to point to the good work of Vedanta/Sterlite-supported NGOs and portray Adivasi as being in favor of mining development and that Vedanta is really 'Mining happiness for the people of Orissa' [corporate slogan] and to dismiss our protest as the work of anti-national [instigating] NGOs. And with all this good and bad NGO talk, NBA's real demands and anti-mining position is ignored and the public is misled about our views on this matter (SM, NBA movement activist, Interview notes, February 2011).

This state propaganda is utilized to bolster pro-mining/industrial development politics and public misperceptions around the same in urban middle class constituencies predictably sympathetic to urbanization and industrialization but also increasingly cognizant of India's political image abroad in relation to human rights and ecological considerations (such as the 'India Shining' goverment campaign to promote India internatiionally).

These class constituencies are subsequently keen to sanitize social and ecological exploitation implicating mining and other industrial development activity in rural contexts through such convenient explanations for the apparent political unrest.

The above scenario could perhaps still absolve NGOs of any direct complicity in an obscurantist displacement politics, i.e., this is state politics and has nothing to do with the *real* work of NGOs (just being used as red herrings by the state). But it is the *real* work of NGOs that is also called into question in relation to undermining and obscuring movement political aspirations in these contexts through shape-shifting or drastic changes in political positioning of NGOs with respect to these movements. For instance, according to LAM social movement activists, seemingly supportive NGOs not averse to social activism of a certain political ilk (or 'social action groups/ NGOs', Kamat, 2002, p.9–13) are unable to, or do not, maintain their stand for various reasons including: state pressure and control through the FCRA (Foreign Contribution Regulation Act) mechanism and the threat of de-registration (which would make them financially inoperable); being blacklisted as anti-industrial NGOs (168 NGOs in Orissa were de-registered in 2012); and due to state-corporate intimidation. These NGOs then move towards questionable positions and roles (from a movement perspective) that misrepresent (to the public and movements alike) and indirectly undermine or abruptly ignore movements they once supported. According to LAM movement activists, it was not uncommon for these NGOs who originally claimed to be with the anti-mining/anti-industrial movement to change their position to one in favor of displacement and negotiation (shapeshift) and in the process begin to confuse and derail movement opposition by attempting to motivate people in the opposite direction. As movement activist PM points out, 'In the beginning there were no people called *sapakhsyabadi* or pro-displacement but after these so-called activist-NGOs worked to raise the amount of compensation, people withdrew from the movement and formed the pro-displacement forum' (PM, Kalinganagar movement activist – Bisthapan Virodhi Manch, Interview notes, April, 2010).

This shape-shifting is also evident in the case of the movement in Kashipur (against Utkal Alumina/UAIL bauxite mining), where four such popular movement-sympathetic social action NGOs – AG, AK, L and W (acronyms are used here at the request of the participants who felt these state and national level NGOs could cause 'trouble' for them) – were deregistered (lost their Foreign Contribution numbers and ability to receive foreign funds for 1998–99). While AG even had its premises overturned by *goondas* (goons) and 'at least 3 of these NGOs initially raised awareness, promoted organizing activities and organized resistance to the UAIL mine', today 'AG is involved with mega international funding for watershed development while AK is busy implementing JFM (Joint Forest Management) with Japanese funding and neither have any apparent interest in anti-mining/anti-industrial development movements' (VH, Orissa Adivasi Manch movement activist, Interview notes, March 2010). In fact, according to an NGO-insider, one of these NGOs 'promised the government to help contain the movement in return for rescinding its decision to deregister the NGO' (Focus group notes, February, 2008). Speaking in reference to the Indrāvati reservoir project (funded by the World Bank in the 1980s and 90s with at least 40,000 people displaced, 80 percent of whom were Adivasi), Indrāvati Vistapita Lokmanch movement activists[1] who once viewed AG as an activist NGO supportive of the anti-dam movement, now perceive it to be 'colluding with dam builders and INGOs [funding agencies] like Action Aid for whom they have become surveyors of displacement after having started off as people's activists against displacement' or 'who have taken on the role of government by taking responsibility for DDPs' (AG did receive Action Aid funding for this project from 1993–2002 – Padel & Das, 2010, p. 99). Similarly, anti-UAIL (Utkal Alumina bauxite mining) movement activists from the Prakritik Sampad Suraksha Parishad (PSSP) question AG's initial role in working with the International Fund for Agricultural Development (IFAD)[2] and its entity – Orissa Tribal Development Project (OTDP) – for the Kashipur project in the late 1980s. Activists believed that the project's infrastructure (e.g. roads) as being developed for mining companies (and industrial development), even though IFAD was supposed to be funding agricultural development. Other NGOs similarly scrutinized by LAM activists as having changed colors/sides (shape-shifters) include GR, now in the 'sold out to aluminium' category. GR is seen as an Indian NGO that ignores popular movement activism espoused by movements like those in LAM, and instead accepts funds from the likes of mining giant BHP Billiton for mini-hydropower in Kalahandi district and remains content to promote the use of bio-gas cookers in Orissa. According to an ADEA (Adivasi-Dalit Ekta Abhijan Land, Forest and Unity Movement) movement activist,

> . . . such so-called activist NGOs (*andolono-badi sanstha*/NGO) backtrack when people's movements become a reality taking up land, forest and water claims – they develop cold feet (*seethiro hoi janti*) and change their programs to child education, anti-malaria, anti-tobacco campaigns, vocational training, SHG (Self-Help Groups) promotion and flood villages with so many programs that we don't have time to think collectively or to fight for our claims (focus group notes, April 2009).

> Even in Kalinganagar, Action Aid-supported NGOs started SHGs and confused the women about the movement . . . At a meeting in Muniguda, Action Aid's women's representative was thrown out of the people's meeting . . . we don't allow them to come in to our anti-POSCO process (PP, POSCO Pratirodh Manch movement activist, Interview notes, March 2010).

An OAM (Orissa Advasi Manch) movement activist, VH,[3] and activists from the NBA[4] suggest that these NGOs are milking (in terms of funding and NGO institutional consolidations) multiple position-alities (the 'many faces approach') in relation to movements. That is, the process of moving from active supporters of movements to state-pariahs (deregistration and anti-industrial black-listing), to becoming state-compliant service-provider NGOs now benefiting from multi–lateral or bilateral aid, state and donor funding, are all beneficial for the NGO. They suggest, for example, that when allegedly 'supporting' the movements, these NGOs experience a spike in donor support and cite the case of Action Aid's purportedly successful publicity and fundraising campaign around demolishing St Paul's Cathedral as akin to Vedanta/Sterlite's (UK) bid to mine bauxite from the Niyamgiri hills (Lanjigarh) revered by the Dongria and Kutia Kondhs. Once deregistered and blacklisted, these NGOs then secure the sympathy and support of outraged donors (supporting David in the battle against Goliath) and finally, when re-deployed by the state after being chastised into submission, continue to receive state, corporate and donor support for service provision in a state-corporate-sanctioned politics. For example, AG and AK projects today are relatively oblivious to social action in the region, while the latter, according to an ex-Vedanta Foundation employee[5] has accepted Vedanta/Sterlite funds to promote micro-credit and SHG schemes in the regions, as has GR (from BHP Billiton) for water and sanitation programs in Karlapat, a mining area where industrial activity is partially responsible for water shortages in the first place. In shifting their politics from one position to another as suggested, according to APDAM activists, these NGOs instrumentalize the movements at various points in time for their own political ends by for instance: (i) showcasing the movement for foreign visitors/NGOs ('he made us sit and chat with them about the movement and then they were never to be seen again'); (ii) using the members of the movement as workshop participants ('photos would be displayed of our movement, we would be asked to narrate our problems as a movement and then be sent off after a nice lunch and they would never be seen around our movement thereafter') and respondents for surveys/monitoring reports around displacement ('the agenda was to show us as the outcome/results of his NGO's project'); and (iii) using movement members/villages for various peripheral projects/information ('e.g. Dalit atrocity cases or police torture and abuse of communities') that were not the primary focus of the movement.

NGO partnerships with corporates and corporate-friendly state institutions also confound understandings of their political stance and commitments, adding to the charge of NGO obscurantism when the same NGOs claim to be acting in solidarity with the movement. Action Aid, which has figured prominently in the Niyamgiri conflict, for instance, is funded by – and is subsequently a 'stakeholder' of DFID, a majority of whose funds go to companies. Action Aid formed a Corporate Partnership Unit in 1993 (called Partners in Change or PIC since 1995) after the 1991 neoliberal turn in India (New Economic Policy), which enabled Action Aid MoUs with Sterlite, ICICI bank and other corporate houses. Such partnerships understandably raise critical questions about Action Aid's involvement in the movement to save Niyamgiri from a Vedanta/Sterlite bauxite-mining project.

Demobilizing and immobilizing movements: NGO involvements in derailing, obstructing, diverting and depoliticizing popular movements Movement activists identified and discussed several ways in which NGOs actively demobilized and immobilized movements by: (a) being engaged as corporate spies, (b) sowing seeds of division in the project-affected communities which in turn helped derail or obstruct movement politics, (c) acting as corporate persuaders who moved astutely to projectize dissent, (d) utilizing staged politics to disrupt movement politics and (e) failing to act on their promises of solidarity, i.e., disappearing in times of grave conflict demonstrating little concern for reciprocity in social action relationships.

1. *Corporate espionage*

LAM movement activists accuse big NGOs (international funding agencies or INGOs) and CONGOs for spying on communities for mineral extraction corporations, especially in the pre-displacement phase. Given the financial stakes involved, there is good reason for this as POSCO's interest in the Khandadhara mountain in Sundargarh, for instance, is a 600 million ton iron-ore deposit worth USD 108 billion (at 2007 prices of USD 180/ton) (Padel & Das, 2010, p. 562). Referring to a report by Tata on DPs (Displaced Persons) and PAPs (Project Affected Persons) at its Kalinganagar steel plant site – coincidentally commissioned just 4 months after thirteen people from these villages had been killed by police on 2 January 2006 – Padel and Das (2010) suggest that NGO surveys and reports are not just part of corporate espionage but more significantly, are used to promote 'a widespread NGO discourse which constructs a false and alien knowledge about tribal people geared towards controlling and dispossessing them' and 'making displacement seem voluntary and inevitable when it is not'. In their estimation, this positioning has become 'part of a terrifying uniformity in NGO discourse' (pp. 519–521).

Several LAM activists from the various movements and regions of displacement provided similar insights regarding NGOs and corporate espionage:

NGOs come quietly in the name of conducting surveys, but are engaged by the corporates to find out about people's sentiments and strengths, so that they can use this information accordingly to suppress the movement. Sometimes in the name of entitlements or *panchayati raj* [local government] or education or health, they survey entire areas like Sundergarh to expose all the secrets of the villages regarding people's views on such development. Companies even form their own NGOs to do this or hire well-known NGOs. Sometimes they come saying it is for skills development and collect 10–15 girls and start sewing classes for a few days, or come with medicines promising health check-ups. With their help they find out village facts and views and after collecting their report, disappear. In this technical way, NGOs are helping the corporates to snatch people's land, forest and water and livelihoods (NB, Santal Adivasi, Khandadhara anti-POSCO movement activist, Interview notes, January 2012).

NGOs also conduct workshops on industrialization to begin the process of penetration for corporate groups. International Watch and Xavier Group (CENDERET) or Tata Social Sciences have tried to get into our area for survey and workshops but have not succeeded as we have not allowed them. They speak of neutrality but quietly promote industrialization and create favorable opinions for business. They are trying the same tricks in Kalinganagar (PP, POSCO Pratirodh Manch movement activist, Interview notes, March 2010).

2. Sowing the seeds of division

LAM movement activists shared several examples of how NGOs work to divide and create conflict in the movement constituency along the lines of gender, caste, class, ethnicity, age, and project beneficiary/non-beneficiary.

They have the skill of dividing people (*se mano koro lokho koo bhago koribaro kaushala achi*). They use divisive tactics and take sections of people into their fold – their own beneficiaries and restrict their concern for these people while others do not exist

– false concern is reserved for non-beneficiaries who are predictably against the corporate and government project interests or
just stay away. They breed small hopes, solve small issues and
take small actions (*chotiya chotiya kamo ko somosya koo samadhano
koru chonti*) while the movement process is attempting to address
the larger issues of displacement facing all our people, NGO
beneficiary or not (MB, Upper Kolab Basachyuta Mahasangh,
Focus Group notes, February 2009).

When the Kalinganagar killings by police took place, many NGOs
came into the picture like Action Aid and Development Initiative.
After a while they all disappeared as usual, except one NGO who
is working with women's SHGs and providing Rs. 5000 to each
woman member as a loan. This NGO is acting like a *hatho barisi*
[planer of rough wood] after the police killings and women in these
SHGs are gradually moving out of the movement process. . . .
SHG meetings are held in Tata company facilities and often government officials are present. Every week there would be a meeting
for 3–4 groups and all the members would be provided with Tata
transportation with great fanfare as they were picked and dropped
back at their village doors. A pre-condition of these meetings was
that you could not talk of the movement or people's rights. Those
who attend these meetings get plenty of sweets to eat and get new
saris, blouses, *saya*, shoes, vanity bags, etc. My own daughter is an
SHG leader – when I ask about the movement she just keeps quiet.
Slowly, lots of people are going away through this process (NS,
APDAM movement activist, Focus Group notes, March 2010).

Speaking in relation to the same gendered-approach to dividing the
movement, (while simultaneously promoting neoliberalism from below
or small-'c' capitalism), an NBA activist shares the following:

There are many women's SHGs that have got *saris* and loans
from Vedanta through these NGOs. They promise to link these
groups to Banks and Micro-credit companies. . . . they take away
the women luring them with free *saris* and sometimes the women
say 'so what if we take just a *sari* – you men can have your
meetings'. . . . To tell you a fact, this has been a very difficult
struggle – sometimes when we hope 50 persons will show for a

meeting, 20 or so may turn up because the rest are at SHG meetings. The Vedanta people and their NGOs are always tempting people with their money (KM, NBA movement activist, Interview notes, February 2011).

According to an ex-Vedanta Foundation employee,[6] 10–15 percent of the Vedanta budget is marked for 'corporate social responsibility' (CSR)/ social work activities to be channeled through NGOs. However, a large percentage of these funds go to 'bogus NGOs/vested interests' who may be petty traders and local politicians who then use the money in the name of social work to hire goons to intimidate the movements. Often, for example, youth from the movement villages are lured by such payments, like motorcycles and TVs. The Vedanta social work program also uses 'real NGOs' to penetrate the movement villages; NGOs that appeal to youth to form sports clubs (under 'Right to Play' advocacy, for instance) and SHG groups for young girls along with the promise of jobs, bikes, educational programmes in the city/abroad. 'The idea is to make them shut their mouth and make them feel happy' (*pati bond kori khushire basiro honthu*). Or as KJ[7] adds, 'Some NGOs have taken our youngsters out of the area in the name of providing education and help, and that is how they have tried to weaken our movement'. IM[8] also shares, 'Through these youth they are trying to introduce ideas and values that do not fit with our traditions'.

In terms of the politics of mining project persuasion, Vedanta-supported NGOs like Niyamgiri Adivasi Vikas Parishad and Shakti are also being implicated by LAM activists as pitting landless and small peasant classes and rural castes and ethnicities, such as Dalits or Dongria/Kutia Adivasis, against unemployed labor classes, mainly migrant workers from out of state, in addition to some locals from the movement area. These unions (such as the Alumina Refinery Union – since the refinery has been set up prior to plant site mining activity) are being encouraged to threaten or bribe the movement. At the instigation of the company and these company NGOs they have said,

> . . . They won't hesitate to kill movement leaders and supporters. . . . The way they have been trained in attacking others like us, it may well be possible that they will unleash terror and killing in our communities . . . they have ganged up and are trying to occupy the political space in the locality. Bred

and fed by the company and their NGOs, they have said they will also provide financial support to the communities through their NGO if the people go along with the project (L, NBA movement activist, Interview notes, February 2011).

3. Corporate persuaders, propaganda merchants and the projecti-zation of dissent

It is apparent that CONGOs and 'real NGOs' (including funding agen-cies or INGOs) initiating SHG/micro-credit programmes and providing health and educational services are using their social, ethical, moral and financial capital to persuade movement constituencies to avoid confron-tation and struggle, see the benefits of the project and accept better/ compensation packages (Relief and Rehabilitation bargaining with NGOs at their side who 'prepare better compensation packages for victims' – PP, POSCO Pratirodh Manch activist, Interview notes, March 2010). As villages capitulate, according to LAM movement activists, more and more services and projects (real and fabricated) flood the region to continue processes of distraction and inundation, suffocation of dissenting positions and confusion until such time as displacement is realized. APDAM activists for instance, referring to Kalinganagar, paint a stark picture of NGOs showing people the way out of villages (post-compensation), while Tata bulldozers flatten their homes in front of their very eyes:

> 'When our people leave their homes with utensils and baggage on their heads in a long line while the company bulldozers knock down their houses, we can't stop our tears' (*amo loko jethebare basono kosono mundeyi dharire jeeba pai bahar onthi, avom ghoro dwaro* company bulldozer *re bhangi diye jai, amo luho bond kori paroo nah*) (B, APDAM movement activist, Focus Group notes, March 2010).

NGOs like Shakti which are Vedanta-NGOs, and even INGOs doing micro-credit and SHG work, are promoting all kinds of small business activities like leaf plate making, broom-making, and rope-making to help people make money. They use this relationship with the people to create a favorable opinion for

Vedanta and the project – they are saying, if the factory will come up it will be good for you all. You will learn more if Vedanta comes, like tailoring, making phenyl (cleaners) and they will buy this from you, so you should not be opposing Vedanta (L, NBA, Interview notes, February 2011).

They are trying to take us away from our traditional ways of cultivation and our own ways of feeding our communities by introducing blackberry cultivation among a few farmers, blackberries for Vedanta/outsiders to buy at Rs. 500/kg. All these SHG activities are also about money only – can we eat money? If we keep doing this, we will soon have to leave the mountains and the land to work in the towns to make whatever money we can to buy what we need from the city markets and that is surely going to be the end for us. Who wants to give work to Adivasis and what work can we do in their machine businesses? (KM, NBA, Interview notes, February 2011).

Micro-credit, as acknowledged by activists, is the ultimate de-politicizing intervention since it enmeshes communities into the market through individual debts to banks and promotes neoliberalism from below or small-'c' capitalism which undermines collective movement interests (by promoting the conception of the rational profit-seeking individual) and rural reliance on known modes of production (hence the struggle to maintain control over land, forests and water for subsistence cultivation, hunting-gathering and horticultural work). Subsequently, as Padel and Das (2010, p. 518) have noted, the World Bank and associated corporates like Citibank and Monsanto (who have supported key micro-credit summits organized by the World Bank) take a great interest in these schemes, especially after Mohammed Yunus was awarded the Nobel in 2006 for the Grameen model in Bangladesh. According to the Bank's recommendations, NGOs need to be integrated with finance markets by: (a) developing an appropriate regulatory framework for financial operations of the NGO sector (b) encouraging large NGOs to establish themselves as banks; (c) encouraging wholesaling of credit to established NGOs; and (d) using smaller NGOs as brokers to mobilize self-help savings groups. In KJ's[9] words, 'education, health, SHG has no relevance at the moment when we are in the process of losing everything' (*ame shobu haraiba avosthare ehi prokaro kamoro kaunasi artha nahi*).

As anti-displacement positions soften through such penetrations, NGOs step up their traditional role of charity work (*unoyono anudan kajyo*) and become doling-out institutions (*datobyo anushthan*). They start to flood the place with goods and programs to

'create a culture of dependence (*eha eko nirbharotharo sanskruti*) as yesterday's missionaries did . . . so much so that people start to bargain and ask, request and beg (*patchariba, anurodho kaoriba abom magiba*) – people begin to forget to assert themselves and to take on the injustice that is displacement' (ADEA movement activist, Focus Group notes, April 2009).

They ask us not to proceed further with confrontational approaches (*sangharsha kori aroku jeeba theek nahi*) after we faced police bullets and the country started talking about Kalinganagar and Tatas . . . they said you should not fight with the government or you will be in big trouble. You are poor people. You cannot fight with the rich and the mighty. You say yes to this process and you will get a lot of benefits. They promised us rice, wheat and polythene shelters. . . . They even used local school teachers to motivate us to allow all the industrial plants, to sell our land and accept compensation packages. Most of these teachers are plant contractors today and making lots of money (KJ, APDAM movement activist, Focus Group notes, April 2009).

The companies and their NGOs also make false promises about activities in the name of CSR or 'Resettlement & Rehabilitation'. As KM and SM from the NBA point out, it is only after public pressure and false reports that have been exposed, that they start doing the minimum on some fronts.

Otherwise we cannot see where there are schools or health centres as everything happens only on paper. . . . In some villages they have constructed small concrete houses and put up boards like tailoring centre, leaf plate making centre, etc. but when the Central Empowerment Committee from the Ministry of Social Justice and Empowerment came, they found nothing behind these signs which were only boards hanging and swinging in the air (SM, NBA, Interview notes, February 2011).

4. Disrupting movement politics with staged politics: Parallel events, photo-ops/media events, fake leaders and individual/shareholder activism

When asked to consider the role of Action Aid, an NGO that has internationalized their struggle in Niyamgiri, NBA activists acknowledged the initial role that this INGO had played in putting them on the international map and then began to share problems with its role and methods, warranting the conclusion 'no more Action Aid':

We are not clear about what they are up to. We don't know when they are coming and going until they just show up. Once we arranged a meeting at Ijurupa village and then we find that they have organized another meeting with dal, rice and cooking utensils for the village in Ambaguda on the same day. They have done this often – setting up parallel programs with the NBA programs and we ask the question, if you are doing this, are you not disturbing our process and dividing people? What is your agenda?

Action Aid was also accused of using the movement for photo/media promotional opportunities and superficial engagements for their own publicity and for self-promotion.

We had organized a meeting in Muniguda and on the same day as usual, Action Aid had organized a procession on the other side of the meeting place. Without warning, two of their staff showed up with Action Aid banners and stood behind us and started taking photographs. I got annoyed and asked them what they were doing and they said it was part of their evaluation process and that is when I told them to leave (KM, NBA, Interview notes, February 2011).

Survival International and Action Aid came and made documentary films about the Lanjigarh movement or about the Kutia Kondh ways of life and Amnesty International also visited – they kept appearing and disappearing and even after asking Action Aid representatives lots of questions about their work, I could not get a clear picture of what they really do for the movement. I have just come to know that Action Aid has won an award for their documentary on Niyamgiri[10] . . . and this is after they staged an event where people were saying prayers on Niyamgiri and used even non-Dongria to play representative roles for the movement. Action Aid is also, like the government's latest manipulations, helping to brand some people's leaders and the movement as Maoist and making indirect claims to represent the movement – one of their representatives told me that they are getting good support because of this struggle from human rights donors and that fundraising has become like a tiger – if we get off it, it will eat us (KM, NBA movement activist, Interview notes, March 2010).

An ADEA movement activist[11] sums up this aspect of NGO-movement relations as follows,

Big NGOs often join up to put up a collective front and bring people's movements behind them to gain international attention. . . . In my 25 years of experience as a social activist I have observed many NGO-promoted movements starting with high hopes but slowly just becoming vehicles for creating an international name for promoting NGOs. They become like engines of vehicles driven by NGO persons and the speed and direction is controlled by the NGO. When these types of movements come out on the streets, they don't do things that would shake up the administration in Bhubaneswar or New Delhi but only create sound bytes (*huri koronthi*) – just enough to draw the attention of INGOs [funders]. These become events for taking photos and making reports and calling meetings to enhance the image of NGOs as promoters of movements (NGO *manokoro nijero prathi chabi koo barhai sohayoko bhabe*).

Action Aid was also called on its approach to, if not dubious practices pertaining to the selection of leaders and movement representatives, an individualist approach (leader-centered) to campaigning, as well as an ineffectual and remote/distant (from the scenes of mining/industrial conflict) shareholder activism. This is also construed by activists as an attempt to play all sides (pro- and anti-, again causing confusion about the NBA's positioning) and an attempt to put themselves forward as the key movement leaders and representatives with corresponding social capital in movement constituencies. This enables them to bring leaders, including non-representative ones, to London.

Even in the case of Lanjigarh we don't see Action Aid or Survival International doing any positive service for the communities being displaced. When individual leaders are taken to shareholder meetings in London to talk to [Vedanta CEO] Anil Agrawal, what can you expect from this? Can they really challenge or stop him this way? We feel this is an advertising exercise for these funding agencies and NGOs (PP, POSCO Pratirodh Manch movement activist, Interview notes, March 2010).

As far as the locally recognized leaders from the NBA were concerned, Action Aid, by taking false leaders (people who have had nothing to do with long-term organizing work) to London (or not bothering about who they took) were making 'a fight that was about life and death for the Adivasi in Niyamgiri' into a 'fake fight for their experiments of NGO promotion'.

I was motivated to go to London when they said the money Vedanta is getting from its partners (shareholders) to destroy your God's abode can be stopped if you attend this meeting. I went to London twice. I found that along with me, on both times, they were taking another person who would support the Vedanta project. After I shared this with our movement, we collectively decided not to participate – no more Action Aid (KM, NBA, Interview notes, February 2011).

It was shocking and we felt that if Action Aid could project a person outside the movement as movement leader, it can very well say everywhere that it is running the movement. Tomorrow it can tell the world the leaders have surrendered to the project (L, NBA, Interview notes, February 2011).

5. Disappearing acts: Solidarity? Reciprocity?

Movement activists shared several examples of development displacement-related direct action and protest, and related violence across the board. This often involved the state/police and corporate mafias and the violation of people's rights – situations of conflict and direct action or visible and vocal protest where and when NGOs consistently perform the vanishing act.

They show up when we are having meetings or our own rallies but they disappear when we call them to stand with us when we are fighting. We don't see them around during those crucial times of movement action . . . after the police firing and after our people were killed and they cut off the hands of the dead, NGOs came and some expressed solidarity and took photographs standing with us but they never returned . . . we needed them the most when the government attacked our movement and the industries were pouring money into hiring local goondas and police but they were nowhere to be seen (KJ, APDAM movement activist, Focus Group notes, April 2009).

In Baliapal we fought against the missile testing range against the government during my youth. Here I learnt that NGOs are slaves of the system – they bring people on to the roads for small issues, within the system issues and not system challenging issues like what we are talking about here today. . . . Ours is collective action from the people's identified issues and problems – our action is from outside the institutions and NGO action is institutional action (C, Adivasi Dalit Adhikar Sangathan activist, Focus Group notes, April 2009).

NGOs were generally seen as 'taking half-hearted stands' (*asompurno bhumika*) or as being unwilling to take 'proactive and open stands with the movements in times of great conflict'. These and other examples shared here suggest that the NGO discourse around human rights is 'a discourse concerning justified violence' (Rajagopal, 2003, p. 174; Williams, 2010) evidenced by the inability or unwillingness of NGOs to stand up against such market/development-violence (Kothari & Harcourt, 2004) in solidarity with popular movements.

The above list of possibilities pertaining to the uncivility of civil society in contexts of development displacement and dispossession is in no way intended to be exhaustive. For instance, participating leaders and representatives from several movement contexts also spoke to the tendency for NGOs to monkey-wrench dissent through the push towards the abyss or quagmire of litigation as a means for resolving displacement-related issues; the role of alien or imported modes of elitist decision-making and organizational technologies and ways of thinking (e.g. self-seeking rational individualism or entrepreneurialism; nature as property and commodity form for market exchange; eschewing attachment to place and spiritual ontologies etc.) which divided movement ways of organizing and thinking/acting; and the move by NGOs and corporations to channel the movement and emphasize the avenue of local village-level 'autonomous' government (*Panchayati Raj* institutions), which are easily manipulated by state-corporate-feudal interests in these displacement projects. This includes the privatization of resources like water through *pani panchayats* for instance, as the forum for decision making and constructive approaches to resolving project disputes/movement possibilities. Activists questioned NGO-led and induced forms and expressions of dissent (language and forms of dissent like exclusive or restricted meetings and staged-with-permission campaigns), including a heavy reliance on human rights-based approaches (Kapoor, 2012; Williams, 2010) as the only effective option for voicing popular resource and cultural claims. As has been acknowledged, there is an urgent need to re-examine the politics of human rights given the 'ascendancy of rights as the privileged discourse for the symbolic articulation of international justice in an era of advanced global capitalism' (Williams, 2010, p. xv).

From NGOization to social action: Prospects, possibilities and concluding reflections

Given the tenor of the analysis shared by LAM activists and movement constituencies that are unequivocally engaged in an anti-mining/anti-industrial displacement politics, it is unsurprising to note a general reluctance to suggest or consider the prospects and possibilities for NGO-movement relations. While there are myriad politics around development displacement and dispossession that would consider such a possibility, the level of skepticism if not bitterness about NGO politics in relation to anti-mining/anti-industrial movements should be self-evident in this exposition. Viewed as an agent of displacement and dispossession or an accomplice of state-corporate-UN sponsored capitalist development initiatives that disregard the interests of these rural movement constituencies (hence the opening reference to capitalism and colonialism accounting for the dispossession of subordinate rural social groups including Adivasis and Dalits), NGOs were referred to as institutional actors engaged in an institutionally defined politics, i.e., as anti-politics machines wedded to a neoliberal state-corporate-civil society circumscribed politics (Kamat, 2004; Petras, 1997), contrary to the so-called apolitical or neutral stance prescribed by the state and often alluded to by NGOs (Goonatilake, 2006). These NGO politics were seen to be colonial in material (e.g. forcible introduction of petty capitalist modes of production and exchange through SHGs and subsequent merging into the networks of finance capital and credit markets while semi-agrarian and hunter-gatherer modes are threatened through the act of displacement and dispossession from the natural base – neoliberalism from below) and cultural terms (e.g. penetration of other ways of thinking, valuing, organizing, doing, resisting and expressing dissent etc.). Given the stakes involved – the radical dissolution of centuries-old ways of being and living in some cases, and the relatively flippant (e.g. publicity fixations, shape-shifting and experimentation with the lives of villagers about to experience a socio-physical lobotomy or development triage) and ambiguous role being played by NGOs referenced in this exposé, it is hardly surprising that NGOs are viewed with suspicion, if not resentment.

The analysis raises several pointed questions for NGOs engaged in rural contexts of displacement and dispossession that NGOs may or may not be able to address. For instance, can NGOs work outside hegemonic structures and relationships to embrace an anti-colonial and anti-capitalist movement politics and teleology? Does the class-caste (mainly urban) positioning of NGOs/civil society already compromise them in such class-caste (urban-rural) conflicts? What might a class-caste compromised or circumscribed role for NGOs look like? Are NGOs prepared and able to increase their role in a confrontational and conflict-politics (with state-capital), which begs NGO political-economic and socio-cultural hegemonic location (Fernando, 2011; Petras, 1997), by engaging in these struggles on movement terms? If NGOs are going to relate to the politics of LAM movement networks so that they are taken seriously, they will clearly have to find ways to be less complicit with, and swim a lot harder against, dominant political-economic and cultural currents and their colonial import in contexts of rural displacement and dispossession.

Table 2.1: Lok Adhikar Manch (LAM)

Movement participant (Year established)	Location/operational area	Social groups engaged	Key issues being addressed
1. *Kalinga Matchyajivi Sangathana* (Kalinga fisher people's organization) (Early 1980s)	Gopalpur-on-sea (centre) including coastal Orissa, from Gopalpur in Ganjam district to Chandrabhaga and Astaranga coast in Puri district	Fisher people (mainly Dalits) originally from the state of Andhra Pradesh called Nolias and Orissa state fisher people or Keuta/ Kaivartas	Trawler fishing, fish stock depletion and enforcement of coastal regulations/zones (Transnational and National Corporate (TNC/ NC) investments) Occupation of coastal land by defense installations (e.g., missile bases) Hotel/tourism industry developments along coast (TNC investment) Special economic zones (SEZ) and major port projects for mining exports (TNC investment) Pollution of beaches and oceans Displacement of fisher communities related to such developments
2. *Prakritik Sampad Suraksha Parishad* (PSSP) (Late 1980s) Approximately 200 movement villages	Kashipur, Lakhimpur, Dasmantpur and adjacent blocks in Rayagada district of Orissa	Adivasis including Jhodias, Kondhs and Parajas and Pano/ Domb Dalits	Bauxite mining (alumina) (TNC investments) Industrialization, deforestation and land alienation/displacement People's rights over 'their own ways and systems'

Movement participant (Year established)	Location/operational area	Social groups engaged	Key issues being addressed
3. *Jana Suraksha Manch* (2007)	Adava region of Mohana block, Gajapati district including sixty or more villages	Saura and Kondh Adivasis and Panos (Dalits)	Government/local corruption Police brutality/atrocities Deforestation and plantation agriculture (National Corporate investment)
4. *Adivasi Dalit Adhikar Sangathan* (2000)	Jaleswar, Bhograi and Bosta blocks in Balasore district and Boisinga and Rasagovindpur blocks in Mayurbhanj including over 100 villages	Dalits, Adivasis, fisher people and Other Backward Castes (OBCs)	Dalit and Adivasi land rights and land alienation Industrialization, port development and displacement of traditional fisher people (TNC investment)
5. *Adivasi-Dalit Ekta Abhiyan* (2000)	Twenty panchayats in Gajapati and Kandhmal districts including 200 plus villages (population of about 50,000)	Kondh and Saura Adivasis, Panos (Dalits) and OBCs	Land and forest rights Food Sovereignty/plantation agriculture ((National Corporate) NC investment) Industrialization, modernization and protection of indigenous ways and systems Communal harmony Development of people's coalitions/forums (no state, NGO, corporate, 'outsider', upper/middle castes participants)

6. *Indrāvati Vistapita Lokmanch* (Late 1990s)	Thirty villages in the district of Nabarangapur	Several Adivasi, Dalit and OBC communities	Dam displacement (Indrāvati irrigation and hydro-electric project) (TNC/NC investment) Land and forest rights Resettlement, rehabilitation and compensation for development displaced peoples (DDPs) Industrialization and modern development and protection of people's ways
7. *Orissa Adivasi Manch* (1993 to 1994)	State level forum with an all-Orissa presence (all districts) with regional units in Keonjhar and Rayagada districts and district level units in each district	Well over forty different Adivasi communities	Adivasi rights in the state Tribal self-rule, forest and land rights and industrialization (SEZs) (TNC investments)
8. *Anchalik Janasuraksha Sangathan* (2008)	Kidting, Mohana block of Gajapati district including some twenty villages	Kondh and Saura Adivasis and Panos (Dalits)	Land and forest rights Conflict resolution and communal harmony between Adivasis and Dalits over land and forest issues

Movement participant (Year established)	Location/operational area	Social groups engaged	Key issues being addressed
9. *Dalit Adivasi Bahujana Initiatives* (DABI) (2000)	Five blocks in the Kandhmal district with ten participating local movements (networks)	Kondh Adivasis, Panos (Dalits) and OBCs	Land and forest rights Food sovereignty and livelihood issues Communal harmony
10. *Uppara Kolab Basachyuta Mahasangh* (Late 1990s)	Umerkote block, Koraput district (includes thirty villages displaced by the upper Kolab hydroelectric and irrigation reservoir)	Paraja Adivasis, Panos and Malis Dalits and OBCs	Displacement due to the upper Kolab hydro-electricity and irrigation reservoir (TNC/NC investment) Compensation, rehabilitation and basic amenities for DDPs Land and forest rights
11. *Jeevan Jivika Suraksha Sangathan* (2006)	Three panchayats in the border areas of Kandhmal and Gajapati districts including fifty or more villages with a population of 12,000 people	Kondhs and Saura Adivasis and Panos (Dalits) and OBCs	Land and forest rights/issues Communal harmony Food sovereignty and livelihood issues

12. *Adivasi Pachua Dalit Adhikar Manch* (APDAM) (2000)	Kalinga Nagar industrial belt in Jajpur district (twenty-five or more villages, along with several participants in the Kalinganagar township area)	Adivasis, Dalits and OBCs	Industrialization and displacement (TNC investment) Land and forest rights Compensation and rehabilitation Police atrocities/brutality Protection of Adivasi-Dalit ways and forest-based cultures and community
13. *Janajati Yuva Sangathan* (2008)	Baliapal and Chandanesar block in Balasore district including thirty-two coastal villages being affected by mega port development (part of SEZ scheme).	Dalit fisher communities and OBCs.	SEZs (TNC investments) Industrialization and displacement Land alienation and marine rights of traditional fisher communities

Note: In addition to the above LAM movements, leaders from 2 other movements were also included in the research, both of which have expressed an interest in joining LAM. These include: (i) The Niyamgiri Bachao Andolan (NBA), a Dongria and Kutia Kondh (Adivasi) movement against the Vedanta/Sterlite (UK) bauxite mine/refinery in Lanjigarh, and the (ii) anti-POSCO (South Korea) movement, Santal Adivasi wing from the Khandadhar region and the parent POSCO Pratirodh Manch which includes several wings including small and medium farmers (e.g. Betel leaf farmers), Adivasi, Dalits and fisherfolk affected (or potentially affected) at the plant site or due to port development (Jatadhar river basin area; this includes the Paradip Port Trust which would have to handle iron ore exports) and water-affected areas/groups in Cuttack district as water for irrigation and drinking in these areas is channeled through a proposed canal (going through 5 districts) to the POSCO plant.

Source: Kapoor (2011), p.132–134.

Notes

1 Focus group notes, February, 2009.
2 AG disengaged from IFAD in 1993.
3 Orissa Adivasi Manch movement activist, Interview notes, March 2010.
4 KM, Niyamgiri Surakhsha Samiti movement activist of the NBA, Interview notes, February 2011.
5 RM, Vedanta Foundation, Interview notes, March 2010.
6 RM, Vedanta Foundation, Interview notes, March 2010.
7 APDAM activist, Focus Group notes, April 2009.
8 IM, OAM movement activist, Interview notes, March 2011.
9 APDAM movement activist, Focus group notes, April 2009.
10 L, NBA, Interview notes, February 2011.
11 KP, Focus Group notes, April 2009.

References

Alvarez, S. & Billorey, R. (1987). 'Damming the Narmada: The Politics Behind the Destruction'. *The Ecologist, 17*(2/3), 62–75.

Alvarez, S. E., Dagnino, A., & Escobar, A. (Eds.) (1998). *Cultures of Politics and Politics of Cultures: Re-visioning Latin American Social Movements.* Oxford: Westview Press.

Araghi, F. (2010). 'Accumulation by Displacement: Global Enclosures, Food Crisis and the Ecological Crisis of Capitalism'. *Review: A Journal of Fernand Braudel Centre, 34*(1), 113–146.

Araghi, F. & Karides, M. (2012). 'Land Dispossession and Global Crisis: Introduction to the Special Section on Land Rights in the World System'. *Journal of World Systems Research on Land Rights, 18*(1), 1–5.

Barua, B. (2009). 'Participatory Research, NGOs and Grassroots Development: Challenges in Rural Bangladesh'. In D. Kapoor & S. Jordan (Eds.) *Education, Participatory Action Research and Social Change: International Perspectives* (pp. 239–250). New York: Palgrave Macmillan.

Baviskar, A. (1995). *In the Belly of the River: Tribal Conflicts Over Development in the Narmada Valley.* New Delhi: Oxford Publications.

Bevington, D. & Dixon, C. (2005). 'Movement-relevant Theory: Rethinking Social Movement Scholarship and Activism'. *Social Movement Studies, 4*(3), 185–208.

Bharati, S. (1999). 'Human Rights and Development Projects in India'. *The PRP Journal of Human Rights, 3*(4), 20.

DeMars, W. (2005). *NGOs and Transnational Networks: Wild Cards in World Politics.* London: Pluto Press.

Fernandes, W. (2006). 'Development Related Displacement and Tribal Women'. In G. Rath (Ed.) *Tribal Development in India: The Contemporary Debate* (pp. 112–132). New Delhi, India: Sage.

Fernando, J. (2011). *The Political-Economy of NGOs: State Formation in Sri Lanka and Bangladesh.* London: Pluto.

Ghai, D. & Vivien, J. (1992). *Grassroots Environmental Action*. London: Routledge.

Ghosh, K. (2006). 'Between Global Flows and Local Dams: Indigenousness, Locality and the Transnational Sphere in Jharkhand, India'. *Cultural Anthropology, 21*(4), 501–534.

Goonatilake, S. (2006). *Recolonisation: Foreign Funded NGOs in Sri Lanka*. New Delhi: Sage.

Harvey, D. (2003). *The New Imperialism*. Oxford: Oxford University Press.

GRAIN. (2012). *The Great Food Robbery: How Corporations Control Food, Grab Land and Destroy the Climate*. Cape Town, Dakar, Nairobi and Oxford: Pambazuka Press.

Indian People's Tribunal on Environment and Human Rights (IPTEHR). (2006). *An Inquiry into Mining and Human Rights Violations in Kashipur*. Mumbai, India: IPTEHR.

Kamat, S. (2002). *Development Hegemony: NGOs and the State in India*. New Delhi: Oxford University Press.

Kamat, S. (2004). 'The Privatization of Public Interest: Theorizing NGO Discourse in a Neoliberal Era'. *Review of International Political Economy, 11*(1))February), 155–176.

Kapoor, D. (2009). 'Participatory Academic Research (par) and People's Participatory Action Research (PAR): Research, Politicization and Subaltern Social Movements (SSMs) in India'. In D. Kapoor & S. Jordan (Eds.) *Education, Participatory Action Research and Social Change: International Perspectives* (pp. 29–44). New York: Palgrave Macmillan.

Kapoor, D. (2011). 'Subaltern Social Movement (SSM) Post-mortems of Development in India: Locating Trans-local Activism and Radicalism'. *Journal of Asian and African Studies, 46*(2), 130–148.

Kapoor, D. (2012). 'Human Rights as Paradox and Equivocation in Contexts of Adivasi (original dweller) Dispossession in India'. *Journal of Asian and African Studies, 47*(4), 404–420.

Kothari, S. & Harcourt, W. (2004). 'The Violence of Development'. *Development, 47*(1), 3–7.

Levien, M. (2012). 'The Land Question: Special Economic Zones and the Political Economy of Dispossession in India'. *Journal of Peasant Studies, 39*(3–4), 933–969.

Manji, F. & O'Coill, C. (2002). 'The Missionary Position: NGOs and Development in Africa'. *International Affairs, 78*(3), 567–583.

McMichael, P. (Ed.) (2010). *Contesting Development: Critical Struggles for Social Change*. New York: Routledge.

McMichael, P. (2012). 'The Land Grab and Corporate Food Regime Restructuring'. *Journal of Peasant Studies, 39*(3–4), 681–701.

Menon, N. & Nigam, A. (2007). *Power and Contestation: India Since 1989*. London: Zed Books.

Nag, S. (2001). 'Nationhood and Displacement in the Indian Subcontinent'. *Economic and Political Weekly*, March 1.

Nandy, A. (1998). *Exiled at Home*. New Delhi: Oxford University Press.

Oliver-Smith, A. (2010). *Defying Displacement: Grassroots Resistance and the Critique of Development*. Austin: University of Texas Press.

Oxfam. (2011). *Land and Power: The Growing Scandal Surrounding the New Wave of Investments in Land*. Retrieved from www.oxfam.org/en/grow/policy/land-and-power.

Padel, F. & Das, S. (2010). *Out of This Earth: East India Adivasis and the Aluminium Cartel.* New Delhi: Orient Blackswan.

Patnaik, U. & Moyo, S. (2011). *The Agrarian Question and the Neoliberal Era: Primitive Accumulation and the Peasantry.* Cape Town, SA: Pambazuka Press.

Petras, J. (1997). 'NGOs: In the Service of Neoliberalism'. *Journal of Contemporary Issues in Asia, 29*(4), 429–440.

Petras, J. & Veltmeyer, H. (2001). *Globalization Unmasked: Imperialism in the 21st Century.* New Delhi: Madhyam Books.

Quijano, A. (2000). 'Coloniality of Power and Eurocentrism in Latin America'. *International Sociology, 15*(2), 215–232.

Rajagopal, B. (2003). *International Law from Below: Development, Social Movements and Third World Resistance.* Cambridge: Cambridge University Press.

Shivji, I. (2007). *Silences in NGO Discourse: The Role and Future of NGOs in Africa.* Cape Town: Pambazuka Press.

Walker, K. (2008). 'Neoliberalism on the Ground in Rural India: Predatory Growth, Agrarian Crisis, Internal Colonization, and the Intensification of Class Struggle'. *Journal of Peasant Studies, 35*(4), 557–620.

Wallerstein, I. (2012). 'Land, Space and People: Constraints of the Capitalist World-Economy'. *Journal of World Systems Research on Land Rights, 18*(1), 6–14.

Williams, R. (2010). *The Divided World: Human Rights and its Violence.* Minneapolis: University of Minnesota Press.

3

NGOs, Indigenous Peoples and the United Nations

Sharon H. Venne

Introduction

A non-governmental organization (NGO) cannot represent the rights of Indigenous Nations. Indigenous Nations must speak for Indigenous Peoples in any international and national gathering that affects our rights. State governments at the United Nations (UN) and other international gatherings have tried to corral Indigenous Peoples into an NGO system and away from our Nationhood. This chapter will explore these and many other issues related to our quest for our rights to be decolonized and to be free to have our own nations as intended by our Creation.

In order to understand an Indigenous relationship with an NGO, it is important to start at the beginning. Here I look at NGOs from our point of view as an Indigenous person who is part of an Indigenous Nation.[1] It is sufficient at this point to write that our nations are not non-governmental. We are not an organization. We are not advocating anything in the traditional sense of the word. Indigenous Peoples are not arguing for a cause or pushing an agenda. We are Nations who have been colonized. Indigenous Peoples are trying to free ourselves from colonization. Our road to freedom does not come wrapped in NGO packaging.

Indigenous Nations: Inherent rights

It is always a direction from our ancestors to remind the reader that Indigenous Nations continue to exist on Great Turtle Island.[2] Each of our Indigenous Nations has our own laws, our own government, and our own territories that have been in existence since our Creation. There are hundreds of Indigenous Nations residing on Great Turtle Island. In our territories, we have responsibilities to the lands and resources based on our laws. In our own ways, we lived in harmony with the Creation.[3] In our territories, our clans set out their jurisdiction and responsibilities to the lands and resources. Our Clan Mothers carried the law of our Peoples. The Clan Mothers ensured that there was harmony and balance in the lives of all our Peoples. The harmony between Nations was the highest priority of our Peoples. When we refer to Nations, we are referring to all living and non-living entities. It is a worldview that guides and protects our lives for the future generations. Our ancestors based their decisions on the effect it would have on the seventh generation. This is not an ideal lifestyle. It is the laws of our Peoples. These are the laws that are overtaken by the work of NGOs.

During our time on Great Turtle Island, we made many contributions to our wellbeing. We had secure food sources, clean waters and good relations with all of Creation. There has been much written about starvation amongst our peoples. These stories usually end with the arrival of the visitors who supposedly saved us. Starvation did not occur until after the arrival of the visitors to our Island. The non-Indigenous visitors without any knowledge of the laws of the land destroyed the land, water and the resources.

Very extensive trade routes crisscrossed Great Turtle Island. In the east, the people grew corn and tobacco, a necessary element of certain ceremonies. Our ancestors would trade goods from our area for their goods. It was on these trade routes that the visitors were able to find their way across our Island. Then, the non-Indigenous person put their name on the route as if they had found it. The whole of Turtle Island is covered by these false names. Our goal as Indigenous Nations is to remember and honor our own names for our territories.

In our history, as told to us by our Elders, there are references to journeys from the east to the west, from the north to the south. Our Nations crossed our Island without any harm, as there were numerous peace and friendship treaties amongst the Nations. The Cree Nation has treaties with the Blackfoot Confederacy, the Dene Nation, the Lakota Peoples, and the Ojibway Peoples. This is a sample of our extensive treaty relationships. These Peace and Friendship Treaties were marked by certain exchanges that are a visual reminder of the relationships made by our ancestors. A couple of years ago, there was a ceremony with the Lakota Peoples to confirm the peace and friendship treaty made by our ancestors. This Treaty is important to our peoples. It deals with peace and friendship over large areas of central Turtle Island where our buffalo relatives roamed prior to the arrival of the visitors on our island.

Colonization

This changed with the arrival of the non-Indigenous People on our island. It is really amazing that the arrival of a sailor lost on the big waters would have such a dramatic effect on our Nations. The arrival of the visitors brought death, disease and destruction to our territories. We have been engaged in a battle of survival of our Nations as colonization runs amok amongst our peoples and our lands. For nearly five hundred years, our voice was not heard. We were too busy trying to survive.

Indigenous Peoples and Indigenous Nations of Great Turtle Island[4] began the long journey back to our rightful place as Nations among the family of nations. This long journey began in the 1920s with the attempt by Deskaheh of the Haudenosaunee to speak at the League of Nations in Geneva (Venne, 1998; Lyons, 1993). At that time, Canada did not have a voting seat within the League of Nations because, as a colony of Great Britain, it had no real international personality. With the formation of the League of Nations, the British Empire inscribed itself. Under the British Empire were many commonwealth entities including Canada, India, New Zealand, Australia, South Africa and many others. The British Empire had one vote. There were no votes for the different entities of the 'Empire'. The confusion of rights at the League of Nations led to a commonwealth conference to resolve the issues. Despite the work of the commonwealth, the issue remains that Canada is a colonizer. Under international law, colonizers do not have a right of self-determination, whereas the colonized do.[5] Deskaheh, living within a colonizer state, was able to lobby the Netherlands, based on Treaties made with his ancestors. As a result, he was given permission to present a petition to the League of Nations – until Canada approached Great Britain to stop Deskaheh from speaking in Geneva. The petition was brought from Great Turtle Island to have the League of Nations recognize the Indigenous Nations like all other nations of the world. Canada did not want the Indigenous Nations to be recognized. If Deskaheh was allowed to make a presentation as a member of an Indigenous Nation, the whole question of the state of Canada would be raised. This was Deskaheh's goal. Canada's goal was to ensure that he would not address the League as an Indigenous Nations representative.

There followed a volley of lobbying between states within the League. Deskaheh received support from the Netherlands, Estonia, Ireland, Panama, and Persia. However, Canada and Great Britain strongly opposed Deskaheh's attempts to be received by the League of Nations. Great Britain regarded support for Deskaheh as interference in its domestic affairs, and lobbied Deskaheh's supporters to back down. Canada and Great Britain's efforts to prevent Deskaheh from appealing to the League of Nations succeeded (Titley, 1986, pp. 91–100; Veatch, 1975, pp. 121–124). The League of Nations tried to silence Deskaheh, but the Canton of Geneva recognized Haudenosaunee Peoples' right to self-determination. In 1923, Deskaheh was invited by the Canton of Geneva to give a landmark address that would be remembered by citizens in 1977. In 1977 when the Haudenosaunee came back to the United Nations for an NGO conference, the mayor of Geneva, who had been a young boy in the 1920s, remembered that Deskaheh spoke. He remembered that the city of Geneva gave permission for the future generations to come back using their own passports. In 1977 and until this date, Haudenosaunee Peoples travel on their own passports into the canton of Geneva to attend meetings of the United Nations.

The colonial state of Canada, by contrast, took increasing action to stop the assertion of nationhood by Indigenous Nations throughout the 1920s. In the case of the Haudenosaunee, Canada made special efforts by attacking the traditional council. The traditional councils are comprised of the men and women of Indigenous societies. These Councils conduct the business of the Nation, including use and allocation of resources within their territories. In early August 1924, Canada 'moved quickly to secure an order-in-council authorizing the change to an elective form of government for the Six Nations' (Titley, 1986, pp. 110–134). The state took action in Geneva and in Canada to stop the assertion of Indigenous nationhood. Canada went one step further to impact all the Indigenous Nations living within Canada by changing the *Indian Act*[6] in 1927 to prohibit Indians from raising money to defend themselves against the action of the state, or taking legal action against Canada.[7] These are but a few examples in the long history of Canada denying Indigenous Nations our rightful place among the family of nations.

United Nations

It would take a new institution – the United Nations (UN) – and sixty-six years[8] before Indigenous Nations could try to address an international meeting in our own voices. When the UN was established in 1946, there were many goals and objectives to achieve lasting peace. The UN Charter sets out this goal:

> To develop friendly relations among nations based on respect for the principle of equal rights and self-determination of peoples, and to take other appropriate measures to strengthen universal peace.[9]

With this goal, what has the UN done to support Indigenous Nations to gain our rightful place among the family of nations? Indigenous Nations have been asserting our rights as Nations while state governments who sit on our territories have resisted our attempts. Indigenous Nations have been determined to maintain peace since contact with the settlers. When our ancestors made treaties with the British Crown, it was for peace and friendship. Our Indigenous Nations continue to live in a peaceful way despite all the attempts by the state of Canada to dispossess and use our resources without our free, prior and informed consent. These are our rights as Peoples and Nations. The UN Charter supports our rights to assert our right of self-determination. Yet this remains a goal not realized, and in large part frustrated by, the work of NGOs in recent decades.

The road is no easier now than it was in 1946. Indigenous Nations struggle to survive. Same story – same process. Colonization continues. The NGO process has a lot to answer for because of its role in the continued denial of the voice of Indigenous Nations. We are not sitting at the table in our own right as Nations.

It is important to remember the history of the UN's creation. The League of Nations failed to secure peace and harmony in the world. With the horrors of the Second World War, the 'winning' side decided to recreate an international organization. In the formation of the organization, there was an addition of a new entity – Non-Governmental Organizations (Jones, 1989, pp. 154–162). Within the rules of the organization, the criteria for being recognized by the UN system were set out through an NGO accreditation process. In applying to be recognized, there are rules for their participation set out in Article 71 of the Charter (see Appendix 3.1):

> The Economic and Social Council may make suitable arrangements for consultation with non-governmental organizations, which are concerned with matters within its competence. Such arrangements may be made with international organizations and, where appropriate, with national organizations after consultation with the Member of the United Nations concerned.

There are three important criteria set out in Article 71 that limit Indigenous Nations in being classified as an NGO. First, an NGO has to be a national organization; second, there needs to be consultation with the member state. In the case of Indigenous Nations, we are not a single nation. There are numerous Nations across Turtle Island. It is the wish of the colonizers that we would be classified under one nation or organization. In Canada, the state enacted the *Indian Act*. The Act applies uniformly across Canada to many diverse Nations who have our own unique laws and governmental structures. However, the state of Canada wanted one form of government and one legal system. For a colonial power, this is easier to manage and sell to settler citizens. When Indigenous Nations complain about the legal structure imposed on us, the state easily points to the supposed 'lack of cohesion' that existed before. This is the same argument put forth to demand a single NGO represent all the diverse Indigenous Nations across our Turtle Island. But one NGO does not offer a solution to us under the rules of the UN. Thirdly, a significant aspect of the establishment of the criteria for the UN is a reference to 'competence'.[10] What is a matter of competence for Indigenous Nations? It is simple really: we are colonized since 1492. Where can Indigenous Nations go to gain peaceful decolonization? It should be the United

Nations that was established to build and secure peace amongst the world's Nations and Peoples. Instead, the states have used NGOs to manipulate and control the process to deny our rights as Nations.

Non-governmental organizations

Under UN rules, an NGO is a legally constituted organization created by natural or legal persons that operates independently from any government. The NGO office has specific criteria that have to be followed. Consultative status is granted by the UN Economic and Social Council (ECOSOC) upon recommendation of the ECOSOC Committee on NGOs, comprised of 19 Member States.

In this process, there are three categories of status: General consultative status, Special consultative status and Roster status. General consultative status is reserved for large international NGOs whose area of work covers most of the issues on the agenda of ECOSOC and its subsidiary bodies. Special consultative status is granted to NGOs that have a special competence in, and are concerned specifically with, only a few of the fields of activity covered by the ECOSOC. Organizations that apply for consultative status but do not fit in any of the other categories are usually included in the Roster. The Roster lists NGOs that ECOSOC or the UN Secretary-General considers can make 'occasional and useful contributions to the work of the Council or its subsidiary bodies'.

In order to be eligible for UN consultative status, an NGO must have been in existence (officially recognized by a government) for at least two years, must have an established headquarters, a democratically adopted constitution, authority to speak for its members, a representative structure, appropriate mechanisms of accountability and democratic and transparent decision-making processes. The basic resources of the organization must be derived in the main part from contributions of the national affiliates or other components or from individual members.

In the many years that I have attended various meetings at the UN, NGO representatives have been subjected to various restrictions. In meetings, the time for NGO presentations can be cut from ten minutes down to two minutes. This is designed to silence the NGO representation. Of course, state representatives would argue that the time was running out and that NGOs are in the room to assist in the work, not to control it. It is a constant struggle. As a means to control the role of the NGO, state representatives suggest that NGOs should work together to produce an omnibus statement. It is another way to control the role of the NGO. Many NGOs happily go along with the process. Larger NGOs have more capacity to draft and lobby their statements; so smaller NGOs lose their voice in the process.

A state can also make a complaint to the ECOSOC Committee on NGOs against a particular NGO. Such a complaint when investigated could lead to suspension or loss of consultative status. If an NGO does not follow the rules as set out, they can find themselves suspended and unable to participate in meetings of the UN. In addition, NGOs must adhere to guidelines on speaking and materials submitted to the various bodies. For example, there is often a limit of one speaker per NGO under an agenda item, which causes great problems for diverse Indigenous Nations.

Many NGOs are funded totally or partially by governments. Indigenous Peoples refer to those as 'GONGOs' – Government Controlled Non-Governmental Organizations. Those NGOs have a lot of cash to travel and attend meetings. They cooperate closely with state governments by receiving funds directly or indirectly from state institutions. When an NGO takes funds from a state government, restrictions are placed on the funds. The deliverables become the goals of the state. These organizations set themselves up under the laws of the state. They attract individuals to their boards who do not represent Indigenous Nations but rather sit in their capacity as individuals. This dramatically destroys the voice of the Indigenous Nations. These kinds of NGOs do not report to the Indigenous Nations. They report to the funders. These organizations need to keep people employed and struggle to find those funds to stay afloat. In this atmosphere, it is easy to compromise the rights of Indigenous Nations.

There is no standard definition of 'NGO', unlike the term 'intergovernmental organization' that has a legal definition. The term that is often interchanged with NGO is 'civil society'. Again, Indigenous Nations are not civil society. Indigenous Nations might develop our own intergovernmental processes but not as organizations. This is the general state of affairs that Indigenous Peoples encountered at the 1977 NGO conference.

1977 NGO conference

In the 1970s, the UN started to look into the problem of discrimination against Indigenous communities, Peoples and Nations as having political organizations and a historical continuity with pre-invasion and pre-colonial societies on our territories. The UN Sub-commission on the Prevention of Discrimination and Protection of Minorities named José Martinez Cobo to undertake a study on this, which took twelve years to complete. Meanwhile, the UN was in its second decade dedicated to eliminating racial discrimination. At the same time, Indigenous Nations in Canada and the United States were experiencing serious difficulties. In 1969 Canada issued the 'White Paper' policy with the ultimate objective of getting rid of its constitutional reference to Indians and terminating the treaties made with the Crown.

The National Leader in Canada was George Manuel – president of the National Indian Brotherhood (NIB). He started to travel outside of Canada to other areas of the world where Indigenous Peoples faced similar problems. In October 1975, he was instrumental in organizing the first international conference on Indigenous Peoples in North America in Port Alberni, Vancouver Island. From this conference, an Indigenous NGO was created: the World Council of Indigenous Peoples (WCIP). Prior to the creation of WCIP, the NIB had an agreement with the UN from 1974 to allow them accreditation to attend meetings within the UN system. There was a condition to their accreditation. The NIB had to be engaged in seeking to establish an international organization. The WCIP received its UN consultative accreditation in 1979.

For many years, this NGO was situated in Lethbridge, Alberta. Indigenous Peoples used to come to Lethbridge to work at the NGO. The organizational structure of the WCIP was designed to mirror the Indigenous Nations with a rotating chair and board members. This was a good idea, but hard to organize on a long-term basis. Due to funding problems, the WCIP moved to Ottawa under the NIB. Once there, an office manager was installed who also made decisions on the organization's direction. Since funding came from government, the organization was overtaken by the work of the Indigenous Nations in the meetings at the UN. Over the years, the NGO lost its credibility with Indigenous Peoples and slipped from the international stage.

In the United States, there were land issues and violation of treaties.

The Wounded Knee Occupation in 1973 led to the push for International work. The confrontations between Indigenous Peoples and US federal authorities at Wounded Knee led to the creation of the International Indian Treaty Council (IITC). It applied for accreditation from the UN, which was received in 1977. The Treaty Peoples of Canada joined with the American Indians to go to the United Nations.

A conference was organized by several organizations in Geneva as part of the activity around the second decade against racism. The Conference on Discrimination against Indigenous Peoples of the Americas drew 82 representatives of Indigenous Nations. In 1977, Indigenous Peoples travelled to the Palais des Nations to bring their voices forward. It was a call for action on racism and discrimination experienced by Indigenous Nations.

The most significant event there took place before the first official meeting. The Elders from our Nations gathered on the grass in front of the Palais des Nations and had a pipe ceremony, following the protocol of our Nations. The Elders carrying the pipes with the drummers singing walked onto the grounds of the UN. The main speaker for our Peoples is our sacred pipe given to us by the Creation. It leads the way. We used our own laws and traditions to enter that meeting. We were not bound by the protocols of the UN to enter quietly and without ceremony. Our Nations walked proudly.

It was clear to the Indigenous Nations present at that meeting that no instrument existed within the UN system to promote and protect our interests. Our rights are held collectively for the future generations. Indigenous Nations do not put an individual ahead of the collective. It is the collective that has to survive. An individual's action can be very destructive to collective rights. So in those meetings, Indigenous Peoples started to draft our own declaration of our rights. It seemed to the delegates that many speakers who were familiar with the UN system kept talking about various UN instruments. In those speeches, Indigenous Peoples did not hear their voices. In the end, it was decided that Indigenous Peoples would draft our own Declaration of our Rights as recognized by our Elders and Leaders. The drafting started in 1977 as an Indigenous initiative, not a state process. That process with the states came much later in the history of our relationship at the UN.

In that instance, some NGOs were able to assist Indigenous Nations to voice their concerns within the confines of an NGO conference. This kind of conference had less restrictions than a UN meeting.

Representatives of the Indigenous Nations were able to speak and bring their issues to the front. There was a call for the UN to do more to promote the rights of Indigenous Peoples. Indigenous Nations wanted to be recognized as all other nations of the world. The delegation gathered at the large globe in front of the Palais des Nations for a photograph to show the world that we were like all other nations. From this heady meeting, the UN did nothing.

Cobo's final report would take another five years. Martinez Cobo was bound by the United Nations when he started the report. The working definition of Indigenous Peoples was set out in his final report:

Indigenous communities, peoples and nations are those which, having a historical continuity with pre-invasion and pre-colonial societies that developed on their territories, consider themselves distinct from other sectors of the societies now prevailing on those territories, or parts of them. They form at present non-dominant sectors of society and are determined to preserve, develop and transmit to future generations their ancestral territories, and their ethnic identity, as the basis of their continued existence as peoples, in accordance with their own cultural patterns, social institutions and legal system.

This historical continuity may consist of the continuation, for an extended period reaching into the present of one or more of the following factors:

a) Occupation of ancestral lands, or at least of part of them;
b) Common ancestry with the original occupants of these lands;
c) Culture in general, or in specific manifestations (such as religion, living under a tribal system, membership of an indigenous community, dress, means of livelihood, lifestyle, etc.);
d) Language (whether used as the only language, as mother-tongue, as the habitual means of communication at home or in the family, or as the main, preferred, habitual, general or normal language);
e) Residence on certain parts of the country, or in certain regions of the world;
f) Other relevant factors.

On an individual basis, an indigenous person is one who belongs
to these indigenous populations through self-identification as
indigenous (group consciousness) and is recognized and accepted
by these populations as one of its members (acceptance by the
group).

This preserves for these communities the sovereign right and
power to decide who belongs to them, without external interference.[11]

It was this definition of Indigenous Nations and Peoples that was
accepted. We were from lands that were colonized and have had no
means to decolonize ourselves. The working definition had some
difficulties but Indigenous Peoples and Nations had 'a historical continuity with pre-invasion and pre-colonial societies that developed on
their territories, consider themselves distinct from other sectors of the
societies now prevailing on those territories, or parts of them'.[12] Indigenous Nations continued to dialogue with the supporting NGO in an
attempt to create an atmosphere where the rights of Indigenous Peoples
would be taken up as a serious area of concern to the UN.

1981 NGO conference

In the four years after the 1977 conference, Indigenous Peoples
continued to organize themselves. From the western part of Turtle
Island, we initiated a major lobby in London on the Patriation process
of Canada's Constitution. In the course of the lobby effort, we encountered many organizations in London and elsewhere in Europe. Some
were willing to assist us in our struggle for the recognition of our
treaties and our rights to our resources.

A second NGO conference was organized in 1981 at the UN offices
in Geneva, Switzerland, starting in the same way as the 1977 conference with a pipe ceremony and the walk into the building with the
pipe. This conference focused on the rights of Indigenous Peoples,
especially treaty rights. The Treaty Six, Seven and Eight Chiefs of
Alberta made major interventions calling for a process to recognize
our treaties.

At the same time that conference was taking place, the UN was
moving through its Commission on Human Rights[13] to create a working

group within the UN system to deal with the rights of Indigenous Peoples.

The significance of the NGO-organized meeting was simple to our way of thinking. We were able to address the meetings in our own right. We were not restricted in our presentation based on UN rules. At that time, our Elders and Chiefs did not know how the UN really worked. It was a place that we could voice our concerns about our treaties and try to find a place to get some measure of support for our rights as Nations.

We were as green as grass. We did not know how to make interventions. We did not know how the documentation worked. We did not know the language of interventions. We did not know how to articulate our plight within the terms of the UN. We knew one thing: our Nations were occupied by colonizers and our treaties were not respected.

We continued to draft our Indigenous declaration in the evenings and at coffee breaks. As we discussed various topics at the workshops, the work on the issues to be included in the declaration advanced. In the evenings during our internal meetings, there were long discussions on the clauses for inclusion. If it was agreed, then a clause was drafted and added to the growing declaration.

Working Group on Indigenous Peoples (WGIP)

The UN Commission on Human Rights' staff person Augusto Willemsen-Diaz was charged with researching and drafting the Martinez Cobo report and worked with Theo Van Boven, director of the Division of Human Rights to push a draft mandate for a working group. They developed the terms of reference for the Working Group on Indigenous Populations (WGIP). It had a two-fold mandate: to receive information on recent developments amongst Indigenous Peoples and to develop standards on the rights of Indigenous Peoples. The mandate gave Indigenous Peoples a place to bring information regarding their situation. On a yearly basis from 1982 until the end of the WGIP in 2006, Indigenous Peoples by the hundreds brought information to the UN. It was the highest attended meeting next to the General Assembly.

Almost immediately after the UN created the WGIP in 1982,

Indigenous Peoples referred to the Working Group as one on Indigenous Peoples and not 'populations'. We are not objects of international law. We are subjects. A population refers to insects, deer or lions. We are not like the wildlife of the state to be controlled and managed. The term 'population' was always offensive to the Indigenous Nations.

It was clear from the first meeting of the Working Group in 1982 that there were other problems, such as conforming with the NGO system and the rules of meeting procedures within the UN. In the UN system, there is only one speaker per NGO under an agenda item. If there was more than one Indigenous Nation represented at the meeting who wanted to speak, they were prohibited due to the rules of procedure. This was a cause of great concern. The members of the working group who represented the five regions as designated by the system were lobbied by Indigenous Peoples to open the process. The main argument was simple: we have travelled from our territories to the meeting. We are delegated by our Nations to make statements about the situation in our homelands. One of the WGIP's mandates was to receive information about recent developments within Indigenous territories. The only way that the UN could fulfill that mandate was to hear directly from Indigenous Peoples and Nations. Within two years of the WGIP's initial meetings, Indigenous Peoples were allowed to make presentations in our own right. In the WGIP's first years, the items for discussion were setting up the future agenda. Meanwhile, Indigenous Peoples continued to work on our declaration. By the end of the 1985 session, the number of sections in the declaration had grown to twenty-two. Then, an NGO did something without the consent of Indigenous Peoples.

Declaration drafting by the WGIP

In the 1985, the Four Directions Council – an NGO with consultative status – took the work of the Indigenous Peoples and Nations and submitted the draft sections to the members of the Working Group. The representative of the Four Directions Council was a non-Indigenous person who was observing the working meetings of Indigenous Peoples. During the discussions on the draft sections, there were non-Indigenous Peoples in the room who listened to the discussions as they had requested. They said that they wanted to support the initiatives of

Indigenous Peoples and needed to hear their concerns in order to accomplish more comprehensive support. The introduction of the work done by Indigenous Peoples started us on a trek that would take us away from our main agenda. We went to the UN to promote our rights as Nations and Peoples. The drafting of a declaration within the Human Rights area of the UN system moved us towards a 'state managed' process. The drafting process also consumed large amounts of resources of Indigenous Nations. At one point, the Working Group met for ten working days. Meetings always occurred in Geneva. There were attempts over the years to move the drafting to the other countries where the UN has regional offices. This did not happen.

Indigenous Peoples were forced to defend our original work. Indigenous Peoples were pushed into actions to maintain our voice as the state governments used their considerable resources to try to torpedo the process. Each year, state representatives presented papers on various topics related to the drafting. Indigenous Peoples were forced to try to respond to those papers and positions. In those years, hundreds of Indigenous Peoples came to the Working Group and their voices were added to the drafting of an instrument. The final product of the Working Group was the effort of hundreds if not thousands of Indigenous Peoples.

In the normal course of events, the draft declaration would have gone to the Sub-commission then to the Commission on Human Rights as it made its way through the system. However, the course of things did not go smoothly, as will be discussed below. The Commission on Human Rights threw a curve ball into the mix, by deciding to create a new body: an intersessional working group. Although it is now a common practice, there was no previous history of UN intersessional working groups. Indigenous Peoples would be dragged through yet another drafting process. State governments wanted to take another opportunity to change the wording. Indigenous NGOs would participate, but the process was going to be closed to Indigenous Nations and Peoples. The hundreds of Indigenous Peoples and Nations who participated in the original drafting would be excluded by the resolution passed by the Commission on Human Rights. Indigenous NGOs working with non-Indigenous NGOs would take the voice of Indigenous Peoples.

Intersessional Working Groups

State governments in the Commission on Human Rights made the argument that they needed to participate in the elaboration of a declaration on the rights of Indigenous Peoples. The one big problem with their argument was that during the work of the Working Group, state governments were already involved on a yearly basis in the drafting process. They had their input. The actual problem for the state governments was their inability to convince the expert members of the Working Group that their positions were correct. So at the first opportunity, state governments struck, by creating a new process.

The open-ended inter-sessional Working Group on the declaration was established in 1995 in accordance with Commission on Human Rights resolution 1995/32 and Economic and Social Council resolution 1995/32 (see Appendix 3.2). The Working Group had the sole purpose of elaborating and formalizing the draft contained in the annex to resolution 1994/45 of 26 August 1994 entitled 'draft United Nations declaration on the rights of Indigenous Peoples'. The draft was prepared for consideration and adoption by the General Assembly during the International Decade of the World's Indigenous People (1995–2004).[14]

The Working Group on the declaration was an organ of the Commission on Human Rights and was composed of representatives of Member States. The relevant sections of the resolution are:

6.   Requests the Committee on Non-Governmental Organizations to meet as necessary to examine the applications and, having considered all relevant information, including any views received from the States concerned, to recommend to the Economic and Social Council those organizations of indigenous people which should be authorized to participate in the Working Group, including at its first session in 1995;

7.   Decides, on the basis of the recommendations of the Committee on Non-Governmental Organizations, to authorize the participation in the work of the Working Group of interested organizations of indigenous people, in accordance with rules 75 and 76 of the rules of procedure of the functional commissions of the Economic and Social Council;

XIII. CONSULTATION WITH AND REPRESENTATION OF NON-GOVERNMENTAL ORGANIZATIONS

Representation

Rule 75

Non-governmental organizations in category I or II may designate authorized representatives to sit as observers at public meetings of the commission and its subsidiary organs. Those on the Roster may have representatives present at such meetings when matters within their field of competence are being discussed.

Consultation

Rule 76

1. The commission may consult with organizations in category I or II either directly or through a committee or committees established for the purpose. In all cases, such consultations may be arranged on the invitation of the commission or at the request of the organization.

2. On the recommendation of the Secretary-General and at the request of the commission, organizations on the Roster may also be heard by the commission.

After years of participation in the drafting of the declaration in our own right as Nations and Peoples speaking for our peoples, we were being pushed into the accreditation system and away from our right to speak from our Nations. The Commission on Human Rights resolution 1995/32 also sets out a procedure for participation for Indigenous 'organizations without consultative status'. Those 'organizations', not Nations and Peoples, would be accredited following the standard NGO process. The General Assembly, in its resolution 50/156 of 21 December 1995, decided that the UN Voluntary Fund for Indigenous Populations should also be used to assist representatives of indigenous communities and organizations *authorized* to participate in the deliberations of the Working Group on the elaboration of the declaration. This gesture amounted to a very small carrot; the whole process would be limited to organizations of Indigenous Peoples approved under the procedure established by Commission resolution 1995/32, or with ECOSOC status.

At the first meeting of the intersessional working group, Indigenous Peoples and Nations arrived. There was a concerted effort to change the rules of procedure to allow Indigenous Nations and Peoples to participate in the elaboration of a declaration on our rights. In the first days of the session, Indigenous Peoples refused to participate in the meetings without the recognition of their inherent right to participate in our own right. The system ground to a halt. The state governments refused to meet without Indigenous Peoples in the room, as they needed to have Indigenous Peoples to give legitimacy to their own created process. Indigenous delegates also came to a consensus decision. There would be no participation in the session until Indigenous Peoples would be allowed to participate in our own right.

A dialogue was opened with the state governments concerning the issue of representation in the process. Things were proceeding along as Indigenous delegates continued to remain outside the room. The bells would ring to start the meeting and no Indigenous Peoples were in the room, so the session would be adjourned. This continued until one afternoon when the representative of an NGO – the International Indian Treaty Council – walked into the session and made a statement. When she was confronted by Indigenous Peoples, she said: 'My board of directors instructed me to go into the room and make a presentation'. Indigenous Peoples questioned if the board was aware that a consensus had been reached amongst the Indigenous Peoples to stay together. Once the NGO went into the room, other NGOs started to participate. In the end, consensus was broken. The intersessional work would grind on for years, eventually being overtaken by the restructuring of the Human Rights section of the UN. The Commission on Human Rights was reorganized into the Human Rights Council that adopted a Chairman's view of the declaration. It was eventually taken to the General Assembly.

Concluding remarks

In the General Assembly, accredited Indigenous and non-Indigenous NGOs made decisions about the declaration without the input of the Indigenous Nations. Many non-Indigenous NGOs constituted a major influence in the final outcome. Those NGOs did not report or ask permission of the Indigenous Nations to make the changes to the

Declaration as it was drafted by the hundreds of Indigenous Nations and Peoples who participated in their own right in the Working Group. NGOs are not a friend of Indigenous Nations. They report and get their direction from their funding agencies. In their work, the rights of the Nations and Peoples do not matter. The goal of the NGO is to survive and ensure that their staff are paid on a regular basis. This is a goal of the colonizer: the voice of the land and the nations are not heard. We continue to live in colonial states.

Appendix 3.1

REPERTORY OF PRACTICE OF UNITED NATIONS ORGANS

SUPPLEMENT No. 7
(Revised advance version, to be issued in volume IV of Supplement No. 7 (forthcoming) of the Repertory of Practice of United Nations Organs)
Volume IV
ARTICLE 71

Text of Article 71

ARTICLE 71
TEXT OF ARTICLE 71

The Economic and Social Council may make suitable arrangements for consultation with non-governmental organizations, which are concerned with matters within its competence. Such arrangements may be made with international organizations and, where appropriate, with national organizations after consultation with the Member of the United Nations concerned.

INTRODUCTORY NOTE

1. The structure of the present study for Article 71 remains the same as those for supplements 5 and 6.

I. General Survey

2. During the period under review, the relevant United Nations Organs, as their subsidiary bodies (notably the Council Committee on Non-Governmental Organizations) continued to interpret and apply Article 71 in similar manner as in the past. Cited repeatedly during the period, as in the past, was Council resolution 1298 (XLIV).

**A. The purpose of consultation

**B. Establishment of consultative relationships

II. Analytical Summary of Practice

The Council Committee on Non-Governmental Organizations

3. During the period under review, the Council Committee on Non-Governmental (the Committee) continued to meet biennially and to conduct its work in the same manner as in the past. The

Committee did, however, recommend to the Economic and Social Council (the Council) that the committee should schedule its future sessions in such a manner as not to coincide with those of other subsidiary bodies.

B. Admission to, and review of, consultative status

4. During this period, one recurring issue was that of the Committee's review process for applications to consultative status with the United Nations, and its power, under Council resolution 1296 (XLIV), to withhold consultative status from some organizations and to withdraw it from others.

5. In 1985, the council decided to withdraw the consultative status of the International Police Association. The Association had been found to have connections with apartheid South Africa, since 850 policemen from apartheid South Africa had been granted membership to this NGO. '[M]ost delegations supported the decision because of the active link between the International Police Association and the Government of South Africa; other delegations supported the decision because the organization had provided misinformation to the committee'.

6. The resultant Draft Decision which read: 'The Economic and Social Council decides to withdraw consultative status from the International Police Association', was adopted without vote as Council decision 1985/114.

7. In 1987, the Committee reported that one delegation had raised the issue of hidden funding being given to NGOs by governments. The governments in question would then use these organizations to promote their foreign policy. Such activity, according to this delegation, would be in contravention of Council Resolution 1296 (XLIV). The delegation therefore urged the Committee to be more careful in reviewing future applications and to withdraw consultative status from any such organization.

8. 'The Committee concluded its consideration of the item by appealing to all non-governmental Organizations in consultative status with the Economic and Social Council to respect the sovereignty, independence and territorial integrity of Member States and to accept and carry out the decisions of the Security Council in accordance with the provisions of the Charter of the United Nations'.

9. Also of note, during the period, was the Committee's rejection of the Sikh Commonwealth's application for consultative status. 'The Committee considered that the unanimous rejection of the application of the Sikh Commonwealth reflected the Committee's strong belief that the goals and objectives of that organization were incompatible with the purposes and principles of the United Nations and the provisions of Economic and Social Council resolution 1296 (XLIV)'. That resolution outlined grounds for withdrawal of consultative status, one of which was evidence of governmental financial influence to induce an NGO to undertake acts contrary to the purposes and principles of the United Nations.

Appendix 3.2

Establishment of a working group of the Commission on Human Rights to elaborate a draft declaration in accordance with paragraph 5 of General Assembly resolution 49/214 Economic and Social Council resolution 1995/32

The Economic and Social Council,

Recalling Commission on Human Rights resolution 1995/32 of 3 March 1995, 1/,

Reaffirming its resolution 1296 (XLIV) of 23 May 1968, on arrangements for consultation with non-governmental organizations, in particular its paragraphs 9, 19 and 33,

Recalling the mandate of the Committee on Non-governmental Organizations, especially as contained in paragraph 40 (e) of resolution 1296 (XLIV),

1. Endorses Commission on Human Rights resolution 1995/32 of 3 March 1995;

2. Authorizes the establishment, as a matter of priority and from within existing overall United Nations resources, of an open-ended intersessional working group of the Commission on Human Rights, operating in accordance with the procedures established by the Commission in the annex to its resolution 1995/32, with the sole purpose of elaborating a draft declaration, considering the draft United Nations declaration on the rights of indigenous peoples annexed to resolution 1994/45 of 26 August 1994 of the Subcommission on Prevention of Discrimination and Protection of Minorities, for consideration and adoption by the General Assembly within the International Decade of the World's Indigenous People;

3. Also authorizes the open-ended Working Group to meet for 10 working days at the earliest possible date in 1995;

4. Invites applications from organizations of indigenous people not in consultative status with the Economic and Social Council that are interested in participating in the Working Group;

5. Requests the Coordinator of the Decade, in accordance with the procedures established by the Commission on Human Rights in its resolution 1995/32 and following consultations with the States concerned, and in accordance with Article 71 of the Charter of the

United Nations, to forward all applications and information received to the Committee on Non-Governmental Organizations;

6. Requests the Committee on Non-Governmental Organizations to meet as necessary to examine the applications and, having considered all relevant information, including any views received from the States concerned, to recommend to the Economic and Social Council those organizations of indigenous people which should be authorized to participate in the Working Group, including at its first session in 1995;

7. Decides, on the basis of the recommendations of the Committee on Non-Governmental Organizations, to authorize the participation in the work of the Working Group of interested organizations of indigenous people, in accordance with rules 75 and 76 of the rules of procedure of the functional commissions of the Economic and Social Council;

8. Requests the Commission on Human Rights at its fifty-second session to review the progress of the Working Group and to transmit its comments to the Economic and Social Council at its substantive session of 1996;

9. Requests the Secretary-General to provide the necessary services and facilities for the implementation of the present resolution.

Notes

1 In all my work, the Elders have directed that I speak about our rights as Nations. In this regard, the reference to 'our' means our Indigenous Nations. It is not as an individual that I write. I write as a collective.

2 In our Creation Story, we were placed on our Island (Great Turtle Island) since the beginning of time. We did not move from another place on earth to our present place. It is the colonization process that changed the name of our Island. Indigenous Nations know that we are floating on the back of a turtle. This is based on our creation stories.

3 Indigenous Peoples from my Nation (Cree) refer to the Creation rather than the 'Creator'. We do not believe in one Creator – that is a Christian value. There is a male and female spirit who came together to make life. So, we refer to the Creation.

4 America is not an Indigenous name. It is the name of an Italian mapmaker who wanted to leave his name somewhere. He put it on our lands. Indigenous Nations know that we are floating on the back of a turtle. This is based on our creation stories. We are neither from the garden nor descendants of inbreeding. Our Creation story is different.

5 Nirmal's (1999) *The Right of Self-determination in International Law* has a detailed description of the development of the international law concept of self-determination and its application. See also Sharon Venne's *Our Elders Understand Our Rights – Evolving International Law Regarding Indigenous Rights* (1998, p. 119–122). Venne also sets out a number of General Assembly Resolutions dealing with the issue of non-self-governing territories and their right to self-determination within international legal norms (footnote 31, p. 99). There have been a number of studies done by the United Nations on the issue of self-determination, particularly by Special Rapporteur Aurelieu Cristescu (E/CN.4/Sub.2/L.641) and Hector Gros Espiell (E.CN.4/Sub.2/405).

6 The parliament of Canada enacted legislation called the 'Indian Act' to initially control their administration of issues related to Indians but it quickly became a legal instrument to control the lives of Indians from birth to death (Venne, 1981). There is still an *Indian Act* in Canada.

7 *Indian Act*, R.S.C. 1927, c.98, s 141.

8 The first Working Group on Indigenous Peoples (Populations) was held on 9–13 August 1982. The previous meetings where Indigenous Peoples participated (1977 and 1981) were called Non-governmental Organization (NGO) Meetings.

9 Charter of the United Nations, 1 United Nations Treaty Series xvi; (1946). These documents are available on the general webpage of the United Nations.

10 The UN Competency Framework is outlined in their handbook, available from: http://un.org/staffdevelopment/DevelopmentGuideWeb/image/OHRM_CDG.pdf

11 *Supra* 1, paragraphs 379–382.

12 Cobo Report E/CN.4/Sub.2/1986/7/Add.4. The Cobo report that took Martinez Cobo twelve years to complete started in 1974, and was based on this definition of Indigenous Peoples as set out in the resolution for Cobo's work. This definition has not been changed.

13 As a procedural UN body, the UN Commission on Human Rights was

replaced by the UN Human Rights Council in 2006. As discussed below, this structural change was an added impediment to the progress of Indigenous self-determination at the UN level.

14 There is a long history of the decade which will not be reviewed in this chapter. It is another story of how state governments tried to diminish Indigenous Peoples (see for example, Churchill, 2011; Schulte-Tenckhoff, 1998; Schulte-Tenckhoff & Khan, 2011; Venne, 2011; Watson & Venne, 2012).

References

Churchill, W. (2011). 'A Travesty of a Mockery of a Sham – Colonialism as "Self-Determination" in the UN Declaration on the Rights of Indigenous Peoples'. *Griffith Law Review, 20*(3), 526–556.

Jones, D.V. (1989). *Code of Peace Ethics and Security in the World of the Warlord States.* Chicago: University of Chicago Press.

Lyons, O. (1993). 'Panel Discussion at the American Society of International Law'. *American Society of International Law – Annual Proceedings of the 87th Annual Meeting* (195). 31 March – 3 April 1993, at 195. (Remarks by Oren Lyons, Faithkeeper of the Onondaga Nation).

Nirmal, B.C. (1999). *The Right of Self-determination in International Law.* New Delhi: Deep and Deep Publications.

Schulte-Tenckhoff, I. (1998). 'Reassessing the Paradigm of Domestication: the Problematic of Indigenous Treaties'. *Review of Constitutional Studies, 4*(2), 239–89.

Schulte-Tenckhoff, I. (2012). 'Treaties, peoplehood, and self-determination: understanding the language of indigenous rights'. In E. Pulitano (Ed.) *Indigenous Rights in the Age of the UN Declaration* (pp. 64–86). Cambridge: Cambridge University Press.

Schulte-Tenckhoff, I. & Khan, A.H. (2011). 'The Permanent Quest for a Mandate: Assessing the UN Permanent Forum on Indigenous Issues'. *Griffith Law Review, 20*(3), 673–702.

Titley, B. (1986). *A Narrow Vision: Duncan Campbell Scott and the Administration of Indian Affairs in Canada.* Vancouver: University of British Columbia Press.

Veatch, R. (1975). *Canada and the League of Nations.* Toronto: University of Toronto Press.

Venne, S.H. (1998). *Our Elders Understand Our Rights: Evolving International Law Regarding Indigenous Rights.* Penticton: Theytus Press.

Venne, S.H. (2011). 'The Road to the United Nations and the Rights of Indigenous Peoples'. *Griffith Law Review, 20*(3), 557–577.

Venne, S.H. (Ed.) (1981). *Indian Act and Their Amendments (1868 – 1975) An Indexed Collection.* Saskatchewan: University of Saskatchewan Press.

Watson, I. & Venne, S.H. (2012). "Talking up Indigenous Peoples' original intent in a space dominated by state interventions'. In E. Pulitano (Ed.) *Indigenous Rights in the Age of the UN Declaration* (pp. 87–109). Cambridge: Cambridge University Press.

4

From Radical Movement to Conservative NGO and Back Again? A Case Study of the Democratic Left Front in South Africa

Luke Sinwell

The relationship between social movements and non-governmental organizations (NGOs) has recently been called into question by a number of radical authors who have pointed out that 'the revolution will not be funded' (INCITE! Women of Color against Violence, 2007). With the proliferation of NGOs internationally, struggles for social change risk becoming nine-to-five jobs that benefit the pockets of careerists, and thereby hold little hope for bringing about fundamental social change. Drawing from the Latin American context since the 1980s, Petras (1997) demonstrates that there has been 'a direct relation between the growth of social movements challenging the neoliberal model and the effort to subvert them by creating alternative forms of social action through the NGOs'. He further laments a situation in which 'NGOs became the "community face" of neoliberalism' (p. 1). In NGO discourse and even in the public's mind, NGOs were closer to 'the people', had the answers and were good. This was counterposed to the state, which was perceived as evil and the enemy. Terms such as 'popular power', 'empowerment', and development from the 'bottom-up' have been employed, increasingly from the 1980s, by a wide range of actors – the World Bank, social movements, NGOs, local governments and national states themselves. It is therefore vital to closely investigate the politics of those NGOs, social movements, states and others that have a relationship to popular organizations or communities and often wield power over them.

In South Africa, the time for (Nelson) Mandela-mania has long ended,[1] inequality between races has increased (South Africa is now considered one of the most unequal countries in the world) and a new wave of resistance movements like the Anti-Privatization Forum, the Landless People's Movement and Abahlali baseMjondolo (shack dwellers movement) have emerged arguably to contest the legitimacy of the state. Bond (2007) has argued that South Africa is the home of the most protests per capita in the world: ten thousand per year. One analyst has called a recent wave of service delivery protests, whereby communities have risen up to demand access to basic services such as water, electricity, and housing, and also to hold the local authorities accountable, the 'Rebellion of the Poor' (Alexander, 2010). In part, this is intended to signify the insurgency of primarily localized protests that tend to operate rather independently from any umbrella organization and, in many instances (at least initially), claim power from the state on their own terms. Sinwell et al. (2009) have traced the historical process through which four communities, having been excluded from the institutional channels provided by the government such as ward committees and development forums, then resorted to other more contentious tactics including direct action utilizing marches, boycotts and road occupations – leading to a heavy state response in the form of police repression.

Social movements have emerged in opposition to neoliberal policies, to meet basic needs, to address socio-economic rights, or to resist government's attempts at repression (Ballard, Habib, & Valodia, 2006, p. 2). Because social movements put forth alternative ideas of development, they are often stigmatized by the ruling African National Congress (ANC) government. According to Desai (2002), leaders of these movements in South Africa are labeled 'agitator, radical, and counter-revolutionary' (p. 16). Social movements therefore represent alternative sites of power. While initially activist writing and scholarship viewed social movements in binary opposition to the state, increasingly scholars have problematized this relationship given the power of the state to control militant communities who rise up to challenge specific local interventions of the hegemonic and ruling ANC (Sinwell, 2011). Furthermore, the demands of social movements often fit within the neoliberal parameters of the ANC.

This chapter uses a case study of the Democratic Left Front (DLF) to investigate alternatives to the NGOization of movements in post-apartheid South Africa. The DLF is a self-funded initiative established in South Africa in October 2008 in the context of the global economic crisis. It seeks to create a united anti-capitalist front of action, which is rooted in labor and community-based struggles. While NGOs have tended to assist movements in fighting legal battles within the confines of the constitution, they have also criticized communities' use of contentious tactics like the burning of property and the occupation of houses and roads. In contrast, the DLF has publicly indicated that the tactics of direct action and civil disobedience are necessary and legitimate forms of protest under a neoliberal state, but little is known about the politics of the DLF's actual practices and future trajectory. Drawing from interviews and participant observation, this chapter explores the relationship between local community-based organizations and the DLF. It questions the extent to which the DLF is able to build a counter-hegemonic force and thereby to offer a viable alternative to the NGOization of struggles in post-apartheid South Africa.

A number of questions have been raised about the NGOization of local struggles in post-apartheid South Africa, where neoliberal policies have been adopted since 1996 by the ANC. Referring to the late 1980s and early 90s, Hlatshwayo (2009) writes that NGOs shifted from 'popular struggles to policy-making' (p. 24). With the transition to democracy in 1994, NGOs, which were largely oppositional (to the state) during the anti-apartheid struggle, have had to redefine their role and now act primarily as service delivery agents for the ANC. In this context, some have warned that the reformist character of NGOs may have led to the containment of militant and potentially counter-hegemonic struggles in communities. In this regard, Mueller-Hirth (2009) explains that:

> NGO staff distanced themselves from social movements . . . by pitting 'constructive engagement' with the state against 'marching on the street'. Institutionalized politics, the media and the courts were in some interviews portrayed as the legitimate and proper channels through which policy can be impacted in the democratic era. Conversely, mass mobilization was portrayed as outdated, with the effect of it seemingly being no longer acceptable to use what was constructed as backward apartheid-era struggle tactics (p. 431).

In this chapter I suggest that, in the South African context, the NGOization of movements arises not only through the agency of NGOs, but also through various other social interactions with so-called 'outsider' academics, lawyers, the employment of the ruling ANC alliance, or even through local activists that carry with them conservative or liberal political agendas. These agents have expectations that social change must occur in the institutional spaces prescribed, and largely controlled, by the state. NGOization therefore occurs when agents intervene in local struggles undertaken by the working class or poor and have the effect of making them less militant. In other words, they shift the terrain of struggle from using direct action, at times illegal, to softer struggles in courts, more 'controlled' marches or even negotiations and workshops which are largely displaced from the realities of popular struggles. The following section discusses the politics of grassroots struggles in South Africa and critically reflects on how umbrella movements have engaged with them. The chapter then hones in to assess the DLF's relationship to grassroots struggles and seeks to understand the extent to which the DLF contributes to the NGOization of movements, or potentially offers a counter-hegemonic alternative through its engagement with these struggles.

Politics and interventions in grassroots struggles in South Africa

The relationship between so-called outsiders such as academics, NGO officials, and lawyers to grassroots organizations has been hotly debated in the South African context. One radical political activist and academic, Ashwin Desai (2006), has suggested that intellectuals bring their 'political diseases' (p. 2) to community-based organizations, thus indicating the negative and perhaps exploitative role that academics play in movements. He later wrote that social movements in post-apartheid South Africa have become a 'spent force', 'more like a conservative NGO, than a radical movement' (cited in Bohmke, 2010, p. 1). In a recent paper entitled 'Combined and Uneven Marxism', which attempts to come to grips with the limitations of community-based organizations to achieve a radical alternative, Bond, Desai, and Ngwane (2011, n.p.) have indicated that, 'in many cases what started out as insurgencies outside the control of the [ANC] Alliance were siphoned off into calls for participation, legal challenges, "voice"'.

Nevertheless, several attempts have been made to coordinate local protests in a way that challenges the ruling ANC and advances beyond the NGOization of struggles. Founded in Johannesburg in 2001, the Anti-Privatization Forum (APF) is an overtly anti-capitalist social movement which provides an important space in which communities can come together to learn about the power of the working class, and in doing so strategize ways to force the government to listen to the demands of the people. At its peak, the APF consisted of about 35 affiliates, mostly from poor communities who were fighting for basic services. The APF regularly held socialist education campaigns bringing together many of the affiliates. In the Gauteng province, the APF assisted communities, particularly those using direct action (such as marches, community controlled electricity, and water reconnections) and the courts, to fight for their rights – thereby providing a much-needed political home for these new civic formations.

One of the central affiliates within the APF, the Soweto Electricity Crisis Committee (SECC), is a good example of this. SECC emerged as a result of cost recovery schemes that have been implemented in Soweto. When people's electricity is shut off as a result of their inability to pay the power utility company ESKOM, members of the SECC have illegally reconnected them in order to claim what they believe is their right to electricity. Within a six-month period in 2003, SECC claims to have reconnected 3000 households (Ngwane, 2003, p. 47, cited in Egan & Wafer, 2004, p. 9).

Elsewhere however, I have argued that there is a disjuncture between the socialist ideology of the APF and its local affiliates (Sinwell, 2011). I suggest that local movements, which appear initially to hold a radical politics because of the militancy which they exert, often die out as a result of minor state, or ANC, concessions in the form of very basic service delivery. The APF has lost its public face and is now moribund.

The Anti-Eviction Campaign (AEC), also formed in 2001, is part of a broader campaign to 'resist disconnections and evictions as well as to intervene in city policies pertaining to housing and public services' (Oldfield & Stokke, 2006, p. 111). The AEC understands that it is unlikely to be effective in the institutional spaces provided by the government. Two AEC activists explain that:

Council doesn't listen to us if we go through the right channels. They don't listen. They make as if they listen if you go through the right channels. They don't take notice of us. But, if we do what we do, then immediately they respond . . . If they take too long, then we do our own thing. (Interview, Anonymous, 14.08.03, in Oldfield & Stokke, 2006, p. 118)

When resisting against evictions and claiming their right to water and electricity, the AEC uses the combination of institutional engagement with authorities, and non-institutional mechanisms such as popular protest and legal routes to meet their demands. Abahlali baseMjondolo, a social movement in Durban, has also attempted to open up alternative spaces in which marginalized groups can influence government policies. Referring to Abahlali's use of popular protest, Pithouse (2006) has noted that 'this kind of direct popular confrontation with official power is where we should invest our hopes for democratization' (p. 7).

In by far the most critical academic piece of writing on Abahlali, which has often been written up in popular writing as a radical democratic umbrella movement of the poor (see Bohmke (2010) for more details), Walsh (2008) has argued that Abahlali's emphasis on service delivery protests in its early stages shifted to an emphasis on 'voice' as academics became more involved with the movement. She argues that the 'favored academics' of the movement position themselves as supporters, who are involved with the movement, but who claim not to take power. Specifically, she quotes Rhodes University academic Richard Pithouse who said that:

Abahlali's founding protest was not a service delivery protest, but a bid to be heard, to be given a voice . . . Abahlali don't want to be represented by elites. They want to have their own voice. They want a say in government' (Walsh, 2008, p. 263).

Like the World Bank's discourse, the politics of the poor's voice are taken out of the equation and it is assumed that poor people's organizations will necessarily 'advance the cause of freedom' (Desai, 2006). The poor are virtuous because of their poverty – 'to be poor is to have power' (Walsh, 2008, p. 264). However, this is problematic since, according to Russell (1980), 'if virtue is the greatest of goods, and if subjection makes people virtuous, it is kind to refuse them power, since it would destroy their virtue' (cited in Walsh, 2008).

Notwithstanding its close connection with grassroots movements, one of the limitations of Abahlali is that it accepts struggles on the ground as an end in itself and does not seek to offer a radical critique of the politics of struggling communities and their relationship to the ANC (Sinwell, 2010).

Adding further depth to this debate, Desai criticizes the proliferation of lawyers and other leaders (lawyers also sometimes position themselves as leaders even if unintentionally) in movements more generally when he states that '[i]t is not their legal or academic work and acumen we must oppose. This may come in useful from time to time. Rather it is the subordination of a political discourse to a legal discourse, the subordination of a radical discourse to a liberal one, the subordination of fist to voice that must be opposed' (Desai, 2010, n.p.). Here, Desai is concerned not only with those leaders that turn militancy and protest into 'voice', but with those outside leaders in general who seek reformist agendas without adequately considering the necessary strategies and tactics to overthrow neoliberalism. The politics of leadership is important here since the strategies that leaders bring to movements 'carry with them a discourse, a certain way of seeing things, of doing things, a value system' (Desai, 2010, n.p.).

On 30 November 2009, at a workshop which brought together activists from struggling communities as well as scholars to discuss the nature of protest in South Africa, Desai noted how lawyers who work directly with communities, 'intervened' in debates about the strategies and tactics of communities. He later wrote that lawyers and other outsiders 'are keen to enter the political debates of their clients with a pompous tone of mastery and to recommend strategies'. Referring to lawyer Stuart Wilson's response to revolutionary impulses 'as always entailing bloodshed. They have gained nothing', Desai has countered that Wilson 'forgot about the spirit of ungovernability that brought the new South Africa into being' (Desai, 2010, n.p.). Offering an alternative to the attempts made by lawyers to soften or NGOize community organizations, the suggestion here is that radical tactics are still necessary and perhaps even efficient at bringing about change in the post-apartheid period. Society is not in equilibrium, but rather remains in constant class conflict between the poor and the rich, who are clearly favored by the law and the constitution. From this perspective, law and order may need to be subordinated to justice.

The mere attempt to bring together community-based organizations under a common development banner, or to assist them in meeting their basic needs, is not enough to extend beyond the NGOization of movements. Rather, far more depends upon the extent to which movements shape the strategies and tactics of organizations, and the outcome of this shaping can be progressive or regressive. The DLF represents one of the first attempts at bringing together a national front that could provide such a radical alternative but, particularly given that its leadership is derived mainly from the middle class, one that could also tame the militancy which currently exists in communities across the country.

The DLF's relationship to grassroots organizations

While the main umbrella organizations in post-apartheid South Africa had previously emerged from below, through struggle, the DLF was formed from above and seeks to connect its socialist political programme to grassroots struggles,[2] something which previous movements arguably fell short of doing. Furthermore, the DLF aims to bring together all progressive organizations struggling for social change locally, including existing social movements, under one development banner nationally. The main campaigns that the DLF has engaged with are workers' struggles, community-based struggles for service delivery, opposition to police and state repression, and climate justice. The DLF, initially called the Conference of the Democratic Left (CDL) was established in October 2008 in the context of the world economic crisis. It was formed primarily by middle-class, left-leaning intellectuals at universities and within NGOs. It is in part self-funded, though for national events it obtains funding from donors (including NGOs) as well.

From its genesis, the DLF held the position that the crisis in the world and, indeed, in post-apartheid South Africa was due to neoliberal globalization. More specifically, the DLF has argued that:

The old apartheid pattern of development has continued with a few elites (and now Black elites) benefiting while the majority are enduring profound suffering. Deepening poverty, inequality, hunger, homelessness, unemployment and ecological destruction are affecting the working class and the poor the most. We believe this has to be confronted to ensure our post-apartheid democracy works for all (DLF, 2011a, p. 2).

At its first national conference held at the University of the Witwatersrand on 20–23 January 2011, 250 delegates from one hundred civil society organizations converged under the CDL in order to extend (thereafter the name was changed from the CDL to the DLF) the DLF's process and to deepen its relationship to civil society organizations. In particular, the DLF has remained committed to grassroots mobilization and a belief that direct action and civil disobedience are necessary and legitimate methods to be employed under a repressive neoliberal state. It has essentially argued that the local government is in crisis – unaccountable to its constituency, lacking adequate resources, and unable to deliver much-needed services to poor communities. The immediate objectives of the DLF in this respect have been to reclaim local government through people's power and to transform communities through democratic alternatives (DLF, 2011a, p. 2).

The DLF has astutely started from the assumption, highlighted above, that 'organizations of the working class and the poor have been weakened, divided and have generally found themselves in a state of desperation' (DLF, 2011b, p. 2). Members of the National Convening Committee (NCC) of the DLF, of which there are now several, have consistently stated that the process of the DLF must be driven from below. Mazibuko Jara, formerly a staunch leader of the South African Communist Party, stated at a DLF Gauteng Forum that, 'If we have to take forward anything, it has to be where people are'.[3] Another NCC member, Noor Nieftagodien, a progressive academic at Witwatersrand University, further referred to a common dilemma that the DLF has faced in relation to community-based organizations when he remarked that, 'from the point of view of local social movements, there is a contradiction between building the DLF [as an organization] and building local struggles'. He concluded: 'I see them as complementary'. On the one hand, building the DLF, an anti-capitalist front, would have the effect of empowering working class organizations while, on the other hand, building local struggles would strengthen the DLF.

The Socialist Civic Movement (SCM) is a small socialist political party in a community called Balfour, Mpumalanga, which emerged out of mass-based protest in the area. Importantly, the protests in Balfour led to ANC President Jacob Zuma visiting the area twice since 2009 after these protests erupted. Dumisani Zwane, co-founder of the SCM, has been involved in the DLF since 2011. He optimistically explains that, 'since our participation in a number of activities organized by the DLF, we have a growing sense that it [the DLF] is fast becoming an alternative movement for many activists and socialists . . . who are involved in grassroots struggles'.[4] However, he offers a counteropinion by pointing out that the relationship between grassroots organizations that fight for service delivery locally and the DLF itself has led to certain problems. He understands that the DLF is a quite new initiative and reflects that 'at the moment, the DLF has only been able to have existence at a removed level from the core struggles of the people that are on the ground'. He adds that the workshops held by the DLF at the University of Witwatersrand and the University of Johannesburg (largely funded by NGOs), while intended to show solidarity and support (to struggling communities), are in fact part of an 'elitist approach'. Rather than being used to strengthen mass struggles locally, he says that they:

> drain our activists . . . it has a tendency of producing a liberal element. They are no longer as militant as before, they are taught to toe the lines, are given a lot of rules and procedures, so it takes the steam out of their engine.

Similarly, the Zabalaza Anarchist Communist Front (ZACF) issued a critical statement after the DLF's first national conference, which indicated that they had been 'cautiously involved' in the discussions regarding the DLF since its inception in 2008 (ZACF, 2011, p. 1). They further argued that the DLF's 'commitment to grassroots struggle stands in welcome contrast to the CDL's [now DLF's] origins':

> The process of holding the conference was initiated and long driven by middle-class left intellectuals associated with Universities and NGOs, many of them coming from a Marxist background. Now, the ZACF cannot object to the involvement of middle-class intellectuals in struggle . . . But we firmly believe that unity-in-struggle can only come from below, from those fighting for their immediate needs. A project of unity led exclusively by intellectuals at a distance from the grassroots would lead nowhere (ZACF, 2011, p. 2).

They then suggested a concrete proposal that would enable the NCC to be elected, driven and held accountable by the grassroots.

Indeed, there has been heavy dissatisfaction on the part of community-based organizations with the role of the DLF in their local struggles, some even feeling that their organization is used to promote the interests of the DLF. One activist from the Anti-Eviction Campaign, an umbrella community-based organization in Cape Town fighting against water and electricity cut-offs and resisting against evictions lamented that 'this year must be the year of action! DLF is a talk-show. We don't want a talk show' (anonymous activist). This points to the fact that, in reality, there is no organic or assumed link between building the DLF and building local struggles.

Progressive academics, activists with previous involvement with the APF and also a revolutionary reading and activist group called Keep Left have arguably been at the forefront of trying to shape the DLF and its relationship to grassroots organizations, at least in the Gauteng region. Rather than building and developing the DLF's capacity and public image from above, they have focused on building and connecting grassroots struggles. Trevor Ngwane, a founder of the SECC, states that:

> Let's start with just solidarity and then if we immerse ourselves in solidarity then . . . we'll find ourselves over time. Then what will come out will be more healthy because if the struggles get strong, whatever we create will be based on something strong. (Interview, 15 September 2011)

The case of Ficksburg, where, in April 2011 a then-unknown activist named Andries Tatane who held literacy campaigns in his community was murdered by the police, is an important example of attempts at solidarity. The Meqheleng[5] Concerned Citizens (MCC) began to organize at the end of 2010 and was officially launched in February 2011. The first march that they held raised their demands to the municipality – the primary one being access to water. The second march gathered more than 2000 residents. It is there that Tatane was killed and Ficksburg received national attention, as the murder was caught on film.

After the killing of Tatane, DLF activists (primarily from the University of Johannesburg, Keep Left and APF) rushed to Ficksburg to find out what happened and also to recruit MCC leaders. Later in April, the MCC joined an emergency meeting, led by the DLF, at Khanya College in Johannesburg to confront the question of police brutality against protestors. The main speakers were from Ficksburg and they spoke about their protests and the particular context in which Tatane was tragically killed. One of the activists from the MCC stayed for three nights in Johannesburg and, each day, attended meetings with Operation Khanyisa Movement (OKM)[6] to learn about how they organize, and also to link them to the idea of the DLF. The leader left with a passionate commitment to forward the struggle of the DLF and OKM in Ficksburg. Since April 2011, the Department of Water Affairs has intervened by making plans to upgrade water, and also, apparently, to provide some of the leaders of the MCC with jobs. One of the OKM leaders, Bobo Makhoba, who has subsequently visited Ficksburg to engage directly with the leaders there, called this action by the government bribery – describing a process through which the government would pay off the MCC so that it would not engage in any further 'disruptive' activities. The same OKM leader later acknowledged that 'we don't have regular visits of the DLF' to places like Ficksburg, thus suggesting that the coordination of struggles by the DLF is insufficient.[7] Today, members of the DLF are in touch with leaders from Ficksburg and elsewhere, but the DLF is not intimately linked to the everyday struggles that are being waged there, nor have they really joined together in a collective campaign. The danger, according to Ngwane, is not only that DLF leaders do not understand the politics of these movements but that, given their limitations and embryonic nature, leaders are not in any position to shape their politics,[8] or to suggest strategies and tactics that might be more effective to challenge the neoliberal enemy that the DLF claims to be fighting.

Conclusion

The NGOization of movements, whereby movements become de-radicalized, cannot be counteracted without critically engaging with where movements are going politically, strategically and tactically. It cannot happen without a sober understanding of the ways in which their struggles engage or do not engage with broader processes of power. Indeed, power will remain in the hands of the elite few, and neoliberalism will remain intact, until the DLF or another set of agents is able to intervene effectively in such a way that struggles are coordinated under a broad socialist platform.

As pointed out earlier, there is a wide range of organizations internationally that support the idea of popular mobilization and empowerment of grassroots organizations. Most notable here is the World Bank. The World Bank's practice and understanding of popular mobilization, empowerment and participation by ordinary citizens is directly linked to implementing neoliberal policies of governments. As Cooke (2004) points out, 'the World Bank is an organization that sees more neoliberalism as the remedy for the problems it has visited on the world's poor' (p. 43–44). Grassroots organizations can become involved in determining decision-making, but the process is depoliticized and a technical fix that leaves the systemic relations of global and national inequality untouched.

This chapter has suggested that the role of social movements and other agents that intervene in local struggles is always political. Furthermore, it has provided a nuanced approach to the understanding of NGOization by identifying a broader definition that views NGOization as undermining the militancy of movements and ignoring, or inadequately addressing, the systemic and global force called neoliberalism. The relationship between movements and struggles must be carefully delineated and unpacked if scholars and activists are to understand whether or not, or the extent to which, the NGOization of movements has the potential to be counteracted.

The question of power is central here, both in terms of the relationship between umbrella movements and local struggles, and also in terms of the relationship between the two with international forces. Militant communities have used a variety of tactics including road barricades and stay-aways (from schools and work) to effectively challenge the local ANC and, in some instances, obtain concessions from the state, which can then be delivered to the community. However, the national policies of the ANC remain intact as the party re-manages the limited resources it can give to poor communities within the physical restraints of a neoliberal framework. The ability of umbrella movements like the DLF to extend beyond NGOization involves not only assisting communities to force the state to deliver through the use of direct action (rather than turning to the courts or negotiations), but also upon their capacity to create a counter-hegemonic force that is controlled and rooted in communities, and which is based upon the centrality of the action and interests of the working class.

Notes

1 In an analysis of the political economy of the South African transition, Bond (2003) illustrates the process through which the African National Congress (ANC) adopted neoliberal policies of the International Monetary Fund (IMF) and the World Bank, further arguing that more radical development approaches put forth by civil society had been denuded by these forces. According to Marais (1998), there were two key reasons for this. Firstly, he points out that the ANC did not 'sell out' to capital, but rather it was not 'equipped to wage battle on technical grounds, a direct consequence of the democratic movement's historical neglect of the social and economic spheres'. Secondly, conservative personalities within the ANC 'steered' the ANC in favor of big business, leaving policy-making 'dislodged from the social and political objectives proclaimed by the ANC, and increasingly impenetrable to activists' (p. 158).
2 This insight was drawn from an interview with Trevor Ngwane on 14 September 2011, at SECC offices in Soweto.
3 This quote and the following are from a DLF Meeting on 19 June 2011.
4 This quote and the following are from a phone interview with Dumisani Zwane on 27 December 2011.
5 Meqheleng is the township in Ficksburg.
6 The OKM is a socialist electoral front in Soweto linked to the SECC. These two community-based organizations have been at the forefront of building the DLF in Gauteng, as well as linking various community-based organizations to each other in Soweto and elsewhere.
7 Interview with Bobo Makhoba on 3 January 2012 at Makhanya Mall in Soweto.
8 Interview with Trevor Ngwane on 14 September 2011, at SECC offices in Soweto.

References

Alexander, P. (2010). '"Rebellion of the Poor": South Africa's Service Delivery Protests, a Preliminary Analysis'. *Review of African Political Economy*, *37*(125), 24–40.

Ballard, R., Habib, A., & Valodia, I. (Eds.) (2006). *Voices of Protest: Social Movements in Post-Apartheid South Africa*. Pietermaritzburg: University of Kwa-Zulu Natal Press.

Bohmke, H. (2010). 'The Branding of Social Movements'. Unpublished paper, on file with the author.

Bond, P. (2003). *Against Global Apartheid: South Africa Meets the World Bank, IMF and International Finance.* Lansdowne: UCT Press.

Bond, P. (2007). 'Volatile Capitalism and Global Poverty'. Paper presented at explanation Poverty Challenge Conference, 26–29 June, Durban, South Africa.

Bond, P., Desai, A., & Ngwane, T. (2011). 'Uneven and Combined Marxism within South Africa's Urban Social Movements: Transcending Precarity in Community, Labor and Environmental Struggles'. Presented to the conference 'Beyond Precarious Labor: Rethinking Socialist Strategies'. Center for Place, Culture and Politics and *The Socialist Register.* City University of New York Graduate Centre, 13 May 2011.

Cooke, B. (2004). 'Rules of Thumb for Participatory Change Agents'. In S. Hickey & G. Mohan (Eds.) *Participation – from Tyranny to Transformation?: Exploring New Approaches to Participation in Development* (pp. 42–56). London and New York: Zed Books.

Democratic Left Front. (2011a). *First Democratic Left Conference Report: 20–23 January 2011*, University of Witwatersrand, South Africa.

Democratic Left Front. (2011b). *Invite to a National Activist Workshop on People-Driven Transformation of Local Government: 29–31 July 2011*, Johannesburg, South Africa.

Desai, A. (2002). *We are the Poors: Community Struggles in Post-Apartheid South Africa.* New York: Monthly Review Press.

Desai, A. (2006). 'Vans, Autos, Kombis and the Drivers of Social Movements'. Paper presented at the Harold Wolpe Memorial lecture series, International Convention Centre, Durban, 28 July.

Desai, A. (2010). 'Legalism, Pragmatism and Community Revolts'. Unpublished paper on file with the author.

Egan, A. & Wafer, A. (2004). 'The Soweto Electricity Crisis Committee'. Centre for Civil Society, School of Development Studies, University of Kwazulu-Natal, Durban. Retrieved from: http://ccs.ukzn.ac.za/files/Egan%20Wafer%20SECC%20Research%20Report%20Short.pdf

Hlatshwayo, M. (2009). 'The State of NGOs'. *From: Advancing a Human Rights Agenda in South Africa: Perspective from Civil Society.* Johannesburg: Foundation for Human Rights.

INCITE! Women of Color Against Violence. (2007). *The Revolution Will Not be Funded: Beyond the Non-Profit Industrial Complex.* Cambridge, MA: South End Press.

Marais, H. (1998). *South Africa, Limits to Change: The Political Economy of Transformation.* London and New York: Zed Books.

Mueller-Hirth, N. (2009). 'South African NGOs and the Public Sphere: Between Popular Movements and Partnerships for Development'. *Social Dynamics, 35*(2), 423–435.

Oldfield, S. & Stokke, K. (2006). 'Polemical Politics, the Local Politics of Community Organizing, and Neoliberalism in South Africa'. In J. Peck, H. Leitner, & E. Sheppard (Eds.). *Contesting Neoliberalism: The Urban Frontier* (pp. 139–156). New York: Guilford Press.

Petras, J. (1997, December). 'Imperialism and NGOs in Latin America'. *Monthly Review, 49*(7). Retrieved from: http://monthlyreview.org/1997/12/01/imperialism-and-ngos-in-latin-america.

Pithouse, R. (2006). 'Rethinking Public Participation from Below'. *Critical Dialogue*, 2(1), 24–30.

Sinwell, L. (2010). 'Defensive Social Movements Need to Engage with Politics'. *Labour Bulletin*, 34(1), 37–39.

Sinwell, L. (2011). 'Is Another World' Really Possible? Re-examining Counter-Hegemonic Forces in Post-Apartheid South Africa'. *Review of African Political Economy*, 38(127), 61–76.

Sinwell, L., et al. (2009) 'Service Delivery Protests: Findings From Quick Response Research on Four "Hotspots" – Piet Retief, Balfour, Thokoza, Diepsloot'. Report produced by the Centre for Sociological Research, Faculty of Humanities, University of Johannesburg. Retrieved from: http//www.uj.ac.za/EN/Faculties/humanities/researchcentres/csr/research/Documents/Quick%20response%20research%20into%20Service%20Delivery%20Protest%20Hotspots.pdf.

Walsh, S. (2008). '"Uncomfortable Collaborations": Contesting Constructions of the "Poor" in South Africa'. *Review of African Political Economy*, 35(116), 255–279.

ZACF – Zabalaza Anarchist Communist Front. (2011). 'The "Democratic Left": A Small Step Towards Uniting Working Class Struggle'. Retrieved from: www.anarkismo.net/article/18858.

5

Philippine NGOs: Defusing Dissent, Spurring Change

Sonny Africa

The Philippines has one of the longest-running, and what is reputedly among the largest and most active, civil society movements in the developing world.[1] Millions of Filipinos now participate in, or are influenced by, citizen-based organizations amid the right to assembly, free speech, a lively press, open elections and a market economy. Mirroring global trends over the last three decades, Philippine non-governmental organizations (NGOs) in particular have multiplied and expanded the range of their development activities.

The supposedly transformative potential of NGOs and of civil society in general should presumably be evident in the Philippines, if anywhere. But there is instead a disturbing lack of progress: widespread poverty and severe inequality, entrenched vested interests in the economy, oligarchic and patronage politics, and tens of millions of Filipinos remaining disempowered with little real control over their economic and political lives. Underlying patterns of socioeconomic backwardness and elite rule persist even if increasingly overlaid with NGO pro-democracy and 'civil society' features.

The Philippine experience highlights the possibilities but also the practical limits of NGOs as opposition to prevailing hegemonies. In the country's specific conditions and historical context the general tendency has been for NGOs to operate in accordance with prevailing political and economic arrangements rather than in sustained opposition to these. Whether consciously or inadvertently, they have aligned with the conservative political program of the established State rather than with that of progressive social movements challenging inequitable structures. This is notwithstanding a brief activist counter-current among NGOs mainly during the Martial Law interregnum.

The chapter begins by tracking Philippine NGO trends over the past decades against the overall backdrop of so-called civil society and the country's major social forces. Of particular relevance is how NGOs increased in number, scope and participation in governance since the second half of the 1980s largely in line with the global neoliberal offensive instead of in resistance to this. This trend continues under the current Aquino government. This is followed by an overview of economic policies and poor development outcomes in the country to emphasize the persistent underdevelopment in the context of decades of NGOization. This discussion points to how NGOs helped create the political conditions for implementing neoliberal policies. Taking all these questions into consideration the chapter concludes by suggesting that NGOs as a whole can at most have only a subsidiary role in the struggle for fundamental social change.

Historical sketch of Philippine NGOs

The Philippines has a long history of civil society organizations (CSOs) dating back to at least nineteenth century Spanish colonial times and early twentieth century American colonization. These organizations include various church welfare groups, charities, cooperatives, anti-colonial/pro-independence resistance, peasant and labor groups, and other service groups (ADB, 2007). The years immediately after the Second World War saw more welfare and civic NGOs formed for post-war relief and rehabilitation for poor communities; many of these focused on children, the elderly, and persons with disabilities. In the late 1940s and early 1950s some community development NGOs were set up in perceived Communist-influenced areas in the country's Central Luzon, Southern Tagalog and Bicol regions to provide health, education and cooperative services and undercut support for the armed struggle. Among the most prominent anti-Communist NGOs set up in this period were the Jesuit-organized Institute for Social Order (ISO) in 1947 and the Philippine Rural Reconstruction Movement (PRRM) in 1952. The early 1960s saw the start of family, corporate, and scientific foundations in the country.[2]

However, the contemporary history of civil society and NGOs in the Philippines can be said to have begun during the Marcos regime from the late 1960s and especially upon Martial Law in the 1970s. While most NGOs remained characteristically welfare-oriented and non-activist social development organizations, a visible sub-section of progressive NGOs emerged in the 1970s and 1980s which did not just implement the usual socioeconomic and welfare projects but also widely propagandized and organized resistance to the regime in close coordination with People's Organizations (POs). The external conditions were set by how revolutionary and anti-imperialist social movements were surging abroad and how the Catholic and Protestant churches adopted more socially progressive orientations after, respectively, Vatican II and exhortations by the World Council of Churches (WCC). Under this influence Filipino church-based NGOs became an important beachhead for the expansion of anti-dictatorship NGOs and POs.

Further momentum came from how the Filipino radical Left at the time did not just wage armed revolt but also underpinned legal aboveground opposition through civil society including NGOs. This period saw the mobilization of wide swathes of the population from the lower to the upper classes that combined with the Communist and Moro armed struggles to weaken and eventually overthrow the Marcos regime. Particularly notable and with implications until this day is how these Left-driven NGO and PO efforts were often expressly couched in terms of a larger struggle for systemic change which injected an activist dynamism and degree of counter-hegemonic ideology into generally conservative civil society and the public in general. For instance, the community-based health programs (CBHPs) set up by the religious Sisters of the Rural Missionaries of the Philippines (RMP) were explicit in their orientation: 'The underlying causes of health problems in society are deeply embedded in the social, economic and political structures . . . The CBHP is [not] the answer to all health problems, but serves as a means to initiate social transformation' (CHD, 1998). The important role that peasant- and trade-union-linked NGOs and POs played in expanding political opposition to the dictatorship and even in supporting the armed struggles exemplifies their mobilizing potential. The late 1970s also saw innovations towards environmental, Indigenous Peoples, women, and migrant workers' issues and even cultural work.

But this was in the specific historical circumstances of Martial Law, an overt dictatorship and a single dominant channel – the radical Left which gave primacy to mass-based POs organized along class lines – to give vent to the impulse for change. The 1986 'People Power' uprising was quickly hailed as some kind of model for a peaceful transition from authoritarianism to democracy. It was also widely interpreted even in sections of radical Leftist circles as changing the nature of the Philippine state into one more pliable to social and economic reforms through the influence of NGOs, POs and civil society in general, for example.

Indeed this was among the major orientational fault lines causing a split within the Communist Left between those who affirmed a 'protracted people's war' strategy and those who entertained other paths to social and political change including, among others, more actively engaging the government to implement reforms in a process of gradually transforming the current elite democracy into a more participatory democracy (see for instance Santos, 2005).

That premise of a more pliable state dovetailed with the emerging neoliberal governance paradigm of civil society as remedying authoritarianism, improving transparency and accountability, and leading to equitable economic development. Together they impelled the emergence of a systematic framework in the Philippines for NGOs to engage and participate in, rather than contest, the state.

This governance concept advanced on two fronts since the mid-1980s. From the foreign side, the United Nations (UN), International Financial Institutions (IFIs), and virtually every major government with neoliberal foreign policy objectives started promoting this notion. NGOs were portrayed as more deeply embedded in communities, and more innovative, cost-effective and development-oriented than government agencies.

IFIs institutionalized mechanisms to engage CSOs and NGOs. The cases of the World Bank and ADB (Asian Development Bank), which are among the Philippines' biggest sources of official development aid, are illustrative. The World Bank (2011a) reports that 'active CSO involvement' in its global operations has risen steadily 'from 21 percent of the total number of projects in 1990 to 82 percent in 2009' and that 'civil society participation occurs throughout the project cycle from the design and planning stages, to implementation and monitoring'. It also reports 'civil society engagement in 75 percent of its loans, 87 percent of country assistance strategies, and 100 percent of poverty reduction strategy papers in the period 2007–2009' (World Bank, 2009). The ADB in turn recently reported that 81 percent of its approved loans, grants and related technical assistance included some form of CSO participation (ADB, 2011a). In 1990, only 5 percent of

ADB loan approvals 'involved NGOs directly in some manner' (ADB, 2011b).

The late 1980s and early 1990s saw tens of millions of dollars in overseas funding going to NGOs through various windows. Among others, the World Bank gave a USD 20 million 'biodiversity conservation grant' for the NGOs for Integrated Protected Areas (NIPAS) programme and access to its Small Grants Fund. The United States Agency for International Development (USAID) had a USD 25 million debt-for-nature arrangement with the Foundation for the Philippine Environment (FPE) in 1993 in addition to over USD 30 million for co-financing NGOs in the period 1989-1996. The Canadian government gave USD 15.3 million for the *Diwata* project (a women's NGO network) and the Philippine Development Assistance Programme (PDAP), the Swiss government gave USD 25 million for the Foundation for a Sustainable Society, Inc. (FSSI) and so on.

On the domestic front, consecutive post-Marcos administrations built up institutional mechanisms for working with NGOs that established a framework for their participation in governance. The Corazon Aquino government (1986–1992) enshrined the role of NGOs and POs in Philippine development in three articles of the 1987 Constitution. Civil society was also formally given a role in local governance through the Local Government Code of 1991 that created local development councils that must include NGOs and POs (composing a quarter of its members). NGOs were given positions in local school boards, health boards, peace and order councils, law enforcement boards, and procurement committees. NGO/PO liaison desks were also set up in government departments of agrarian reform, environment and natural resources and health.

The Ramos government (1992–1998) set up a National Anti-Poverty Commission (NAPC) with formal NGO representation, organized a series of multi-sectoral summits on NGO issues such as the environment, poverty, food, water and peace, and drew up a Social Reform Agenda (SRA) comprehensively covering NGO concerns. CSOs were given spots in the Legislative-Executive Development Advisory Council (LEDAC), which was actively used to coordinate work between these two branches of government. The Estrada (1998–2001), Arroyo (2001–2010) and Benigno Aquino, III (2010) governments did not introduce anything substantially new relative to NGOs, but built on those previous efforts and further institutionalized them.

NGOs and civil society in the Philippines today

Today, NGOs are part of a broader 'civil society' in the Philippines that also includes POs, cooperatives, church groups, professional or business-related associations, academe and assorted other non-state and non-business organizations. From a social change perspective, NGOs and POs are particularly significant not just because development-oriented NGOs generally express links with POs in pursuit of their goals but because together they comprise the largest portion of politically active groups amongst this so-called civil society.

The term 'NGO' is interpreted in many ways from the sweeping 'non-governmental organization', understood literally to include everything outside of the official government machinery, to the more restricted and legalistic 'non-stock, non-profit corporations', to the most limited notion of only referring to expressly social development-oriented NGOs. For consistency this chapter uses 'NGOs' to refer to non-governmental and non-profit organizations – regardless of funding source, ideology (or lack thereof), values and orientation – that provide development-related services to other groups, communities or individuals. This definition covers the likes of charity or welfare groups, social foundations set up by private business groups, as well as more ideologically grounded activist NGOs. All these NGOs are generally staffed by more or less full-time 'professional' NGO workers (as opposed to unpaid volunteer or part-time workers).

NGOs combine to form different kinds of alliances, coalitions and networks. The Caucus of Development NGOs (CODE-NGO) is the Philippines' largest network of NGOs with a membership of some 2,000 and illustrates these diverse combinations. Among others, CODE-NGO includes six national networks and six regional networks. The six national networks each have distinct identities: rural development (PHILDHRRA – Philippines Partnership for the Development of Human Resource), urban development (PHILSSA – Philippines Support Services Agencies), corporate members (PBSP – Philippines Business for Social Progress), services for children and youth (NCSD – National Council for Social Development), cooperatives (NATCCO – National Confederation of Cooperatives in the Philippines) and an association of foundations (AF).[3] The regional networks in turn respectively cover the country's Bicol, Cordillera, Eastern Visayas, Western

Visayas, Central Visayas and Mindanao regions, which are among the poorest areas in the country. There are also other permutations in NGO groupings such as the Council for People's Development and Governance (CPDG), a national network of NGOs and POs with programs on poverty alleviation, environmental protection, women, children, disaster risk reduction and aid effectiveness, and democratic governance.

POs, on the other hand, are membership-based organizations of citizens coming together to advance their common/collective interests and welfare and are sometimes referred to as grassroots organizations or community-based organizations. Politically active POs are generally organized along class/sectoral lines (e.g. peasant organizations, trade unions, Indigenous Peoples, youth, overseas Filipino workers), gender (e.g., women), geographical proximity (e.g., village, province), or some permutation or combination of these. Among the largest and most active Filipino POs are the peasant *Kilusang Magbubukid ng Pilipinas* (KMP), fisherfolk *Pamalakaya*, worker *Kilusang Mayo Uno* (KMU), Alliance of Concerned Teachers (ACT), and women's group GABRIELA which are all national formations with local chapters. But there is also *Migrante International*, which has country chapters of overseas Filipino workers around the world. POs can also come together under a multi-PO multi-sectoral umbrella such as the *Bagong Alyansang Makabayan* (BAYAN).

Today, the Philippines has a reputation for having a 'vibrant civil society'.[4] Estimates of the number of civil society groups and NGOs vary widely due to the lack of generally accepted definitions, inadequate monitoring and the fluidity of their operations. An NGO literature review gives an estimate of 'between 249,000–497,000 [non-profit] organizations (Songco, 2007). The Asian Development Bank (ADB, 2007) similarly acknowledges 'up to 500,000' civil society groups but specifies between 3,000–5,000 'development-oriented' NGOs among these. The World Bank (World Bank, 2012) on the other hand cites 'an estimated 18,000 registered NGOs' in the country. The Philippine Council for NGO Certification (PCNC, 2011) mentions 'as many as 60,000 non-profit, non-governmental organizations'. The most recent comprehensive study on the matter compiles figures from various sources and reports that the number of NGOs in the country is estimated to range from 'between 15,000 and 30,000' to 'around 34,000 to 68,000' (Tuaño, 2011).

Regardless of the exact numbers, the Philippine NGO sector is not insignificant – and apparently even relatively large compared to other countries – even as the biggest number of NGOs are apparently small with less than 25 staff and ones which often struggle financially (Tuaño, 2011). Rough estimates of the number of NGO staff in the Philippines place these at around 1 percent of the total 37.2 million employed in 2011 (for comparison, the public sector accounts for some 5 percent of total employment).[5]

There is no direct survey of the ideological tendencies underpinning the country's numerous NGOs but indirect evidence supports the notion that only a minority are actively engaged in mass struggles with POs, national policy reforms, local government and related political activities. Indeed there is reason to suspect that their political views and levels of political engagement are so disparate that they have no qualitative impact as a whole beyond the mere sum of their incongruent parts.

Philippine NGOs chiefly implement projects and provide social development-related services to their chosen constituencies covering education, training and human resource development and community development (AF, 2001; Tuaño, 2011). Taking the CODE-NGO network as an example, a survey of its members found these concentrated in education/training/human resource development (77 percent of NGOs surveyed), health/nutrition (44 percent) and enterprise/livelihood development (43 percent) versus, at the other end of the scale, agrarian reform (18 percent), urban poor (12 percent) and labor organizing (3 percent) (AF, 2001). While such a profile of activities does not necessarily mean political passiveness, the bias towards welfare projects and income-generation is clear.

That result can also be read with how one of the few NGO surveys in the country found that 'few NGO respondents implement asset reform programmes' because they are 'prone to conflict and therefore more difficult to implement' which indicates a tendency to avoid addressing important structural inequities that requires political activism. NGOs' choices of sectoral partners certainly lean towards non-controversial ones: children and youth (57 percent of respondents) and women (53 percent) rather than peasants (35 percent), urban poor (33 percent) and labor (13 percent) (AF, 2001). Taken together, these can be interpreted as indicating how Philippine NGOs are mainly concerned with immediate service delivery rather than long-term struggles mobilizing grassroots sectors against systemic inequities in resources and power.

This characterization is consistent with the results of a recent nationwide survey: while almost half of the population (46 percent) considered themselves active members of at least one civil society organization, only about a quarter (26 percent) considered themselves active members of at least one political organization and just 15 percent participated in political activities (understood merely as attending a demonstration, signing a petition or joining a boycott) (CIVICUS, 2011). The same survey also found that only 5 percent and 10 percent of the population considered themselves to be active members of an NGO and PO, respectively, by comparison with 34 percent for church or religious organizations, 10 percent for sports/recreational organizations and 6 percent for art, music or education organizations.

It can be roughly estimated that there are perhaps only some hundreds or a few thousand NGOs that are more activist in the sense of operating with a more consciously political framework and a self-definition as actively working for more profound social change. Increasing the political power of erstwhile disempowered sectors always figures strongly with such NGOs whether in the sense of being accumulated from the ground up through ever-expanding grassroots organizations, by working within state structures, or via some combination of both. An example of this approach is the Council for Health and Development (CHD) which provides health services and sets up community-based health programs under a framework of the social determinants of health – or where ill-health is rooted in structural poverty and not just the absence of health services. CHD thus also works closely with the Health Alliance for Democracy (HEAD) which is a PO describing itself as 'composed of individuals from the health sector who adhere to the principles of the Filipino people's struggle for sovereignty and democracy'.

The social development and service delivery orientation of NGOs results in a particularly significant characteristic with implications for how they operate as a sector: they are resource-intensive and dependent on external funding. They require continuous and sustained human, technical and financial resources to keep providing services to their chosen beneficiaries while, conversely, they are chronically unable to generate substantial incomes in the normal course of their operations because their beneficiaries are poor communities and sectors. This makes them reliant on external subsidies and correspondingly vulnerable to the priorities, values and orientation of these external subsidizers.

As it is, Philippine NGOs' main funders are foreign (on which 48 percent of NGOs primarily rely), corporate (12 percent) and government (10 percent) sources (CIVICUS, 2011). The foreign sources could be Northern NGOs although a recent trend is for these donors to themselves be tapping official funding in their home countries and hence being drawn into the foreign policy frameworks of their own governments. The European Union (EU) and individual European governments for instance have so-called co-financing arrangements where they fund European NGOs who in turn provide grants to NGO partners in the South according to priorities set by the official agencies that are the primary sources of funds.[6]

Business groups have also become increasingly active in the NGO sector, which further blurs the supposed civil society-market distinction. The Philippine Business for Social Progress (PBSP) was set up in 1970 and describes itself as a corporate-led foundation of more than 240 member-companies pledging 1 percent of their companies' net income before taxes for poverty reduction and committed to corporate social responsibility (CSR). It reports having supported 6,200 projects with 3,300 organizations and 4.5 million beneficiaries in 65 provinces (CODE-NGO, 2012). Since 2000, PBSP has been the most organized expression of the business sector's support for the UN Millennium Development Goals (MDGs). There is also the League of Corporate Foundations which has been growing in number from around 60 members in 2005 to over 80 in 2010, reflecting both their access to corporate financial resources as well as the CSR trend (Tuaño, 2011).

The nature of NGO funding sources and the corresponding process of fund-raising is potentially problematic where NGOs will be predisposed, consciously or unconsciously, to functioning within the political and economic spaces acceptable to the State and private enterprises that sponsor them. Otherwise, these discretionary funds would just go to other NGOs who share the development paradigm espoused by government and big business. The reality is that organizations with the financial resources to spare for NGOs will generally be conservative and disinclined to be counter-hegemonic. Diverse funding sources with respective priorities and requirements will also tend to aggravate the fragmentation of NGOs who are already extremely diverse in their lines of work and political orientation.

The chronic backwardness and underdevelopment in the country are conditions for the rise of radical alternatives outside the more accustomed forms of civil society and NGO social action. The mainstream Left in the Philippines, the 'national democrats', the largest and most organized Left formation in the country, is meaningful for remaining resilient in the face of 'end of history' triumphalism. This bloc continues to work on the basis of an understanding of the structural problems of the country and the crisis of capitalism. It correspondingly still gives primacy to working class politics as the building blocks for wider social change which means a much greater emphasis on ideological work and organizing peasants, workers, national minorities and other oppressed groups into POs towards claiming political power rather than on service NGOs.

It is also important to emphasize that the conventional categorization of social forces being split into state, market and civil society is particularly inappropriate in the Philippine context, which has armed revolutionary movements going back for at least four decades. The influence of these movements includes parallel governance structures in large portions of the country's territory.[7] The biggest and most important are the Communist Party of the Philippines-New People's Army-National Democratic Front of the Philippines (CPP-NPA-NDFP) that operates in 70 of 79 provinces across the country, and the Moro Islamic Liberation Front-Bangsamoro Islamic Armed Forces (MILF-BIAF) that is active in 14 provinces in the southern Philippines (Santos et al., 2010). These radical alternatives are objectively the strongest counterpoint to neocolonialism and capitalism in the country.

The CPP decries the 'semi-colonial and semi-feudal' character of present-day Philippine society in which the Filipino people suffer from 'foreign and feudal domination'.[8] It declares that it is waging a 'national democratic revolution' which, upon victory, will proceed to the 'socialist revolution'. The integral components of its 'protracted people's war' are explicit: 'revolutionary armed struggle, land reform and mass-base building'. The CPP categorically opposes neoliberalism as imperialist globalization. The MILF's struggle on the other hand asserts political and military control over territories in Mindanao based on a legacy of protecting the ancestral domains of Moro sultanates there. The Moro struggle espouses the right to self-determination and the creation of an independent Bangsamoro homeland.

Neoliberal governance and state-NGO ties

Meanwhile, consecutive administrations have given growing numbers of government positions to NGO leaders with long histories of political activism (see for instance ADB, 2007; Racelis, 2000; Wurfel, 2002). These included Cabinet-rank positions in agrarian reform, social welfare, education, health, housing, peace and others aside from various national and regional posts.[9] These NGO leaders kept their ties with NGOs and POs, which served as important means by which to bring civil society on board in official programs and projects and hence give substance to the NGO/PO-related institutional mechanisms being put in place. NGOs were particularly visible in the implementation of agrarian reform communities, health service devolution, housing projects, environmental projects and Indigenous Peoples' programs.

NGOs apparently also financially benefited from such ties. A prominent controversy in this regard was in 2001 when CODE-NGO was accused of using its influence to make a government flotation of Treasury bonds more profitable in favor of a specific purchaser for which it received a large 1.5 billion Philippine pesos (Php) (USD 29 million at prevailing exchange rates) commission for zero cash outlay. This was around the time that key CODE-NGO leaders held the top positions in the government's social welfare department, anti-poverty commission, urban poor commission, civil service commission and presidential management staff (aside from the CODE-NGO chair being the sister of the finance secretary).

The neoliberal governance paradigm, Philippine government civil society mechanisms, and greater NGO openness to work with government were conditions for the proliferation of NGOs in the post-Marcos dictatorship era and by one estimate the number of NGOs increased from an estimated 5,000 in 1986 to over 15,000 by the end of the decade (Management Advancement Systems Association, Inc., 2000).

But it was not only that new NGOs were being formed – even erstwhile protest or activist NGOs were shifting towards socioeconomic programs and participating in government or official aid programs. There was a financial dynamic underpinning this. During the Marcos regime, anti-dictatorship NGOs were able to access foreign funding from politically sympathetic international NGOs, church-based funding agencies, solidarity groups and even political parties. This type of funding dried up in the 'democratic space' of the Corazon

Aquino government – often replaced by official government sources – and the demand was increasingly for so-called concrete or tangible gains that were not always compatible with the priorities of NGOs seeking structural change.

Indeed there was also an ideological dynamic. Left-leaning groups that eschewed armed struggle replaced this with, in effect, an approach of seeking an accumulation of social, political and economic changes through alliances with perceived reformist wings of the local bourgeoisie and landlords as well as through electoral victories.[10] Mass-based organizations are still invoked as the axis of struggles but these are not developed as units of democratic political power for eventually replacing the state but rather as vital points of leverage with which to modify the functioning of the existing elite-dominated state. This trend arguably also reduced the activism and militancy of the portion of the country's social movement that relied on these NGOs for intellectual direction and that correspondingly also bought into the poverty alleviation, sustainable development, participatory democracy and good governance agenda.

In any case it is clear that NGOization in the Philippines occurred mainly upon the initiative and according to the terms set by the government and international agencies, which goes far in explaining the inherently conservative tendencies of NGOs as a whole. Arguably, the way NGOization has developed has created tendencies toward political demobilization and atomistic communities. The first of these relates to how accepting domestic or foreign official funding could, even inadvertently, diminish NGO independence and the taking up of systemic concerns. Second, NGOs may find themselves entangled in the intrinsic bureaucracies of government or official agencies that further strain their already scarce resources and attention. Third, the communities which the NGOs service may find themselves caught up in a reactionary fund-driven dynamic where they become preoccupied with short-term material benefits and disinclined towards the painstaking efforts needed for structural change and longer-lasting gains. Moreover, the bias is for self-help rather than farther-reaching collective efforts. This is reinforced by how the immediate gains from externally funded NGO projects and mechanisms will often surpass those from merely internally financed but collective efforts. And fourth, competition for finite funding means that NGOs and communities are in effect competing with each other for this.

NGOization today

Developments during the current administration of President Benigno Aquino III, which came to power in mid-2010, affirm the continuation of decades-long trends. High-level positions going to NGO leaders include ones in the social welfare department, national anti-poverty commission, human rights commission and presidential adviser for political affairs. The Akbayan Party, which was formed by various NGO leaders – some of whom now hold Cabinet-level positions – is also in coalition with President Aquino's traditional political party, the Liberal Party.

The current government also shows how NGOs and community projects are used against challenges to the state. This phenomenon takes sharpest form in the Armed Forces of the Philippines' (AFP) latest internal security plan for 2011–2016 *Bayanihan*. The plan takes a 'Whole of Nation Approach [and] People-Centred Security/Human Security Approach' with 'community-based peace and development efforts' as one of its four strategic concepts (the others being military operations, peace processes, and internal AFP reforms). 'NGOs, POs and CSOs' are explicitly defined as responders astride the government's military and civilian agencies and are declared 'indispensable [in filling the gaps] in the dispensation of tasks and functions of national government agencies and local government units' (AFP, 2011).

The result is that NGOs are partners in the implementation of the PAMANA (*Payapa at Masaganang Pamayanan,* or Peaceful and Prosperous Community) and KALAHI-CIDSS (*Kapitbisig Laban sa Kahirapan* [or Linking Arms Against Poverty]-Comprehensive and Integrated Delivery of Social Services) community development components of the AFP's counterinsurgency program. PAMANA is a tentatively Php 90 billion (USD 2.1 billion at current exchange rates) four-year program of cash transfers, livelihood projects, post-harvest facilities and road works in armed conflict areas. The World Bank-supported KALAHI-CIDSS is a smaller Php 9.3 billion (USD 216 million) program of community education, health, water, farming, access, electrification, and environmental infrastructure projects.

On the face of it the projects are not undesirable and do meet real local needs. The overall motive becomes suspect though inasmuch as they are implemented selectively in armed conflict areas and in the absence of more far-reaching structural changes with longer-lasting benefits. At the local level, such changes could include speedy and free distribution of land to decisively break rural monopolies. At the national level there could be the reversal of destructive neoliberal policies implemented over decades.

The record of the military itself that NGOs are now working with remains questionable. At the time of writing, human rights group *Karapatan* reports that violations have continued with 99 extrajudicial killings and eleven enforced disappearances so far under the new Aquino administration (between July 2010 and June 2012); the number of political prisoners continues to rise to 385 already. Rural communities continue to suffer forced evacuation due to combat operations with many thousands of families recently displaced from villages in Surigao del Sur, Negros Oriental, Davao Oriental, Agusan del Norte, and North Cotabato. These give rise to criticisms that these projects with NGOs merely seek to undermine community support for the rebel groups and cover up continuing rights abuses by the military.

The Aquino administration's flagship anti-poverty program also shows how NGOs can be used to make neoliberal policies more acceptable. Hundreds of accredited NGOs are participating in a multi-year PHP 307 billion (USD 7.1 billion) World Bank- and ADB-supported *Pantawid Pamilyang Pilipino Programme* conditional cash transfer (CCT) scheme. Beneficiary families will receive cash grants of up to PHP 15,000 (USD 349) per year upon compliance with certain education and health conditions. However this relief for poor families must be seen in the context of unreformed neoliberal economic policies that cause the poverty to begin with, so the net effect is a temporary dole-out to mitigate the adverse social consequences of these policies and rationalize their continued implementation.

The affinity of CCTs to neoliberalism is evident. They are justified as 'efficient' in focusing on 'deserving poor'. Children are 'human capital' to be invested in for their future income-generating capacity, and the role of 'individual responsibility' in social poverty is over-emphasized – while the government is excused for privatizing essential social services because welfare intervention has shifted to selective cash transfers.

It is worth mentioning that the protracted global crisis may have implications for civil society in general and NGOs in particular. There are two contradictory tendencies. On the one hand, the crisis will strain the government funding and private resources that have so far been directed to NGOs in support of state-civil society interaction and 'participatory democracy'.

NGOs as a whole have already been facing an increasingly difficult funding environment since the start of the 2000s. For instance, net official development assistance (ODA) loan commitments to the Philippines that have been a major source of funding for NGOs, directly and indirectly, have fallen by 24 percent between 2001 (USD 13.2 billion) and 2010 (USD 10.1 billion).[11] There are no similarly precise figures for grant funding from Northern NGO donors to Philippine NGOs although the general consensus is that the global funding slump is well-reflected in the country which has driven many NGOs to seek alternative sources and even compete with other NGOs (CIVICUS, 2011; Tuaño, 2011). NGO activities are unfortunately not self-sustaining and dependent on what is essentially discretionary funding and so could be among the first to suffer cutbacks in public and private sector budgets.

On the other hand, civil society and at least some NGOs may yet be encouraged as a countervailing force or social escape valve to undercut the further development of radical alternatives upon worsening social and economic conditions. It is also possible for government-aligned NGOs and POs to be used to justify the imposition of further neoliberal policy programs such as higher taxes ostensibly for state-provided social services and even outright austerity measures targeting public education, health and housing services.

Philippine neocolonialism and underdevelopment

NGOs and civil society are frequently construed as institutional mechanisms by which the poor, vulnerable and marginalized can empower themselves, improve their conditions and even challenge structural inequities and exploitation. An accounting of NGO projects, civil society efforts and community beneficiaries would doubtless show quantitative increases over the past decades. But notwithstanding such an aggregation, overall socioeconomic and political outcomes in the Philippines are consistent with merely narrow and localized

NGO gains in the context of more generalized social, economic and political disempowerment.

Civil society and NGOs have been absorbed into the margins of policy-making and implementation, especially their social welfare and social mobilization components, but the fundamental policies that truly define the economy and its arc remain in the hands of accustomed domestic and foreign power elites. The direction of development policy has not changed hence the persistence of poverty and backwardness.

NGOs have been increasingly involved in the formulation of the country's periodic medium-term development plans. Former president Ferdinand Marcos' 1978–1982 and 1983–1987 plans at most mentioned 'participatory schemes for the broader base of society will be developed, principally through the rural cooperatives, *barangay*,[12] and youth mobilization programmes' (Sicat, 1979). While NGOs grew rapidly under Corazon Aquino, her 1987–1992 plan still only had a generic '[a]ll sectors of society, public or private, shall be consulted to the fullest extent to obtain their opinions and positions on matters related hereto'.[13]

By Fidel Ramos' 1993–1998 plan however, the government declared: 'The plan shall be formulated in close collaboration with other agencies of the executive branch, the legislative branch and private/non-government sectors'.[14] Joseph Estrada's 1999–2004 plan went even further and said '[c]ivil society will complement and possibly substitute for the efforts of government in areas where it is deemed more effective and efficient'.[15] President Gloria Macapagal-Arroyo's 2004–2010 plan mentioned civil society and NGOs prominently in its chapters on environment and natural resources, housing, labor, anti-poverty, elections, peace process, national reconciliation, rule of law, science and technology, culture, anti-corruption, national security and constitutional reforms.[16]

Benigno Aquino III came to power on a platform of 'good governance', which is reflected in the overall thrust of his 2011–2016 plan.[17] His plan declares: 'A big part of the solution to the governance problem however lies outside government itself and involves the active participation of private business, civil society and the media . . . This gives "voice" to people, enables civil society and the media to become partners of government, and makes the government more responsive to the needs of citizens'. The plan was drawn up in close consultation with civil society and NGOs but remains thoroughly neoliberal and proposes even more free market policies for the country (IBON, 2011b).

Economic outcomes have remained poor despite greater civil society and NGO participation and engagement in socioeconomic policy-making – in the periodic medium-term plans, in program and project implementation, in assorted consultative summits, in local government bodies, and actually holding high Cabinet positions.

The Philippines is the twelfth largest country in the world with a population of some 94 million. Though classified by the World Bank as a lower middle-income country it still ranks among the world's poorest by gross domestic product (GDP) per capita at 131st out of 190 countries (World Bank, 2011b).[18] In 2009, some 65 million or 70 percent of Filipinos lived on PHP 104 (USD 2.20) or even much less per day.[19] Inequality remains as bad as in the mid-1980s notwith-standing two-and-a-half decades of supposedly increasing democratization. The highest income 20 percent of the population corners over half of total family income (52 percent) while the remaining poorest 80 percent share the leftover 48 percent. Strikingly, the net worth of the twenty-five richest Filipinos continues to rise and at PHP 1,021 billion in 2009 (USD 21.4 billion), this is almost equivalent to the combined annual income of the country's poorest fifty-five million Filipinos (PHP 1,029 billion).

Filipino producers have suffered under imperialist globalization policies that gave up trade protection and investment support, opened up the national economy, and integrated key sectors into the global economy. The share of manufacturing in the economy is as low as in the 1950s or half a century ago; the share of agriculture is down to the smallest in the country's history. This deprives millions of Filipinos of the opportunity for decent work, livelihoods and their means of subsistence. The period 2001–2010 was the worst decade of jobless-ness in the country's history with average annual unemployment of over 11 percent and underemployment of 19 percent – forcing some 9.5 million Filipinos, or roughly a tenth of the population, overseas for work.

The rural poor meanwhile still suffer backward agricultural systems and feudal relations.[20] Despite decades of successive agrarian reform programs overseen by former NGO leaders, over half of all farms and total farm area in the country remain under tenancy, lease, and other forms of tenurial arrangement (52 percent). Less than a third of landowners still own more than 80 percent of agricultural land. Half of all farms still rely on hand tools, ploughs and water buffaloes, and only 30 percent of the total farm area is irrigated.

If anything, the NGO language of alternative development has been used by the government to embellish its socioeconomic policies and bolster the notion that technical solutions to the intrinsic problems and contradictions of the system are possible and, indeed, can be initiated by the oligarchic state. The 2011–2016 Philippine development plan, for instance, talks about 'human rights, cultural sensitivity, gender equality, people empowerment and sustainable development' and decries the 'perennial condition of poverty, inequity and lagging human development' but seeks to solve this merely through 'massive investment in physical infrastructure [and] transparent and responsive governance'.[21]

Political outcomes have likewise remained poor despite greater civil society and NGO participation and engagement in various aspects of democratic governance. Civil society and the NGO sector have not just been active during national and local elections, including presidential elections, but have also formed new political parties and entered into coalitions with traditional ones. Major NGO networks and prominent leaders actively campaigned for or otherwise supported recent presidents.[22]

Yet political parties still lack substance, the electoral system remains corrupted and shallow, key government positions remain in the hands of local elites, and the military establishment is still tasked to attack the most active democratic forces in the country (as shown in its record of human rights violations discussed earlier). This is not to say that traditional elites have not had to adjust to a situation where civil society and NGOs are marginally more prominent and engaged in governance than before. But despite this situation their hold on power remains consolidated and unthreatened.

The May 2010 national elections, for instance, did not see a significant departure from the country's tradition of elected national and local leaders coming from the ranks of established structures of power and patronage. The popularly elected president hails from one of the country's oldest political and landlord families. The country's peasants, workers, urban poor, Indigenous Peoples and other marginalized sectors meanwhile remain grossly underrepresented in the elected government including the presidency, vice-presidency, Senate, House of Representatives, and local government units.

There is actually even violent resistance to political incursions by the Left at the congressional and local levels – it is telling of the rigidity and resistance of oligarchic rule that, as reported by rights group *Karapatan*, over 200 members of Left-leaning partylist groups have been assassinated in the last decade. The external features of democracy such as regular, high-turnout and citizen action-intensive elections coexist with deep social divisions, economic backwardness and lack of real sovereignty.

It is also noteworthy that United States (US) 'democracy promotion' – a key soft power instrument for stabilizing the global capitalist order – has included support to Philippine NGOs across a wide range of 'good governance' areas. These projects have spanned electoral processes, good governance, anti-corruption reforms, building the legal system, assisting law enforcement agencies, promoting a free press, local governance and decentralization.

All this has given domestic elite economics and politics a human face, more democratic flavor and a development façade. Yet, since 1986 and the end of the Marcos dictatorship, Philippine governments clearly retain their elite character and do not confront the powerful local and imperialist interests that benefit from unimplemented land reform, non-industrialization, wage repression and liberalization of trade, investment and finance. The last three decades of thriving NGOs and increasing state-civil society interaction in the country has seen continued implementation and deepening of neoliberal 'free market' policies of imperialist globalization. The Ramos government, for instance, actively courted civil society, as discussed earlier, but this administration also saw the most extensive implementation of neoliberal policies of any post-Marcos government with liberalization of trade, investments, infrastructure, oil, telecommunications, airways, shipping, foreign exchange and banking. The current Aquino government in turn, despite the accumulated failures of neoliberal globalization globally and domestically, is set to push free market policies even further.

Conclusion

The Philippine experience over the past decades fits well with a view of neoliberalism as post-Cold War neocolonialism and imperialist domination: opening up markets to foreign plunder, consolidating capitalist market processes and structures, and promoting Western liberal democracy and free elections. The civil society and NGO trend has gained much traction in the course of the neoliberal policy offensive since the 1980s and especially after the overthrow of the Marcos dictatorship in 1986. Social forces in the country spanning the traditional to ideologically driven counter-hegemonic movements have all seen opportunities in NGOs. NGOs have accordingly flourished and now provide services and even engage in portions of governance to an unprecedented degree. Yet the country remains deeply underdeveloped.

The Philippine experience with NGOs is illustrative of their dual character in relation to social transformation. On the one hand, they are vehicles for people to mobilize and act on issues and concerns beyond their immediate families and selves. They can potentially support larger struggles for political and economic change as well as deliver concrete benefits at the community level, as they notably did during the Marcos dictatorship. They have a progressive potential to spur change in this regard.

On the other hand, their service character predisposes them to seeking immediate and concrete gains which is not necessarily undesirable in itself but can have unintended adverse consequences. Two possibilities are particularly problematic. First, in terms of orientation, NGOs may give undue emphasis to parochial community concerns rather than real and sustained political engagement whose gains will only be realized over the long-term. Second, in terms of practice, the chronic need for the funding necessary to deliver services could cause undue reliance on conservative funding sources – such as governments and corporations – and result in a correspondingly conservative political stance. These could diffuse dissent where people are diverted from political struggles to NGOs or are reduced to merely seeking marginal benefits amid an enduring inequitable state of affairs.

The crucial element appears to be the extent to which there are genuinely mass-based initiatives, efforts and struggles outside of the unavoidably conformist framework to which NGOs are predisposed. As ever, mass-based organizations are the fundamental dynamic creating the foundations and setting the pace and direction of the overall struggle for social transformation. The challenge is for such organizations to be stronger, have deeper roots among the people, and be more engaged in ideological, political and economic struggles than NGOs whose gains are inherently limited and which can at most have only a subsidiary role.

The global crisis of capitalism is the most important economic feature affecting the Philippine situation in the coming period and aggravates the chronic domestic crisis of backwardness and underdevelopment. These crises create the overall conditions for an accelerated resurgence of social and mass movements struggling against entrenched foreign-backed domestic elites. Long-standing poverty and inequality can only worsen which will further underscore the structural nature of the problem.

The country fortunately remains the site of a vigorous Leftist urban and rural mass movement and of armed revolutionary struggles with embryonic political power in areas removed from government control. Those forces are the most effective counters to any reactionary influence by NGOs and civil society and are the most important means for ensuring that impulses for social reform, such as those which find expression in NGOs, are directed towards struggles for revolutionary change.

Notes

1 See reports by the Asian Development Bank (2007) and the World Bank (2005).
2 See Management Advancement Systems Association, Inc. (2000), 'The roles of Northern NGO activities directed at poverty reduction through service delivery and income generation'.
3 These are the Philippine Partnership for the Development of Human Resources in Rural Areas (PHILDHRRA), Philippine Support Services Agencies (PHILSSA), Philippine Business for Social Progress (PBSP), National Council for Social Development (NCSD), National Confederation of Cooperatives in the Philippines (NATCCO) and the Association of Foundations (AF).
4 This is how Philippine civil society is characterized: USAID (2011), *USAID in the Philippines: 50 Years of Partnership for Peace and Development*, 2011; World Bank (2010), *World Bank Country Assistance Strategy for the Philippines (FY 2010–2012)*; and Freedom House (2007); *Countries at the Crossroads 2007: Country Report-Philippines*.
5 Estimates of NGO employment are from Tuaño (2011). Estimates of public sector employment and total employment are from the 2011 Labor Force Survey (LFS) of the National Statistics Office (NSO, 2011).
6 See for instance European Commission (2002), Participation of Non-State Actors in EC Development Policy.
7 See United Nations Children's Fund (2007), *Uncounted Lives: Children, Women and Armed Conflict in the Philippines* and Human Development Network (2005), *Philippine Human Development Report 2005: Peace, Human Security and Human Development in the Philippines*.

8   This discussion of strategy draws from Armando Liwanag (1993), Chairman, Central Committee, Communist Party of the Philippines (CPP).

9   Some examples of prominent NGO personalities in government included Juan Flavier as health secretary during the Corazon Aquino government, PBSP's Ernesto Garilao as agrarian reform secretary during the Ramos government, PRRM's Horacio Morales as agrarian reform secretary during the Estrada government, CODE-NGO's Corazon Soliman as social welfare secretary, and long-time NGO activist Ronald Llamas as presidential adviser on political affairs in the Benigno Aquino III government.

10 Exemplified by the Akbayan Citizen's Action Party project of the so-called independent and democratic socialists and ex-popular democrats (Santos, 2005).

11 'National Economic and Development Authority' (2011a), *CY 2010 ODA Portfolio Review, 2011.*

12 Smallest administrative district in the Philippines, i.e. neighbourhood, ward, or village.

13 Philippines Office of the President (1986), Memorandum Circular No. 4 – Directing the Formulation of the Medium-Term Philippine Development Plan for 1987–1992, Manila, March 18, 1986.

14 Philippines Office of the President (1997), Memorandum Circular No. 166 – Directing the Formulation of the Philippine National Development Plan for the 21st Century, Manila, August 21, 1997.

15 National Economic and Development Authority (1999), *Medium-Term Philippine Development Plan, 1999–2004.*

16 National Economic and Development Authority (2004), *Medium-Term Philippine Development Plan, 2004–2010.*

17 National Economic and Development Authority (2004), *Philippine Development Plan, 2011–2016.*

18 World Bank (2011b). Data from http://data.worldbank.org/country/philippines, accessed December 29, 2011.

19 Country socioeconomic data in this paragraph and the next are from IBON (2011a, 2011c).

20 Agricultural data in this paragraph from IBON (2011d).

21 National Economic and Development Authority (2011b), *Philippine Development Plan, 2011–2016.*

22 For example PRRM's Horacio Morales campaigned for President Estrada and became agrarian reform secretary, CODE-NGO supported President Arroyo and took a number of Cabinet positions, Akbayan campaigned for President Aquino and its NGO leaders are likewise in the Cabinet.

References

Armed Forces of the Philippines (AFP). (2011). 'Internal Peace and Security Plan "Bayanihan".' Quezon City, Philippines: General Headquarters.
Asian Development Bank (ADB). (2007, December). 'Civil Society Brief: Philippines' [Brochure]. Manila, Philippines: ADB NGO and Civil Society Center.

Asian Development Bank (ADB). (2011a). 'ADB and Civil Society: Overview' [Fact sheet]. Retrieved from: http://beta.adb.org/site/ngos/overview.

Asian Development Bank (ADB). (2011b). 'The Bank's Experience with NGOs' [Fact sheet]. Retrieved from: http://www.adb.org/Documents/Policies/Coopera tion_with_NGOs/ngo_experience.asp?p=coopngos.

Association of Foundations (AF). (2001). *Philippine NGOs: A Resource Book of Social Development NGOs*. Manila, Philippines.

Caucus of Development NGO Networks (CODE-NGO). (2012). 'Members: Philippine Business for Social Progress' (PBSP). Retrieved from: http://code-ngo. org/home/membership/pbsp.html.

CIVICUS: 'World Alliance for Citizen Participation and Caucus of Development NGO Networks'. (2011). *Civil Society Index: Philippines – An Assessment of Philippine Civil Society*. Quezon City, Philippines: Caucus of Development NGO Networks (CODE-NGO).

Council for Health and Development (CHD). (1998). *25 Years of Commitment and Service to the People – Onward with the Struggle for Social Change!* Quezon City, Philippines: Council for Health and Development.

European Commission. (2002, November). 'Participation of Non-State Actors in EC Development Policy. Communication from the Commission to the Council, The European Parliament and the Economic and Social Committee' (COM (2002) 598 final). Brussels, Belgium: European Commission.

Freedom House. (2007). 'Countries at the Crossroads 2007: Country Report-Philippines'. Retrieved from: http://www.unhcr.org/refworld/docid/4738692964. html.

Human Development Network. (2005). *Philippine Human Development Report 2005: Peace, Human Security and Human Development in the Philippines, Second Edition*. Quezon City, Philippines: Human Development Network.

IBON. (2011a, January). 'Year end 2010: Real Change, or More of the Same?' [Briefing paper]. Quezon City, Philippines: IBON.

IBON. (2011b, June). 'The Philippine Development Plan (PDP) 2011–2016: Social Contract With Whom?' [Policy paper]. Quezon City, Philippines: IBON.

IBON. (2011c, July). 'Mid year 2011: Failing Economy, Growing Disenchantment' [Briefing paper]. Quezon City, Philippines: IBON.

IBON. (2011d, November). 'Submission by IBON Foundation, a Philippine NGO, to the United Nations Human Rights Council (UNHRC) for the Universal Periodic Review (UPR) of the Philippines During the 13th UPR Session' (21st May–1st June 2012). Quezon City, Philippines: IBON.

Liwanag, A. (1993, November). 'Marxism-Leninism-Mao Zedong Thought as Guide to the Philippine Revolution'. Paper presented at the International Seminar on Mao Zedong Thought, Gelsenkirchen, Germany.

Management Advancement Systems Association, Inc. (2000, January). 'The roles of Northern NGO activities directed at poverty reduction through service delivery and income generation'. Paper presented at the Danida Seminar on 'Civil Society in the South in the 21st Century: Governments and NGOs, Which Roles?', Copenhagen, Denmark.

National Economic and Development Authority. (1999). 'Medium-Term Philippine Development Plan, 1999–2004'. Pasig City, Philippines: National Economic and Development Authority.

National Economic and Development Authority. (2004). 'Medium-Term Philippine Development Plan, 2004–2010'. Pasig City, Philippines: National Economic and Development Authority.

National Economic and Development Authority. (2011a). 'CY 2010 ODA Portfolio Review, 2011'. Pasig City, Philippines: National Economic and Development Authority.

National Economic and Development Authority. (2011b). 'Philippine Development Plan 2011–2016'. Pasig City, Philippines: National Economic and Development Authority.

National Statistics Office (NSO). (2011). '2011 Labor Force Survey (LFS)'. Retrieved from: http://www.census.gov.ph/data/sectordata/datalfs.html.

Philippine Council for NGO Certification (PCNC). (2011). 'Philippine Council for NGO Certification: Background and Rationale'. Retrieved from: http://www.pcnc.com.ph/bgandrationale.php.

Philippines Office of the President. (1986). 'Memorandum Circular No. 4 – Directing the Formulation of the Medium-Term Philippine Development Plan for 1987–1992, Manila, March 18, 1986'. Manila, Philippines: Executive Secretary.

Philippines Office of the President. (1997). 'Memorandum Circular No. 166 – Directing the Formulation of the Philippine National Development Plan for the 21st Century, Manila, August 21, 1997'. Manila, Philippines: Executive Secretary.

Racelis, M. (2000). 'New Visions and Strong Actions: Civil Society in the Philippines'. In Ottaway, M. & Carothers, T. (Eds.), Funding Virtue; Civil Society Aid and Democracy Promotion. Washington, DC: Carnegie Endowment.

Santos, S.M. (2005). 'Evolution of the Armed Conflict on the Communist Front. Background Paper for the Philippine Human Development Report 2005'. Retrieved from: http://hdn.org.ph/2005-philippine-human-development-report-peace-human-security-and-human-development/.

Santos, S.M., Santos, P.V., Dinampo, O.A., Kraft, H.J.S., Paredes, A.K.R., & Quilop, R.J.G. (2010). 'Primed And Purposeful: Armed Groups And Human Security Efforts in the Philippines'. Quezon City, Philippines: South-South Network for Non-State Armed Group Engagement.

Sicat, G. (1979). 'The Five- and Ten-Year Development Plan, 1978–82 and 1978–87'. Manila, Philippines: Ministry of Labor.

Songco, D. A. (2007). 'The Evolution of NGO Accountability Practices and their Implications on Philippine NGOs: A literature review and options paper for the Philippine Council for NGO Certification'. Retrieved from: www.hapinternational.org/pool/files/philippines-evolution-of-ngo-accountability-implications.pdf.

Tuaño, P. (2011). 'Philippine Non-government Organizations (NGOs): Contributions, Capacities, Challenges'. In Yu Jose, L. N. (Ed.), Civil Society Organizations in the Philippines, A Mapping and Strategic Assessment. Quezon City, Philippines: Civil Society Resource Institute.

United Nations Children's Fund. (2007). Uncounted Lives: Children, Women and Armed Conflict in the Philippines. Quezon City, Philippines: UNICEF & IBON Foundation.

United States Agency for International Development (USAID). (2011). 'USAID in the Philippines: 50 Years of Partnership for Peace and Development'. Retrieved from http://philippines.usaid.gov/newsroom/usaid-philippines-50-years-partner ship-peace-and-development

World Bank. (2005). 'Stocktaking of Social Accountability Initiatives in the Asia and Pacific Region, (The World Bank Institute – Community Empowerment and Social Inclusion Learning Programme)'. Retrieved from: http://siteresources. worldbank.org/WBI/Resources/Sirker_StocktakingAsiaPacific_FINAL.pdf.

World Bank. (2009). 'World Bank–Civil Society Engagement: A Review of Years 2007–2009 (World Bank Civil Society Team)'. Retrieved from: http://siter esources.worldbank.org/CSO/Resources/CivilSocietyBook2009final.pdf.

World Bank. (2010). 'World Bank Country Assistance Strategy for the Philippines (FY 2010–2012)'. Retrieved from: http://www-wds.worldbank.org/external/ default/main?pagePK=64193027&piPK=64187937&theSitePK=523679&men uPK=64187510&searchMenuPK=64187283&theSitePK=523679&entityID=0 00112742_20090519114325&searchMenuPK=64187283&theSitePK=523679.

World Bank. (2011a). 'WB and Civil Society: Frequently Asked Questions' [Fact sheet]. Retrieved from: http://web.worldbank.org/WBSITE/EXTERNAL/ TOPICS/CSO/0,,contentMDK:20093224~menuPK:225318~pagePK:220503~ piPK:220476~theSitePK:228717,00.html.

World Bank. (2011b). Philippines data. Retrieved from: http://data.worldbank.org/ country/philippines.

World Bank. (2012). 'The Role of Non-Profit Organizations in Development: the Experience of the World Bank'. Retrieved from: http://web.worldbank.org/ WBSITE/EXTERNAL/TOPICS/EXTSOCIALDEVELOPMENT/EXTPCEN G/0,,contentMDK:20507529~isCURL:Y~menuPK:1278313~pagePK:148956~ piPK:216618~theSitePK:410306,00.html.

Wurfel, D. (2002, March). 'Civil Society and Democratization in the Philippines'. Paper presented at the Asia-Pacific Center for Security Studies, Honolulu, United States.

6

Disaster Relief, NGO-led Humanitarianism and the Reconfiguration of Spatial Relations in Tamil Nadu

Raja Swamy

Given the plethora of civil society organizations in the contemporary era, including those entities broadly defined as NGOs engaged increasingly in processes of development and relief work on a global scale, some studies have drawn attention to the role these play in facilitating processes that depoliticize populations (Alvarez, 1998; Ferguson, 1990; Fisher, 1997).[1] This disciplining aspect, generally attributed to the insights of Foucault, is assumed to be an extension and generalization on a global scale of neoliberal governance (Foucault, 2009). In recent years, a small but growing body of literature has focused on the nexus of state and private interests in post-disaster reconstruction. Many of these works examine the ways in which disaster situations, either those arising from natural causes, or devastation resulting from warfare, are viewed as opportunities for corporate and state interests to advance strategies of accumulation (Gunewardena, 2008; Klein, 2007; Middleton, 1998). The gradual merging of the field of development with broader processes conventionally associated with the imperatives of global capital accumulation proceeds as notions of security and vulnerability become part of a common discourse justifying new strategies of expansion and control (Duffield, 2007; Fassin, 2007). Thus, responses to disasters today increasingly invoke new strategies of development that rest upon a discursive and practical field merging conceptions of vulnerability, risk, resilience and security. There is therefore an increasing tendency to view the need for humanitarian relief as a simultaneous demand for a distinctly neoliberal form of economic development, one centered on rapidly depoliticizing populations while advancing the strategic imperatives of states on behalf of global private capital. This chapter is a call to develop greater empirical depth in our consideration of NGO humanitarianism. It is proposed here that NGOization as a processual component of radical post-disaster respatialization can result in more complex outcomes than simple depoliticization or 'accumulation by dispossession' (Harvey, 2001). As this chapter seeks to demonstrate, a combination of local resilience articulated in ways that render useless paternalistic conceptions by NGOs of disaster victims as vulnerable subjects, and the stubborn counter-strategies of popularly aligned 'local' NGOs, can result in outcomes radically different from those envisioned in grand schemes of regional post-disaster respatialization.

This chapter is concerned with the dynamics of NGO involvement in the aftermath of the devastating 2004 tsunami in Nagapattinam district, Tamil Nadu, India. Focusing on the specific ways in which the disaster circumscribed a distinct terrain of action for the work of NGOs, I examine the manner in which NGOization itself may sometimes be characterized by an open-ended struggle between different political strategies, shaped by, and in engagement with, complex arrangements tying the interests and goals of the state, multilateral institutions and affected populations. Three features stood out in post-tsunami Naga-pattinam that make this a productive context for the study of NGOization, its outcomes and limitations. To planners and policy makers the tsunami was seen as an opportunity for the acceleration of region-wide transformations that were not possible prior to the disaster, primarily on account of a long history of resistance by the coastal fisher population. Secondly, the involvement of NGOs in reconstruction was unprecedented in scale, with the entire housing construction component undertaken by numerous organizations many of which never had a pre-tsunami presence in the region. This second aspect was directly tied to a strategic distinction drawn by policy makers and their multi-lateral institutional partners between humanitarian aid and economic development which ensured that the crucial question of relocation was removed from its proper political context and rehabilitated within the domain of safety and humanitarian generosity. This strategic move was intended to facilitate the radical respatialization of the coast with industrial, infrastructural and tourist development agendas envisioned for the long-term transformation of the region into an economic zone integrated into a global capitalist economy.[2] Based on ethnographic research on the impact of post-tsunami housing reconstruction on fisher communities in Nagapattinam, I examine in this chapter how the dominant mode of NGO engagement in post-disaster reconstruction advocated political complicity in processes of dispossession, and how the work of another NGO with a long history of political engagement on behalf of artisanal fisher interests played an important role in helping to subvert the goal of mass relocation of the district's fisher communities.

I conducted ethnographic fieldwork as part of my doctoral dissertation research in Nagapattinam in 2007–08, focusing on the impacts of relocation on selected households from the coastal fisher villages of Ariyanattutheru, Kallar, and Keechankuppam. In order to explore the general contours of post-tsunami housing construction I conducted two surveys. A preliminary assessment of the impact of relocation on household incomes, expenditure and credit was conducted among 174 households in the relocation sites of five fisher villages in Nagapattinam Taluk–Kallar, Akkarapettai, Keechankuppam, Ariyanattutheru, and Nambiyarnagar. A second survey involved a region-wide study of relocation and beach-space use in the coastal villages of Nagapattinam and adjacent Karaikal, spread from Kallar to Pazhayar. I utilized a GPS unit to map relocation distances and the spatial dimensions of new locations and villages, as well as beach space use by fisher villages and non-fishing (infrastructural, industrial, tourism, and forestry) activities along the Nagapattinam-Karaikal coast from Kallar in Nagapattinam Taluk to Pazhayar in Sirkazhi, bordering Cuddalore district. Data was also collected on the structural and locational features of new housing as reported by randomly sampled households in each of these villages. I conducted formal and informal interviews, field visits and participant observation with the staff of the NGOs Social Needs Empowerment Humane Awareness (SNEHA) and World Vision.

NGOs in post-tsunami reconstruction

NGOs played a central role in housing construction as a result of an elaborate 'public-private partnership', which emerged through government and multilateral agency initiatives and the pressure represented by the flood of NGOs in the weeks following the tsunami. The manner in which the state government envisaged a central role for NGOs ensured both that the costs of housing reconstruction for the most affected population – primarily marginal coastal fishers – would be externalized to NGOs, and that this process would take place in coordination with state and multilateral agency agendas to respatialize the coast.[3] Thus reconstruction institutionalized a division between economic development and humanitarian aid, and paved the way for a program that consisted on the one hand of infrastructural projects such as port and harbour expansion and construction, while relegating housing construction to an NGO-led effort designed to facilitate the relocation of fisher communities from the coast to inland sites selected and procured for the purpose by the government.

Government Order 25, issued by the Tamil Nadu state government's Revenue Department on January 13th, 2005, called for a 'public-private partnership' between the government, private interests and NGOs to 'participate for the permanent relocation and rehabilitation of people affected by this calamity'.[4] What this meant becomes clear in the specifics laid out in the Order whereby NGOs may take on housing construction as per specific guidelines laid out by the state government, with the latter identifying and procuring land for the purpose.[5] As a result, reconstruction by NGOs effectively meant building and delivering 'quality' housing on location and land that the government decided. NGOs overwhelmingly accepted this condition and commenced building, focusing on their work in terms of meeting deadlines and 'delivering' houses rather than on the substantive question of how location and proximity to the coast are crucial criteria for artisanal fishers.

A second Government Order, G.O. 172 issued on March 30th, 2005 laid out criteria for relocation that served as the basis for advancing mass relocation of the state's coastal communities.[6] Using absolute distances as criteria, without regard to specifics of land – elevation, protective vegetation, structures, etc., and invoking the Coastal Regulation Zone Notification of 1991, the Order proscribed the construction of new houses within 200 meters of the high-tide line, and denied government assistance to those in this category who wished to repair damaged houses. It is well-known that households living closest to the coast tend to be poorer residents of *kutcha* houses, built with locally available materials. Thus the poorest residents of fisher villages living close to the coast were pressured into accepting new housing. Moreover, by stating that for the zero-200 meter category, only 'repair of structures authorized prior to 1991 is permissible and no new construction is possible', the Order blatantly disregarded the *de facto* as opposed to *de jure* nature of property conventions governing the housing practices of marginalized populations such as the artisanal fishing communities of Nagapattinam.[7] Very few structures would have qualified for the simple reason that, in general, housing remains an often locally negotiated state of affairs often straddling state and customary claims. Invariably a great many households in coastal fishing communities live in houses constructed on what is legally speaking state-owned *poramboke* land. Even if a household were able to produce evidence of authorization before 1991, the Order denied government support for necessary repairs, leaving such residents to fend for themselves. The only way out for households in this zero-200 meter category was therefore to accept a new house in a location identified by the government. While requiring proof of prior authorization and denying assistance for repairs constituted the coercive part of the government's strategy, the offer of a new house for even those residents whose houses within the zero-200 meter category were undamaged represented its intentions as benign and generous.

The most contentious part of G.O. 172, however, was the requirement that households accepting new housing give up all rights to their old habitations and legally hand over those properties to the government. The lands thus given up would be entered into a 'Prohibitory Order Book' to ensure that they remain in the hands of the government and not transferred. While stating this, there was no other guarantee provided that the land would remain available to the community for its livelihood needs. This requirement to hand legal ownership of land over to the government confirmed suspicions already rife that new housing was being used to lure the fishing communities of the state out of their coastal settlements. Nagapattinam's District Collector went so far as to threaten criminalization of, and legal action against, anticipated efforts to retain old houses by recipients of new housing, and urged NGOs to 'explain' the Government Order's stipulations in this specific regard to communities who seemed to be 'unable to understand G.O.s properly'.[8] Many NGOs made this part of their engagement with communities as they sought to convince residents of the advantages of accepting new housing and the related requirement to relinquish claims on the coast. The Mata Amritanandamayee organization, an internationally funded Hindu NGO based out of Kerala, went so far as to help its beneficiaries 'voluntarily' demolish their houses on the coast as a demonstration of good faith, while World Vision issued an agreement form that explicitly required residents seeking new houses to formally relinquish all claims on existing houses and lands as per the core demand of G.O. 172. By presenting the 'tsunami house' as a gift, NGOs not only foregrounded their interventions in terms of compassion and generosity, but crucially enabled the alienation of land by tacitly or actively supporting the government's requirement that eligibility for housing be predicated on the relinquishing of all claims on coastal land and properties. As such the NGO gift of housing to fisher communities also served as a means to transfer coastal land to the state government.

World Vision and 'service delivery'

With 990 residents, Kallar is located atop a dune about a kilometer south of Akkarapettai. While there were about 123 deaths due to the tsunami, houses on top of the dune and those behind it were relatively undamaged. The majority of the destruction and damage was in the northern part of the village along a U-shaped road that provides access to the beach, and in the zero-200 meter range. In terms of its location, Kallar is the most rural of all of Nagapattinam Taluk's fisher villages located close to the agricultural village of Poignallur. World Vision, the powerful US evangelical NGO, undertook the construction of more than a thousand housing units for Nagapattinam Taluk's fisher communities of which 240 houses were built for residents of Kallar.[9] The site for construction was located in Papa Koil,[10] an inland agricultural village approximately six kilometers from Kallar by road. The site was flanked by shrimp farms to its east, north and south, and the Velankanni highway to its west. This was the farthest relocation site for any fisher village in Nagapattinam district and the impact of distance was most acutely experienced by men and women accustomed to living in proximity to beaches and landing centers and within short distances of markets and civic facilities.

The site selection process involved little community input and despite misgivings about the distance and location of the new site, the Kallar's *panchayat*[11] agreed to accept new houses in Papa Koil. 'New Kallar', completed in 2007, was soon occupied by Kallar's fishers, many of whom had lost homes and family members in the tsunami. By early 2008 however, the site began to be abandoned, with many units locked up, or occupied by non-fisher households who now 'rented' from fisher owners. The difficulties of trying to sustain artisanal fishing from such a distance proved to be too much for New Kallar's fishers. In addition locational and structural problems such as the lack of fresh water, salinity and pollution from adjacent shrimp farms that tended to corrode the poorly plastered walls of their new houses, the lack of roof tiling which necessitated the consumption of more electricity for electric fans, and the absence of functional septic tanks, indoor plumbing, drainage, and running water were some of the most pressing problems for residents. Income/expenditure surveys which I conducted in this community showed that the cost of living here was prohibitively higher than what most residents were accustomed to on the coast. Unsurprisingly most residents returned to Kallar reneging on their agreements with the government and rebuilding on the coast while renting out or putting to other uses their World Vision 'gifted' housing units. Kallar's experience exemplifies the failure of post-tsunami large-scale reconstruction efforts in addressing the central problems facing the fisher community *vis-a-vis* livelihood and location, and stands as a glaring example of the failure of World Vision's 'service delivery' approach.

As an international NGO with a global focus,[12] World Vision functions like a giant corporation with a complex bureaucracy and division of labour organized around a managerial culture. Its India headquarters, located in Kodambakkam, Chennai, is an imposing building towering above a predominantly middle-class neighborhood. With security guards manning a check-post where they process visitors, and a secured and air-conditioned interior that resembles a busy corporate office with cubicles dedicated to regions around the world, World Vision is an organization with substantial resources and power at its disposal. As a constituent member of the Sphere Project, an initiative that began in 1998 around the establishment of a 'Humanitarian Charter and Minimum Standards in Disaster Response', World Vision's post-disaster interventions invoke international standards informed by years of experience in a wide range of contexts. Guided by a body of best practices arrived at by a group that includes some of the world's largest relief agencies such as Action Aid, CARE, Caritas and Oxfam, the organization's work is representative of the approach adopted by a global conglomerate of funding agencies, NGOs, academics, government and extra-national bodies. Since they seek to ensure that 'all possible steps should be taken to alleviate human suffering arising out of conflict and, . . . that those affected by disaster have a right to life with dignity and therefore a *right to assistance*' (emphasis added), international NGOs like World Vision see themselves as global players engaged in the delivery of 'assistance'.[13] As such their own assessments of accomplishments are grounded in a 'service delivery' model that concerns itself primarily with the number and spread of discrete social goods delivered. However, with no prior presence in Nagapattinam, its programs were temporary in focus and had ended by late 2007, with only 'awareness training' on 'environment, health, garbage disposal and toilet usage' being conducted by two locally recruited field staff (Swamy, 2011, p. 217–19).

Artisanal fishers and SNEHA: A background

From the 1950s, state-led initiatives promoted the technological modernization of fishing, driven by the assumption that mechanization of fishing operations would facilitate the gradual transition away from artisanal fishing. However, two unforeseen outcomes of mechanization shaped the terrain of politics for coastal fisher communities, and set the stage for the entry in the 1980s of SNEHA. First, contrary to planners' expectations, mechanized fishing operations proliferated in the same near-shore zone utilized by artisanal fishers, instead of deeper waters. This was complicated by the fact that most mechanized fishers were from the same communities as their artisanal fisher competitors and set the stage for a distinct set of struggles within the fisher community itself. Moreover, artisanal fishers quickly adapted associated technologies such as better nets and outboard motors, increasing the range and efficiency of fishing operations. This led to an increase in their numbers and contributed to their remaining a significantly large majority in the overall fisher population (Bavinck, 2001; Kurien, 1998). Most importantly, their ability to compete fiercely with mechanized fishers led to a sharpening of boundaries between them, facilitating what some scholars describe as the expression of a notion of 'fisher citizenship', centered on a sense of economic autonomy expressed in the cultural idiom of community (Subramanian, 2009).

Beginning in the 1980s, the Indian government, at the behest of international financial institutions, started the large-scale promotion of shrimp aquaculture, and Nagapattinam district's coast became the locus of a great struggle between shrimp farm operators and fisher communities. Whereas the previous era's struggle was over the marine resource base, the struggle over shrimp farms principally had to do with threats to the terrestrial claims of fishers as shrimp farms instituted sharply demarcated notions of private property on a coastal landscape where customary rights of access and land use prevailed. Moreover, with the pollution of water sources and the release of effluents into the near-shore waters, fishers faced additional threats that soon inspired one of the largest anti-shrimp farm mobilizations in the world.

It is in this latter context that SNEHA emerged as a key player in the coast, mobilizing the fisher communities of Nagapattinam and contiguous Karaikal in a manner that profoundly shaped its post-tsunami engagements with reconstruction. SNEHA has worked with Nagapattinam's fisher communities since 1984 when P. Christy, the founder and director first approached nearby Karaikalmedu's newly formed *Mathar Sangam*[14] and offered to help strengthen it.[15] The primary focus was to strengthen efforts by women to make demands on the local administration. Veteran women leaders recount that this involved first and foremost recognizing that people were actually entitled to something called 'rights' (*urimaigal*), which most directly translated into specific actions and services of the government that were being withheld simply because they neither knew about them nor how to effectively demand them. Key to these efforts was the growing recognition that political effectiveness required building a strong organizational base connecting women across fisher villages. Moreover, the discourse of rights during this period also centered on the key issue of the marginalization of women within staunchly patriarchal fisher communities. Karaikalmedu's men were taken by surprise at first, but could do nothing to stop the *sangam* from growing with an increasing number of women empowered both around improving their own social condition and intervening where common fisher interests were at stake across the Karaikal-Nagapattinam coast. Soon other villages in Karaikal as well as adjacent Nagapattinam became part of an expanding federated structure consisting of several village level women's *sangams*.

With a two-fold mission including on the one hand a social agenda to empower women socially and economically, and on the other a sectoral agenda to defend the economic interests of artisanal fishers, the organization marked a unique space for itself in the region. Reorganized as 'self-help groups' (*kulus*) in the early 1990s, primarily to take advantage of new credit programs linking such entities to banks, SNEHA *sangams* grew rapidly from 20 in 1985 to 638 in 2008, with about 11,565 members. The turn to microcredit did not however reduce the push for both defensive and pro-active political mobilizations. Thus even as microcredit programs expanded, registering impressive savings throughout the two districts, *sangams* simultaneously succeeded in pushing local administrations to install street lamps, introduce bus services, and improve access to drinking water, as well as expanding efforts to address the marginalization of women. These latter efforts included cases involving violence against women in which *sangams* took the initiative to demand and enforce punishment against powerful men, successfully diminishing the impunity that such acts often enjoyed under the umbrella of patriarchal *panchayats*.

As recounted by veteran activists, the initial resistance put up by village *panchayats* towards women's *sangams* underwent a transformation when women took on 'sectoral' issues and rapidly won some significant victories for the fishing communities of the region. For instance in 1991 Karaikalmedu's women intervened forcefully against a polluting PNCB/ONCB[16] manufacturing plant operated by Kothari Sugars and Chemicals located in Vanjore near the Karaikal-Nagapattinam border. By the mid-1990s SNEHA allied with Land and Freedom for Tillers (LAFTI), which organized affected agricultural workers and small farmers, particularly Dalits, in mass mobilizations against shrimp farms. The alliance was significant in light of persistent social discrimination faced by Dalits, even at the hands of fishers. The anti-shrimp farm mobilizations of the 1990s saw SNEHA *sangams* engaging in a vibrant and confrontational politics that ranged from mass rallies and demonstrations to direct action. Women and men courted arrest, endured beatings and villages were threatened by an alliance of shrimp farm operators, local administration, police and company-hired thugs for a period of about five years until a landmark ruling by the Supreme Court of India in 1996 shifted the tide in favor of coastal communities, and against the shrimp industry.[17]

Post-tsunami engagements

Within days of the tsunami, SNEHA began conducting damage assessment and mobilizing resources towards supplying relief materials and
support to the devastated communities of Nagapattinam. By early
January 2005, the NGO Coordination Centre (NCC) emerged as the
coordinating body convened by SNEHA and SIFFS (South Indian
Federation of Fisherman Societies), in coordination with the district
administration, to ascertain the extent of destruction, the immediate
needs of communities, and to match these with an ever-growing flood
of NGO funds and relief supplies. One of the key problems at this
stage was the practice by many outsiders representing NGOs to land
in the district, fan out into accessible areas and lay claim to humanitarian 'territory'. 'Adopting' villages, many NGOs then sought to
exert exclusive control over humanitarian work in their 'territory',
often leading to conflict. Moreover, haphazard efforts at this stage led
to replication, over-supply of often unnecessary materials in some
places, and the neglect of other, less accessible, places. The NCC was
therefore intended to impose a semblance of order on the process of
relief and rehabilitation, and through the leadership of SNEHA, to
ensure that the political rights of the affected communities not be
sacrificed in the name of relief. However, once the state government
exerted greater control on the process by rapidly aligning NGO work
with its own multilateral inspired agenda of mass relocation, SNEHA
withdrew from active involvement in coordination and the NCC
quickly transformed itself into an arm of the district administration,
renamed now as the NGO Coordination and Resource Center (NCRC)
after receiving United Nations Development Programme (UNDP)
funds. Without the active leadership of SNEHA, the NCRC adopted
a less suspicious view of state government motives and focused instead
on NGO compliance with government requirements and criteria,
effectively legitimizing the depoliticized engagement of NGOs on the
crucial issue of relocation.

SNEHA engaged in housing construction knowing full well that it
could not directly defy the state government. Reconstruction of
destroyed houses in the zero-200 meter zone was prohibited by G.O.
172, although repairs of such houses could be undertaken but without
government assistance. This was the negative incentive that drove many
poorer households to seek new houses inland leaving their damaged

houses on the coast. Thus SNEHA sought to assist households with funds that could be used towards repairs of damaged houses, and by stretching the definition of repair, such support could also be directed towards substantial reconstruction of badly damaged, or destroyed houses. Additionally, SNEHA argued that rather than force communities to live in crowded, unsanitary temporary shelters while they awaited completion of new housing by NGOs, households should be allowed to repair their old houses and allowed to stay there temporarily. This provided yet another means by which households could utilize SNEHA funds to repair, reconstruct or even extend and modify damaged houses and remain in their original sites.

In conjunction with this strategy, SNEHA also established a distinct approach to 'ownership' that contrasted sharply with the dominant model adopted by NGOs. Each recipient began the first phase of construction with an initial installment, and upon completion of this phase obtained a subsequent installment for the next phase. With some variation, most housing repair/construction projects financed by SNEHA were spread across four installments. For design and construction, individual owners could utilize their own contractors and labor, or use recommended contractors. In most cases, at least part of the labor was provided by the owners themselves. One drawback of this approach to 'owner-driven' housing was that the pace was slow compared to NGO housing. However, in terms of design specifications, quality and dimensions, these houses were superior. The most common complaint was that recipients had to repeatedly request funds from the organization at each step. SNEHA's coordinators point out that this is a necessary constraint since it would otherwise be impossible to ensure that funds are actually used for building houses and not wasted. Through its core constituency – women members of SNEHA *sangams* – the organization disbursed funds into communities throughout the coast encouraging them to not only rebuild their homes in the way they saw fit, but crucially, it sought to ensure thereby that households exercised their own judgment about remaining or moving out of their villages.[18]

It was in Kallar where SNEHA's intervention most visibly challenged the logic of relocation, and in the process helped encourage relocated residents to return to the village from 'New Kallar.' A grove directly behind the large dune on which the village sits was purchased for the village by the organization, from owners who belonged to some prominent families. With financial support from SNEHA, forty-two houses were built by owners, mostly from poorer families in the village who married after the tsunami and needed new houses. The houses, though in various states of completion as of late 2008, were nevertheless superior in dimensions and design to any houses built in Nagapattinam by NGOs.[19] 'Owner-driven' and conforming to the expected aesthetic and functional needs of fishing households, these houses had sloping tiled roofs, and floor tiling comparable in quality to those found in some of Nagapattinam's middle-class localities. Owners here utilized SNEHA funds, but also over time used their own incomes in small installments, or obtained loans in order to add or embellish design or functional elements, including decorative window frames, door panels, and floor tiles. Each house in Kallar cost SNEHA a minimum total of Rs. 40,000 (approximately USD 1,014 in 2008),[20] with some variation, while the government estimated minimum required cost for NGO-built housing was Rs. 150,000 (USD 3,450 in 2005) in 2005 and increased substantially over the next two years.

Discussion

World Vision's approach to post-tsunami reconstruction effectively kept the focus on efficiency of service with a view to ensuring that its agreement with the state government was honored in a timely fashion. Moreover in its engagement with local communities the organization remained aloof and in some cases adopted a paternalistic attitude, encouraging fishers to accept relocation without seriously considering the implications of such decisions for their ability to sustain livelihoods. On the issue of livelihoods, World Vision adopted the state's argument that the supply of boats and fishing gear would suffice even if recipients were to now face the prospective loss of coastal land. Artisanal fishers rely upon beaches for parking boats and storing fishing gear among other uses, all of which would be rendered useless if they lived far away from beaches now potentially reckoned by the state for other purposes than artisanal fishing. The real problem however was revealed to be the sheer limits of its intended engagement in Nagapattinam. As an organization that merely saw itself as another subcontractor for the state government, its temporary presence in the district precluded any serious efforts at anything more than a superficial engagement with its erstwhile beneficiaries.

How may we assess World Vision's engagement in post-tsunami reconstruction in terms of NGOization? While the organization initiated a series of projects in addition to housing, designed along lines of encouraging modes of self-regulation and individualized discipline (garbage management, toilet usage, etc.), its lack of a long-term commitment resulted in these projects achieving little. The only tangible sign of the NGO's presence that remained were newly built houses that were now treated as assets, as fishers quickly sought new ways to renew their abilities to sustain livelihoods dependent on proximity to the coast. It is only through the 'gift' of housing that World Vision came close to imposing a form of disciplinary control over its beneficiaries, but only because it strictly adhered to the state government's agenda. As noted above, G.O. 172 was intended to ensure that recipients of relinquished rights over the coast in order to qualify for new housing. The Order also imposed a set of requirements on recipients that ensured their compliance with the requirements of relocation. Adherence to these requirements constituted what we may consider a demand of responsibility that sought to discipline recipients of the NGO 'gift' of housing. Ownership implied accepting two conditions. First, only the male and/or female heads of household (in both of whose names a house was formally registered) and their families would live in these houses. Second, these families would not transfer their house to anybody either for rent or as property for sale. This was designed to enforce adherence to the agreement with the government that recipients would not reclaim lands and properties relinquished by the act of accepting new housing. Thus 'responsibility' at the outset implied working within a set of legal limits to ownership. The transformation of people cast as perpetual transgressors living at the literal margins of state sovereignty on lands technically owned by the state, into law-abiding subjects who now owned houses and lived responsibly, was sought to be instituted through the 'gift' of housing. Hence the NCRC, now a quasi-state body articulating the local administration's goals and concerns, repeatedly requested NGOs 'to ensure that the beneficiaries shall not be allowed to enjoy relinquished land/house once moved to permanent houses' (NCRC, 2007).

Here one may consider World Vision's role as a facilitator of, rather than a substitute for, state power. Doubtless the process was imbued with 'anti-politics' – victims of the disaster were cast into recipients of 'gifts' rather than as subjects and constituents of a sovereign state from which they may demand entitlements. Yet, with the rapid exit of most NGOs from the region by the middle of 2008, what remained on the ground was the familiar relationship between an artisanal fisher population once again eager to assert its autonomy and a sovereign forced to turn its grandiose plans for relocation over to multiple locally negotiated outcomes. Large-scale evictions have not taken place in Nagapattinam and fishers retain autonomous though tentative control of their coastal lands, though they remain once again at the literal and legal margins. Recipients of the 'gift' returned the implicit bad faith of the gift explicitly – they renewed their preference for autonomy even if it meant returning to the margins of legality since the promise of the latter turned out to be no more than a means to enforce alienation from their means of sustenance. Thus NGOization in the case of the 'service delivery' model pursued by NGOs like World Vision stands for a temporally bound process whereby state power is sought to be advanced through the agency of the humanitarian imperative centered on the economy of the gift. However inasmuch as recipients have been able and willing to distinguish between the gift economy and the real political economy that centers on their access to resources and land, post-tsunami NGOization has failed in redrawing the balance of power between sovereign and subject.

How may we assess SNEHA's strategies to defend fisher claims on the coast? An NCRC official quipped that SNEHA was not so much a regular NGO but an entity that 'stood outside and shouted slogans.' Yet its engagement with the state demonstrates a keen understanding of how state-subject relations constitute the crux of politics at the local level. If NGOs view themselves as 'civil society' standing separately from the state, and as alternatives to the state, and yet work to promote citizenship and rights as the correct way to become proper subjects of state power, 'political society' is that domain of political engagement where power is contested at the local level between populations and state sovereignty (Chatterjee, 2004). This often works in the course of electoral politics, but also at the level of the myriad local negotiations of power that routinely shape relations between subjects and sovereigns, often in tentative terms. Legality itself is a negotiated state of affairs and not something enshrined in citizenship as assumed by civil society. SNEHA keenly recognized this tentative character of power negotiated between state sovereignty and the autonomous bases of power invoked by fishers. Fishers after all view themselves as a distinct community; a community with its own claims to the coast and the sea, a distinct livelihood that always makes the terrestrially bound state uneasy because it involves constantly traversing the terrestrial-maritime boundary, and a distinct cultural and historical geography. In this sense the organization's local moorings in the ethos of fisher citizenship (to invoke Ajantha Subramanian's (2009) formulation) played a distinct role in shaping an engagement that effectively subverted and undermined NGOization even as it deployed the discourses and practices of NGOs. It is for this reason that SNEHA remains one of the most important organizations in Nagapattinam today.

Notes

1 Sonia Alvarez (1998) is also one of the first scholars to use the term 'NGO-ization' in describing the dual process of transferring the state's social functions to NGOs and the depoliticizing shift from activism to professionalization in Latin America. Kamat (2002) points to similar trends in India as politically engaged organizations became NGOs as a result of professionalization.

2 I provide a detailed explanation of this strategy in my doctoral dissertation (Swamy, 2011).

3 The Order invites NGOs that can construct houses for at least 50 households at the minimum estimated cost of Rs. 75 lakhs (Rs. 7.5 million). A host of NGOs responded to the government call including local, regional, national and global NGOs. A brief survey of NGOs undertaking reconstruction activities reveals that the largest single group were affiliated to religious organizations, although secular organizations were also represented by a large number. The 'local/grassroots' versus 'outsider' distinction is not very useful in distinguishing NGOs involved in reconstruction since financing networks overlap such putative boundaries across the spectrum. Thus while World Vision could bring to bear its immense global resources garnered largely through its affluent donor base in the United States, local NGOs such as SNEHA also relied upon funds provided by European donors such as the Swiss Red Cross. A more useful characterization of differences would focus attention on the willingness and ability of organizations to respond effectively to the political economic needs of their beneficiaries. On this count, the few organizations that did make a difference were those that already had established themselves as political allies of local communities, especially through a rights paradigm rooted in livelihood and communal autonomy.

4 See G.O.Ms. No.25, Dated 13.1.2005. http://www.tn.gov.in/gosdb/gorders/rev/rev-e-25-2005.htm

5 G.O.Ms. No.25, Dated 13.1.2005, Annexure 1.

6 G.O.Ms. No.172, Dated 30.3.2005. Retrieved from: http://www.tn.gov.in/ gosdb/gorders/rev/rev-e-172-2005.htm.

7 *De facto* refers to actual arrangements that have no explicit sanction in law, or sometimes occur in contravention of law, while *de jure* refers to arrangements that are explicitly sanctioned by law.

8 See *Consultation with NGOs on Habitat and Shelter* /5./4.05 (NCC, 2005), *Minutes of Shelter Review Meeting* 11./8.05 (NCRC, 2005b), and *Review of Permanent Shelter Meeting with the Collector* 20.07.05 (NCRC, 2005a).

9 The U.S. Internal Revenue Service identifies World Vision Inc. as a nonprofit [501(c)3] public charity [509(a)1] exempt from taxes under the tax codes applicable to a church [170(b)(1)(A)(i)]. See www.worldvision.planyourlegacy. org/advisors/pdf/tax-exempt.pdf.

10 World Vision named this site 'New Kallar'.

11 *Panchayat* here refers to the *Ur Panchayat* – the traditional council that governs village community. This *panchayat* is distinct from the formal *Panchayat Raj* institution set up as the local administrative apparatus of the government.

12 According to its annual report, World Vision raised USD 2.6 billion in cash and kind, and 'served' more than 100 million people in 98 countries of the world in 2008 (World Vision, 2008).

13 See The Sphere Project's *Humanitarian Charter and Minimum Standards in Disaster Response,* at http://www.sphereproject.org/.

14 In the 1980s *Mathar Sangam* or *Magalir Sangam* were women's collectives often organized locally around rights-based agendas. In the 1990s, these were largely supplanted by or transformed into *kulus* ('self-help groups') which shifted the focus towards microcredit.

15 This account of SNEHA's history draws upon interviews conducted with SNEHA staff including Indrani (Karaikalmedu), Dr. Kumaravelu, Vanaja, S. Rajendran, and Shankar (Nagapattinam), as well as R. Revathi, a Nagapattinam resident who worked closely with the organization in post-tsunami relief and rehabilitation. It also extensively utilizes information from SNEHA's 1997–1999 annual reports (SNEHA, 1997, 1998, 1999), and reports on the organization's impact on women in the fisher community (Sharma, 2007).

16 Para/Ortho Nitro-Chloro-Benzene (PNCB/ONCB) is an intermediary compound used in the manufacture of commercial chemical products.

17 S. Jagannath Vs Union of India and Others, Writ Petition (C) No. 1994 (Kuldip Singh, S. Saghir Ahmed JJ) 11.12.1996. See also campaign documents of CASI (Campaign Against Shrimp Industries, 2004).

18 Without doubt the key strength that enabled such an engagement with the reconstruction regime was the fact that SNEHA enjoys a large membership base within the fisher community. This factor aided in its efforts to take a longer-term perspective than other NGOs.

19 Kallar's SNEHA-financed houses had an area of about 600 sq. feet, significantly larger than the 300–325 sq. feet required by the government in G.O.172.

20 Exchange rates selected by year for consistency.

References

Alvarez, S.E. (1998). 'The "NGOization" of Latin American Feminisms'. In S.E. Alvarez, E. Dagnino, & A. Escobar (Eds.) *Cultures of Politics, Politics of Cultures: Re-Visioning Latin American Social Movements* (pp. 306–324). Boulder, Colorado: Westview Press.

Bavinck, M. (2001). *Marine Resource Management. Conflict and Regulation in the Fisheries of the Coromandel Coast*. New Delhi: Sage.

Campaign Against Shrimp Industries. (2004). 'Peoples's Struggles Against Shrimp Industries and the Role of Campaign Against Shrimp Industries, Nagapattinam District'. Information booklet produced by CASI, on file with the author.

Chatterjee, P. (2004). *The Politics of the Governed: Reflections on Popular Politics in Most of the World*. New York: Columbia University Press.

Duffield, M.R. (2007). *Development, Security and Unending War: Governing the World of Peoples*. Cambridge: Polity Press.

Fassin, D. (2007). 'Humanitarianism: A Nongovernmental Government'. In M. Feher, G. Krikorian, & Y. McKee (Eds.) *Nongovernmental Politics* (pp.149–160). New York: Zone Books. Distributed by MIT Press.

Ferguson, J. (1990). *The Anti-politics Machine: 'Development', Depoliticization, and Bureaucratic Power in Lesotho*. New York: Cambridge University Press.

Fisher, W.F. (1997). 'Doing Good? The Politics and Antipolitics of NGO Practices'. *Annual Review of Anthropology, 26,* 439–464.

Foucault, M. (2009). *Security, Territory, Population: Lectures at the Collège De France 1977–1978*. First edition. New York: Picador.

Gunewardena, N. (2008). *Capitalizing on Catastrophe: Neoliberal Strategies in Disaster Reconstruction (Globalization and the Environment)*. California: AltaMira Press.

Harvey, D. (2001). *Spaces of Capital: Towards a Critical Geography*. New York: Taylor & Francis.

Kamat, S. (2002). *Development Hegemony: NGOs and the State in India*, New Delhi: Oxford University Press.

Klein, N. (2007). *The Shock Doctrine: The Rise of Disaster Capitalism*. New York: Metropolitan Books.

Kurien, J. (1998). 'Small-scale fisheries in the context of globalization'. Center for Development Studies, Trivandrum. Working Papers 289, Center for Development Studies, Trivandrum, India.

Middleton, N. (1998). *Disaster and Development: the Politics of Humanitarian Aid*. London: Pluto.

NCC. (2005). Consultation with NGOs on Habitat and Shelter 5 April 2005. NGO Coordination Center: Nagapattinam, Tamil Nadu, India. On file with the author.

NCRC. (2005a). Nagapattinam, Review of Permanent Shelter Meeting with the Collector. 20 July 2005. NGO Coordination and Resource Center: Tamil Nadu, India. On file with the author.

NCRC. (2005b). Minutes of Shelter Review Meeting. 11 August 2005. NGO Coordination and Resource Center: Tamil Nadu, India. On file with the author.

NCRC. (2007). Minutes of the NGOs Weekly Review Meeting. 3 July 2007. NGO Coordination and Resource Centre: Tamil Nadu, India. On file with the author.

Sharma, A. (2007). 'Enhancement of Women's Livelihoods and Group Solidarity in Karaikal District, Pondicherry. Tsunami Reconstruction / Rehabilitation Initiatives Programme Publication No. 2. Swiss Solidarity, Swiss Red Cross, Initiatives in Development Support'. Retrieved from: http://www.iids.in/pdf/enhancement_of_womens_livelihoods_group_solidarity.pdf.

SNEHA. (1997). Annual Report. Social Needs Empowerment Humane Awareness: Nagapattinam, Tamil Nadu, India.

SNEHA. (1998). Annual Report. Social Needs Empowerment Humane Awareness: Nagapattinam, Tamil Nadu, India.

SNEHA. (1999). Annual Report. Social Needs Empowerment Humane Awareness: Nagapattinam, Tamil Nadu, India.

Subramanian, A. (2009). *Shorelines: Space and Rights in South India*. Stanford: Stanford University Press.

Swamy, R. (2011). 'Disaster Capitalism: Tsunami Reconstruction and Neoliberalism in Nagapattinam, South India'. Doctoral Dissertation. Austin, Texas: University of Texas at Austin.

World Vision. (2008). *World Vision International Annual Review 2008*. World Vision International. Retrieved from: http://www.wvi.org/wvi/wviweb.nsf/C5C75B869 35DAAA88825758900751799/$file/WVI_2008_Annual_Review.pdf.

7

Seven Theses on Neobalkanism and NGOization in Transitional Serbia

Tamara Vukov

As in other post-socialist and 'developing' area contexts, and commencing with the years of political strife and war that led to the dissolution of the Federal Socialist Republic of Yugoslavia, the ongoing transition to capitalism in post-Yugoslav Serbia has been accompanied by the explosion of the so-called Third Sector, civil society, or 'the Other Serbia' ('*Druga Srbija*'). The predominant image presented in the West of the civil society/NGO sector is that of a major progressive force countering the crude nationalism of the general public and leading Serbia on the road to eventual European Union membership. Yet this chapter argues that much of the sector has in fact played a compromised, coopted, and at times destructive role in preparing the ground for and reinforcing neoliberal restructuring, legitimizing the so-called democracy promotion of empire (what Michael Ignatieff (2003) approvingly calls 'empire lite'), and entrenching the political 'dance' between neoliberalism and nationalism that squeezes out all other alternatives from accepted political discourse in the region. Certain actors in this sector have also worked to counter, diffuse, and marginalize grassroots and autonomous resistance to neoliberalism in the region, although growing instances of the latter have emerged and will be something I gesture towards at the end of the chapter.

Building upon the theoretical and political groundwork laid down in a series of panels on 'Balkanism' convened by members of the Global Balkans network at the 2008 and 2009 Critical Race and Anti-Colonial Studies Conferences (held in Toronto and Montreal respectively), this chapter offers seven theses that attempt to elucidate the complex yet intimate relations between the racialized discourse of balkanism, NGOization, and the post-Yugoslav economic and political transition. This reflection piece emerges out of some of the concrete political struggles and organizing dilemmas I have engaged with as a participant in the informal Global Balkans network, as well as a film-maker working on an independent documentary film project in collaboration with Global Balkans and activist groups in the region on how the post-Yugoslav transition is being lived by workers and displaced people in Serbia.

Grounded in my engagement with grassroots movements in Serbia through the Global Balkans network and practices of militant investigation (Shukaitis, Graeber, & Biddle, 2007) that I undertook over the 5 years (2006–2011) I spent filming the documentary film project *Tranzicija/Transition* (forthcoming, 2014), I draw upon interviews with grassroots actors in the region in thesis 5 to weave together some of the primary forms and critiques of this NGOization of social and political space in Serbia over this period. Building on the grounded analysis emerging from these interviews, I sketch out some of the ways through which NGOs have come to act as both the 'swords' and 'soft power of empire' (Bartholomew & Breakspear, 2004, p. 124). I close with a brief consideration of emerging political energies and networks working beyond the compromised model of NGOization to build and support autonomous grassroots resistance to the destructive impacts that balkanism, military humanitarianism, and the neoliberal economic transition have wrought in the region.

The New Balkanism

One particularity of both military humanitarianism and NGOization in the region is the extent to which it has been introduced and buttressed via imperial rhetorics of neobalkanism. Following the works of such writers as Maria Todorova (1997) and Vesna Goldsworthy (1998), balkanism has come to be understood as a persistent and recalcitrant imperialist discourse that frames the Balkan region as a volatile, primitive, and savage land of primordial hatreds and nationalist backwardness requiring some form of imperial oversight. If we trace the history and periodic recurrence of balkanism, it becomes clear that the re-emergence and reactivation of balkanism and a corresponding discourse of humanitarian intervention in relation to the wars amongst the successor states of the former socialist Yugoslavia in the 1990s and 2000s carried specific traits. Tracing the parameters and effects of this 'new balkanism' is a larger project. Two key parallel and symbiotic discourses to the new balkanism of the past 20 years include the 'new' and highly visible politics of militaristic *humanitarianism*, which has operated and been mobilized in close concert with the erasure and invisibility on a global stage of the dramatic impacts of *neoliberalism* in the region. The persistent occlusion of the latter has in many ways been enabled by this spectacle of western military humanitarianism, of a benevolent west bringing order to a chaotic, brutal local culture. This obscures the extent to which the violent neoliberal restructuring of the region from its earlier days in the guise of the shock therapy of the late 1980s and early 1990s (under the counsel of Jeffrey Sachs) has impacted and generated the conditions for war, for the rise of the nationalisms and violent militarisms that shaped the dissolution of the Socialist Federal Republic of Yugoslavia (see Woodward, 1995). Through the lens of the new balkanism, neoliberalism is euphemized into a triumphalist discourse of 'transition', of the coming of humanitarian aid, democracy and progress to the region, a way to cleanse and purify it of its indigenous backwardness by westernizing and promising to bring it into the European family. As Horvat and Stiks (2012) argue, 'the very concept of Transition – as an ideological construct of domination based on the narrative of integration of the former socialist Europe into the Western core – actually hides the monumental neo-colonial transformation of this region into a dependent semi-periphery'.

Empire lite: Military humanitarianism

The post-Yugoslav Balkans have been the testing ground for a series of innovations and shifts in coalescing imperial projects that have played a crucial role in the latest manifestations and mutations of humanitarian imperialism on a global stage. The neoliberal economic program known as shock therapy that was introduced in the region in 1990 was just one of these experiments. The shift from a development-based model of humanitarianism, however paternalistic, to a newly militarized form of humanitarian intervention during the 1999 NATO bombing strikes in Yugoslavia and Kosovo was a key turning point that shaped the trajectory of later military incursions elsewhere in the world (Iraq, Afghanistan, Libya).

One of the key proponents and ideologues of this emergent form of human rights imperialism, Michael Ignatieff, has written quite boldly, some might say triumphally, of the intimate relationship that has developed and been increasingly mobilized between humanitarianism and imperialism. In his paean to what he approvingly calls 'empire lite', Ignatieff is forthright in his assertion that this is a positive thing (2003). As he notes,

> I focus on nation-building in Bosnia, Kosovo, and Afghanistan because they are laboratories in which a new imperium is taking shape, in which American military power, European money and humanitarian motive have combined to produce a form of imperial rule for a post-imperial age (p. 18).

The progression from Bosnia and Kosovo to Afghanistan, and, on the eve of the US intervention when the text was written, Iraq, is important here. The arenas for these humanitarian military adventures are figured by Ignatieff as barbarian frontier zones of failed states and ethnic conflict, zones that will remain ungovernable, prey to disorder and violent chaos, but for the intervention of a benevolent imperial hegemony. This is what he calls 'temporary imperialism', a limited occupation necessary for the establishment of democracy and the imposition of responsibility onto local elites who are otherwise incapable of self-government. Ignatieff argues that 'Bosnia after Dayton offered laboratory conditions in which to experiment with nation-building' that became the precedent for the later interventions into Afghanistan and Iraq (p. 31). Yet he also rather baldly notes that 'the reconstruction of the Balkans has not been an exercise in humanitarian social work, it has always been an imperial project' (p. 27). He does not mean this as a form of critique. In fact, he is quite enthusiastic about the promise of progress that this 'imperial kernel at the heart of the humanitarian enterprise' imposes (p. 36). As he puts it, 'nation-building is the kind of imperialism you get in a human rights era' (p. 90).

Ignatieff's liberal apologetics are bold in their defense of what some would consider a cynical vision of humanitarianism. In this vision, humanitarianism is more or less reduced to imperialism, and the ostensible motive of great powers to 'do good' in the world is always doubled by the convergence between 'doing good' and a calculated self-interest. But Ignatieff's defense of 'empire lite' does have the virtue of directly stating the terms of this approach in an open equation of what he calls 'the humanitarian as imperialist'.

Ignatieff is also clear on the sequence of events called upon in this scenario – beginning with what he terms a barbarian threat in a zone of strategic imperial interest, moving to the need for a humanitarian intervention that is both military and moral on the part of an imperial power (whether in its multilateral or unilateral guise), to the arrival of humanitarian aid, NGOs and nation-building in the liberal democratic image of the intervening power. Nevertheless, this happy scenario of a benevolent humanitarian empire intervening in the name of democracy obscures several critical factors:

(1) firstly, the implication of the same imperial powers in producing conditions that contribute to the destabilization, violence and disorder of the so-called frontier zones;

(2) secondly, the ostensibly surgical yet often brutal violence and 'collateral damage' of militarized humanitarianism;

(3) and thirdly, the extent to which the promotion and advent of liberal democracy, or in the case of the post-socialist Balkans, neoliberal democracy, is motivated by the simultaneous imposition of market capitalism in conditions of what would classically be referred to as primitive accumulation, or what David Harvey (2003) calls accumulation by dispossession.

As Neda Atanasoski has argued (2006), the spectre of Eastern European, and more specifically, Balkan barbarism, re-emerged in the 1990s through a US discourse on Eastern Europe's racial backwardness, whereby an image of primitive racism and ethnic conflicts in Eastern European as well as non-European nations such as Iraq constitute a displacement of the US's anxieties about its own unresolved racial inequalities onto so-called ethnic conflicts in 'underdeveloped' regions. This displacement helped to secure an image of the US's humanitarian role as leader and exemplar of racial tolerance as part of a liberal multiculturalist mode of democracy promotion. At the same time, it obscures the extent to which the 'US promotion of Western human rights ideals [in these regions] goes hand in hand with its stakes in fostering the budding free market economies of Eastern Europe' that only exacerbate existing ethnic, racial, and other inequalities (p. 225).

Swords of empire: NGOization, democracy promotion and the new balkanism

There are many continuities between the new balkanism and its historical forms in the way that both frame the region as a kind of liminal space between Europe and orient, a zone of ethnic impurity, instability and irrationality. But in relation to the post-Yugoslav geopolitical space of the 1990s and 2000s, the new balkanism has its own distinct features and apparatuses that have emerged over the course of the past twenty years. The modes of imperial intervention it has taken are multiple, and include legal, military, economic, academic, cultural, visual and media spheres. The new military humanitarianism has been the vehicle and modus operandi through which a transitional form of imperial governmental oversight has been installed in the post-Yugoslav region, both militarily and politically. Its forms of governance are no less effective or continuous for being heterogeneous (or polyarchic as William Robinson (1996) has argued) and encompassing competing agendas and tensions within the range of national and supranational forms they take: from the new neoliberal and residual nationalist elites governing the successor states, the International Monetary Fund, World Bank, European Union, and special tribunals; to NATO, KFOR (the Kosovo Force of NATO), protectorate forms of governance such as the Office of the High Representative in Bosnia, UNMiK (the UN Mission in Kosovo), and EULEX (European Union Rule of Law Mission in Kosovo, which replaces UNMiK).

Concomitantly, a particularly pervasive and often deceptive agent of the new balkanist humanitarianism comes in the political form of the NGO. Since the emergence of the first NGOs in Serbia in the late 1980s and early 1990s (Vetta 2009, p. 29), the pace of NGOization has accelerated, with 2,000 NGOs registered in the decade between 1990–2000, and a further explosion after the regime change in 2000, when 8,500 NGOs were registered between 2000 and 2006 (Vetta, 2009, p. 29). Steven Sampson (2002) argues that the project teams, directors, and managers of NGO and humanitarian aid projects have become an important component of what he terms the new *comprador* bourgeois elites in 'post-postsocialist' countries. They act as pliable, effective cosmopolitan agents for the political and economic 'democracy promotion' programs of Western metropoles as part of a modernizing mission to propel a 'backward' society (understood in balkanist terms) on the road to democracy and (capitalist) progress (p. 299–300; see also Mandel, 2002). If, as Arundhati Roy (2004) has argued, NGOs are indicator species for the ravages wrought by neoliberalism in non-western countries, the NGOization of the post-Yugoslav space, financed by USAID, the National Endowment for Democracy (NED), Soros' Open Society Institute and various European governments, has played a key role in the cooptation and control of permissible political discourse in the region, largely by controlling and channeling anti-nationalist discourses into a pro-neoliberal, pro-EU (European Union) project that continuously foments balkanist tropes of internal primitivism and barbarism to sustain itself.

In the context of the post-Yugoslav neoliberal transition, the shadow side of military humanitarianism that is rarely spoken of or covered in the Western media is neoliberal democracy promotion by imperial powers (Guilhot, 2005). And central to militarized democracy promotion as an extended project in the region, human rights largely take on the character of what Amy Bartholomew and Jennifer Breakspear (2004) in their critique of Ignatieff call 'swords of empire' in specific instances, and of the 'soft power' of empire in others (and sometimes both simultaneously) (p. 124). While a growing literature is critically assessing the contradictions and limitations (as well as the uses) of human rights as formalistic legal instruments in Western liberal democracies that leave fundamental social and economic inequalities intact (Brown, 2002; Kennedy, 2002a and 2002b), the tactical specificities and impacts of the transposition of Western legalistic notions of human rights into post-socialist contexts can only be fully assessed and grasped in their indissociability from the wider projects of democracy promotion, military cosmopolitanism (Kurasawa, 2006, p. 299) and the neoliberal implantation of market capitalism at play.

It is in liberalism's classical severing of any material considerations of access to food and income from the purview of individual rights that the full irony of the simultaneous legal introduction of truncated formal human rights, and NGOization alongside legal mechanisms for the material dispossession of the majority living in post-socialist contexts becomes most acute. In terms of the historical political enactment of this liberal evacuation of human rights of basic material guarantees, Roxanne Dunbar-Ortiz (2008) has traced the emergence of a humanitarian instrumentalization of human rights for imperialist goals to the Helsinki Declaration of 1975. With the passage of the declaration, previous efforts by 'third world' and socialist countries to entrench the rights to food, guaranteed income, health care, housing and free education as basic human rights in such initiatives as the UN Covenant on Economic, Social and Cultural Rights passed at the UN General Assembly in 1966 (but unratified by countries such as the United States) were politically marginalized and defeated. As Irina Ceric (2009) further argues,

> although it is portrayed as neutral, benevolent international aid, democracy promotion and rule of law promotion, when viewed through the lens of 'balkanism', ought to be understood as intervention which facilitates the linkage of 'freedom and democracy . . . to the presence of markets . . . [T]he invocation of the rule of law, the deployment of the language of rights, and the expansion of NGOs helps cement the connection.

Examining such cases as the introduction of privatization laws into the domestic laws of post-Yugoslav successor states (with wide-ranging oversight and preparation by such international actors as the World Bank's Rule of Law program), Ceric situates this form of rule of law democracy promotion in which human rights constitute the cement binding democracy to market capitalism as a subspecies of legal imperialism that she terms legal balkanism. The special form of chaos and upheaval this has produced for the majority populations on the losing end of these 'democratic' reforms remains largely invisible on a world stage focused on balkanist tropes of their savagery and primitivism.

The dance of neoliberalism and nationalism

The relentless dance between neoliberalism and nationalism that characterized the early years of war and transition is an ongoing reality in the region that suffuses the entire political space and shapes the main parameters of political life. While there are contradictions and differing political actors and alignments at play in both neoliberal and nationalist political factions dominating the political stage, the two sides essentially feed off one another and share a common material base in the scramble for capital accumulation unleashed by the chaos of neoliberal restructuring. In the face of the intensive ideological assault over the past twenty years on leftist political discourse and values in the region, activists who are attempting to construct genuine left political alternatives that reject both the nationalist and neoliberal options operate within a very constrained space for political maneuver, caught between a rock and a hard place in this political dichotomy, attacked and counter-attacked by both sides. This is one of the basic challenges of grassroots organizing.

Given this dynamic, I would suggest that a strictly anti-nationalist political critique or stance towards the post-Yugoslav region is not sufficient, and can in fact serve some counter-productive, indeed destructive, purposes. Those forms of political organizing and opposition that limit themselves to a liberal anti-nationalism, whether of the western neobalkanist variety, or the regional and domestic variants, often produced in urban cosmopolitan NGO circles, tend to both obscure and reinforce, whether tacitly or more actively, the massive damage wrought by neoliberal privatization in the region. The task at hand is how to formulate and operationalize a contextualized yet effective opposition to Serb and other local nationalisms, one that takes into account the factors that contributed to their rise, over and against a demonizing, decontextualized stance towards nationalisms in the region in a way that erases these contributing factors and legitimizes 'international' or humanitarian intervention or imperial oversight in some form. I would argue that such a contextual anti-nationalist politics can only be effective in the context of a wider anti-capitalist, anti-imperialist politics that rejects the dominant neobalkanist narratives, liberal anti-nationalism, and military humanitarianism, while critiquing the political role that much of the established NGO sector has played in reinforcing and ideologically promoting these tendencies.

Critiques of NGOization by activists and organizers in Serbia

It's an apology for capitalism and parliamentary democracy. It's very naive, sometimes interested, sometimes deceptive, that many people who are part of the NGO sector have never uttered a critical word about that system which they are supporting.[1]

This section quotes at length from several interviews with activists in Serbia working both within and outside of the NGO sector, conducted over the course of filming as well as during the summer of 2012, in order to concretely ground the larger analysis this chapter aims to bring forth regarding the role that NGOization has played in the politics of neoliberal transition and dispossession in Serbia and the larger ex-Yugoslav region. I have largely chosen to omit the names of specific NGOs, as my aim is to raise some of the deeper issues regarding the dynamics and impacts of NGOization on politics in the region, rather than to trigger an empirical debate or defensive postures with respect to the work of any particular existing NGO. Several key observations and critiques in the interviews echo one another and have contributed to the analysis emerging throughout this chapter.

To begin with, several organizers/activists noted the extent to which the first wave of NGOs that emerged in the 1990s in Serbia (or what was then still the Federal Republic of Yugoslavia) had their mandates and activities restricted and policed to one narrow goal by the donors they worked with: regime change of Slobodan Milosevic. This only became apparent to several of my interviewees with time, when they either encountered obstacles to their organizing, had their funding cut for attempting to undertake more proactive activities than simple opposition to the regime, and often with hindsight, in encountering the post-2000 accelerated neoliberal economic program and mass privatizations that followed the change in regime.

As one activist who continues to be very active in anti-privatization and workers' movements in Serbia recounts, with regards to a grass-roots network he was involved in that was active during the 1990s, through the days of the NATO bombing in 1999, and past the elections that deposed Milosevic in 2000:

> In the lead-up to the elections of 2000, our network at the time decided we didn't want to join the larger, established NGO umbrella; we wanted to stay autonomous. That was when we first encountered resistance from that older NGO world of the '90s, that kind of human rights-ish anti-war scene, which had already been completely NGOized by that time. As a result, they then attempted to prevent us from receiving funding for a project to develop our initiatives in the lead-up to the elections, due to

the fact that we had no contacts with any donors, and they had contacts with all the donors and had been already working with them extensively for 10 years. Nevertheless, we were able to get support from a specific donor, and the citizen's parliament network was formed out of it.

The first 6 months of the funding we received in 2000; we organized in the way we had envisioned to begin with. To animate a broad conversation and debate bringing in many people from the democratic networks about the changes, because everywhere the topic was the changes, but specifically about the quality of the changes, because we felt it was important that people come out and debate what changes we want, and what is it we are for, and not just for it to be limited to removing Milosevic, which was already understood. Those gatherings were focused on a variety of topics, from education to human rights to the judiciary. We also put out a publication with the conclusions from those various assemblies sent out to a wide public (tens of thousands of copies). . . .

This initiative turned out to be a problem, not because we didn't have the capacity or skills to execute it, which is a common attitude that foreign NGOs tend to take towards local informal groups. We were told by our funder that they were unhappy with the direction of our work, that they didn't understand why we were opening up all those questions that we did to public debate, and why didn't we stick to the same issues we had been working on during the bombing. That we should not enter into larger questions around the quality of changes, but restrict our role to that of protesting and railing against Milosevic. That they wanted to see more activism and less 'philosophizing' (as they put it). We stated our objections and said we didn't feel it was the role of that donor to direct our organizing (which we had clearly outlined in the proposal) in such a manner.

That was in those wild times, when everything functioned differently. For instance, we were registered as an association, but we didn't have a bank account. The funds would basically arrive in bags of cash. Everything was in cash and informal.

We were soon informed that the foundation was unhappy with our work, and that our funding would be discontinued. Actually, no, first they attempted to organize a putsch among the coordinators of the initiative, which was rejected by the network. Then our funding was cut off. We continued with our activities into the election, with seriously reduced capacities.[2]

A second role that the first wave of NGOs played in this phase of political change in the 1990s was, according to several of the activists and observers with whom I spoke, to channel, limit, and coopt broader efforts at political mobilization against the wars in the region, as well as related questions of anti-nationalism and violence. The uneven funding and visibility these NGOs received relative to broader grass-roots efforts limited attempts at building wider social movements, in favor of maintaining the issues under the control and funding of a small cadre of domestic professionals who became the face of antiwar and antinationalist issues, typically framed in ways that were limited and acceptable to the foreign policy objectives of the governments of the countries from which their donors originated.

Ultimately, with the ouster of Milosevic in 2000 and the installation of the new government and political system, the previously oppositional role that many NGOs played was transformed into a more ambiguous, more multivalent and often metamorphic status. Yet nonetheless the NGO sector largely maintained its position in the sometimes tacit, and often open ideological role of promoting the new political system in line with the democracy promotion objectives of their funders (from such backers as the National Endowment for Democracy, USAID and Freedom House to various European NGO donors and Soros' Open Society Institute). In several instances, this led to the metamorphosis of several oppositional NGO organs into private companies, such as the oppositional independent media NGO B92. 'During the 90s B92 worked in some phantom way as both an NGO and a private company, but then after 2000, became exclusively a private media corporation'.[3] In other instances, such NGOs as the G17 PLUS (devoted to economics) and the civic youth opposition movement Otpor, having been funded by the US government through the National Endowment for Democracy and USAID, transformed into political parties that held seats and key ministerial posts directing economic policy (in the case of the G17) in the new regime. It was in the aftermath of 'the changes' and the political disorientation they engendered, that the reasons for the strict monitoring, control, and limiting of the majority of the NGO sector to purely oppositional activities against Milosevic began to become clear to several of the activists I interviewed. As the activist who recounted the defunding of his network above continues:

It was only after the 5th of October, 2000, that we started to really tie together what had happened with regards to our loss of funding. It was in reading Freedom House's report on Serbia for '99 that it really became clear to me. It was shocking for me to realize that for the donors who funded the campaign to replace Milosevic, that they absolutely did not care who would replace him. It didn't matter to them whether it would be some pro-western wing of the SPS party (Milosevic's Socialist Party of Serbia), us, or even some so-called terrorist organization. It then began to dawn on me why all our initiatives around generating discussion about the quality of the changes were considered unnecessary. Everything that was considered useful in bringing down Milosevic was taken and transformed into the campaign that did effectively do so, without any further discussion. Like Otpor's campaign was reduced to something strictly about Milosevic. And that is what was expected of us. Any further discussion was considered unnecessary, a surplus that could hurt the campaign. Any program for further changes beyond regime-change was delegated by foreign donors to the technical experts in the G17 party (former NGO turned political party of neoliberal economists, several of whom, such as Mladan Dinkic, became the new Ministers of Economy and Finance). There was no discussion, they are the expert authorities who will now tell us how the future of Serbia will look like with the expert-driven program they had dictated. So it was clear that in their eyes, we had overstepped our mandate by trying to animate a broader public discussion about the types of changes people wanted to see, that that was not to be a matter for us, and that it was to be turned over to the designated neoliberal experts to carry out.[4]

Another activist working inside the NGO sector put the impacts of the political shift and the disorientation it engendered at that time in the following terms:

What was the political battle of the 1990s? That is the main question. That was a question that only began to be dealt with after 2000 (and the change in regime). Until then, it was understood that everything that is against the rule of Slobodan Milosevic is forward-looking, progressive, and then, once that great common enemy was removed, it became clear that there was a wider confusion in that movement, that it was incredibly heterogeneous, and that that movement had a fairly simple goal, and that it was easy to have such a simple goal. When the situation was settled, then it became clear that it did not have the theoretical or intellectual weapons to carry itself in the new situation, because then the problem became capitalism, no longer the so-called communist regime of Milosevic (I never considered the Milosevic regime communist) . . .[5]

Not accidentally, the transforming NGO sector following the post-2000 regime change and the accelerated privatization program that was put into place at that time, largely maintained a narrow focus on human rights framed in liberal terms and a strict exclusion of any economic questions including ones regarding the status of workers facing mass layoffs, economic dispossession and privatizations of their workplaces in that very moment.

For most of the 1990s and 2000s, there was a complete silence on the part of the NGO sector with respect to the question of workers and economic rights, of the rapidly deteriorating situation for most workers. Until very recently, there was no interest for these questions among NGOs or their donors. There was only an interest that it should be ignored, that it does not exist, and even to speak against them. The neoliberal media was also very effective in gathering neoliberal and NGO intellectuals to shit on workers and their strikes, workers and strikes belonged to the other (enemy) anti-modern side, that are just obstacles on the road to transition. Recently, with the arrival of one left-leaning donor foundation that is interested in funding issues related to workers' struggles, some of the older NGOs have suddenly remembered the workers.[6]

Other activists emphasized the extent to which the bureaucratic and project-driven nature of the work to which the NGO sector is beholden by its donors limits its capacity to engage in any kind of more critical or reflexive work that might provoke a broader questioning of its own role within the capitalist transition or with respect to building a longer-term, broader social base outside of a project-driven logic.

Grants are parceled-up, there no longer exists structure-based funding. Now that it is project-based, we have to write an adequate number of projects to be able to set aside some basic operating costs . . . It's hardest to bring in any kind of analytic or reflexive practice within that. There is always an insistence on an activity basis, like activity 1, activity 2 . . . what are you going to do, what changes are you going to effect. It's a very naive approach. I worry that that managerial logic leads to the awarding of projects that are over-inflated, that promise hills and valleys. . . . We've looked at the fate of some of those NGO projects that, because of those dictates of productivity, a focus on specific themes, actually collapsed on themselves. Because they were in fact trapped in that project-based language. And then they become frustrated, because they have to find a way around what they proposed, and then to find a way to legitimize that work with that project language. That has been cause for questioning, that demand that somehow something always has to be achieved in measurable ways . . .

What I see as the main problem is that anything that is more reflexive, that is rooted in a longer-term strategy, that does not get funded. Only short-term goals get funded, what you are going to do, how many people will change their thinking because of having come to your programming. And that depends on the funding, which has to be adapted to this logic of the market, and to that mercantilism within it.[7]

Ultimately, several of the activists and organizers I interviewed, working both within and outside the NGO sector, argue that, while not playing a totalizing negative role and having achieved some positive initiatives (such as, for instance, building an infrastructure and services for women facing domestic violence), NGOization and the advent of neoliberal economic restructuring (which they also uphold was a major factor in the war of the 1990s) arrived very much hand in hand in the region, and that the NGO sector played a key role in ideologically and more directly promoting the capitalist transition to the detriment of the majority of the population.

The NGO sector did indirectly promote liberal parliamentary democracy and a liberal (capitalist) economy as some kind of ideal paradigm that we should all subscribe to. When that paradigm came into crisis in 2008, then it turned out that that was a superficial politics, and that from that position to criticize the wars of the 1990s without taking into account that the wars were a result of the neoliberalization of the economy in the 1980s, in fact, that it was what opened the space for any appetite for conflict. If people forget that and say, we should have peacefully transitioned into capitalism, that is completely meaningless, out of Yugoslavia that was almost impossible.

There are a small number of NGOs where there is now beginning to form a serious critique of capitalism and of that position towards the war, the naive one, the one that says that we now need truth, responsibility, reconciliation . . . But that critique is not the main focus of the NGO scene at all, and it is not publicly influential. The ones that are much more influential are the standard politics . . . that insist on talk about the wars, civil victims, in a way that terribly irritates people (who are living through extreme dispossession and poverty). But I don't think that for those reasons that is a bad thing. Those are interesting initiatives even if we don't agree with all of their methods, but in any case, they don't deal with any critique of capitalism or how the return/restoration of capitalist relations in the former Yugoslavia led to the opening of the space for those conflicts, that does not cross their minds at all. They deal with it all as forensic specialists, what happened . . . aha, there is a victim, there is an aggressor, and that is that.

Very simply, it's an apology for capitalism and parliamentary democracy. It's very naive, sometimes interested, sometimes deceptive, that many people who are part of the NGO sector have never uttered a critical word about that system which they are supporting. And that is a system of division, exploitation, racism at the end of the day, and they act like it is not happening, as if that system does not constantly generate fascism. Every capitalism generates a fascist ideology. They act like that is not happening, and *then they fight the symptoms, the result of that system. But not against the cause.* That is that liberal antifascism, that is principally against fascism, but not against capitalism, yet fascism will always exist in capitalism [emphasis added].[8]

The remnants of transition: Workers, displaced peoples, and privatization

I want to mention two particular sites that are crucial to and particularly obscured by the modes of operation of balkanism and NGOization in the context of transitional ex-Yugoslav states: the implementation of neoliberal market policies, and secondly, regional and European policies with regards to migration, refugees, and internally displaced people from and within the region, including those displaced during the wars of the 1990s and those minorities displaced following the 1999 NATO intervention in Kosovo.

A specific feature of neoliberal transition and the mass precarity that has been installed in the post-Yugoslav Balkans, one that constitutes both an organizing challenge as well as an opportunity, is the destroyed legacy of workers' self-management. One distinguishing feature of Yugoslav socialism in relation to other socialist systems was the introduction of workers' self-management in the 1950s as an official ideology and practice (see Meister, 1964). The full legacy of self-management in the region remains to be comprehensively assessed, and it certainly had its problems in the ways it was controlled and limited by the authoritarian state. Yet it is significant that with the installation of the mass privatization program in 2000, the self-managed sector of the economy (also known as social property), which is also where a majority of women and Roma workers were employed, was the first sector targeted for mass privatization. The intensity of the assault on the very notion of workers' self-management throughout the years of neoliberal transition has resulted in it becoming an abject and disdained history, just as the heavy ideological and political attacks on the socialist past have left many in the region without an effective political vocabulary to express what is happening to them, although this has begun to change, particularly since 2008.

At the level of daily social struggles of workers facing mass layoffs in the region, this creates a strange yet interesting tension, whereby workers who have organized and fought to overturn the illegitimate means through which their factories have been privatized are politically attacked as self-managers and 'Stalinists'. Often, particularly in the early years of the transition, their only recourse has been to publicly deny that they are self-managers. Yet in many cases, the ethic and attachment they express with regards to the factories they are fighting for very much comes out of a structure of feeling tied to workers' self-management. This gap between the terms and parameters of what is permissible and imaginable with respect to explicit political discourse, and the unspoken, implicit horizons of workers' practices and subterranean memories is very stark, and yet a potent one for new forms of political mobilization that have been slowly yet consistently emerging (see Popov (2011) and Pokret za Slobodu (2011) for further information).

Emergent potentialities, incipient struggles

Through these struggles and the years of transitional upheaval, an emergent yet significant small-scale network of associations, collectives, and movement-based affiliates has worked and coalesced to challenge, counter and resist the effects and policies that have driven mass privatization, displacement and the dispossession of workers, peasants, and displaced people in Serbia and the wider Balkan region. These include such groups as Pokret za Slobodu (pokret.net), Global Balkans (a small-scale activist research, media and organizing network of ex-Yugoslav/Balkan diaspora, globalbalkans.org), independent media such as Kontrapunkt, associations such as Voice of Roma, Ravnopravnost (in Zrenjanin), the Paori peasant association (Crepaja), AZIN (the Association of Autonomous Women's Initiatives), the Coordinating Committee for Workers' Protests, and several related workers' movement networks and mobilizations (such as the Jugoremedija workers in Zrenjanin, Serbia, who, following a 3 year strike and 9 month factory occupation became the first instance of workers' resistance that successfully reversed the privatization of this pharmaceutical company; but also workers from Zastava Elektro, Trudbenik, Sinvoz, Bek, and others). Many of these initiatives and movement-based groups have been working to build an autonomous anti-nationalist, anti-authoritarian, and ultimately anti-capitalist network with a pan-Balkan and internationalist outlook. They have sought to reach out to and organize within social movements and networks both inside and outside the Balkans, including recent initiatives to collaborate and support similar initiatives and mobilizations in other regions of the ex-Yugoslav Balkans (such as the anti-privatization strike of workers at Petrohemija in Kutin, Croatia, as well as the student strike and citizen 'plenum' assemblies in Zagreb, Croatia (see Horvat & Stiks, 2012).

These emerging networks are working to support and actively build solidarity with the former Yugoslav region's slowly (re-) emerging social movements fighting struggles of survival, persistence, and resistance in the face of the dominant neoliberal offensive as well as those of nationalist elites, from anti-privatization and anti-capitalist organizing to peasant organizing (by networks such as Pokret za Slobodu), to support for displaced people and urban poor (particularly Roma) communities facing continual displacement.

The groups and organizations in this loose network largely maintain a critical stance towards the political phenomenon of NGOization and seek to build autonomous capacities to work outside or beyond it, though some are differently positioned in relation to the NGO sector than others. Some maintain an informal, loose presence with little funding, others seek to prioritize a social movement orientation while engaging with donor funding for specific projects (and struggling with the limitations of the project-based logic). Others formally exist as NGOs while attempting to move beyond the limitations of donor imposed top-down structures and ways of functioning (AZIN for example, explicitly structures itself as a horizontal network open to new initiatives and formal or informal sub-groupings who are able to affiliate to the larger network group). In the case of the latter, one organizer who maintains a critical stance while working formally within the NGO sector describes the tactical maneuvers this requires in terms of having to project a double face with respect to donor demands and the actual work a small number of critical NGOs are attempting to do that move beyond the limits of NGOization:

> Some projects, ours included, have acquired a kind of double face. With one face they negotiate with all those funders and NGOs coming from the tradition of the 1990s, and with the other face they have turned towards the true problems of society, which no longer is Milošević; now capitalism is the problem.[9]

The efficacy of this tactical, ambivalent stance remains open to debate and is perhaps yet to be determined (or can only be done so in concrete, specific instances), yet overall the groups composing this nascent network are keenly aware of, and seeking to build broader independent movements that surpass or bypass the limitations of NGOization they have articulated, both substantively (in the content of the issues they address) and structurally. As one Roma association organizer puts it:

> More than anything, I would prefer that our organisation has no need to operate as it does, not just ours but that any organization or NGO need not do this kind of work. That is what I would most wish for. Because before the war we never had a need for any of this. I lived a normal life, and really, no one needed any of these types of things (organizations) we have today.[10]

Workers and displaced migrants in the post-Yugoslav Balkans today are seen as the remnants and remainders of the transition away from the socialist past through the years of war and dissolution, and into the shiny capitalist future that is everywhere promised but rarely evident, except for the new and very small class of super rich so-called *tajkuni* (tycoons) that have emerged in the process. The majority of workers and displaced people increasingly inhabit a state of mass precarity and that of the newly dispossessed, the erased of transition. The incipient and emergent forms their struggles are taking, whether they are more explicit political struggles or the more daily struggle of survival and persistence, also carry ripe potentials for a new and illuminating counterpolitics to the compromised apologetics of NGO-ization and the unhappy triangle of balkanism, nationalism, and neoliberalism that has brought so much devastation to the region.

Acknowledgments

The author wishes to thank members of the Global Balkans network, Pokret za Slobodu, and specifically, Irina Ceric, Milenko Sreckovic, Milica Ruzicic, Ivan Zlatic, and all those interviewed for important dialogue, feedback, and discussion that contributed to this piece.

Notes

1 Interview with NGO organizer, June 29, 2012, Belgrade, Serbia.
2 Interview with Anti-Privatization/Worker's Movement Activist, June 19, 2012, Belgrade, Serbia.
3 Interview with NGO organizer, June 29, 2012, Belgrade, Serbia.
4 Interview with Anti-Privatization/Worker's Movement Activist, June 19, 2012, Belgrade, Serbia.
5 Interview with NGO organizer, June 29, 2012, Belgrade, Serbia.
6 Interview with Anti-Privatization/Worker's Movement Activist, June 19, 2012, Belgrade, Serbia.
7 Interview with NGO organizer, June 29, 2012, Belgrade, Serbia.
8 Interview with NGO organizer, June 29, 2012, Belgrade, Serbia.
9 Interview with NGO organizer, June 29, 2012, Belgrade, Serbia.
10 Interview with Roma association organizer, October 2008, Preoce, Kosovo.

References

Atanasoski, N. (2006). 'Race toward Freedom: Post-Cold War US Multiculturalism and the Reconstruction of Eastern Europe'. *Journal of American Culture*, 29(2), 213–226.

Bartholomew, A. (2006). 'Empire's Law and the Contradictory Politics of Human Rights'. In A. Bartholomew (Ed.) *Empire's Law: The American Imperial Project and the 'War to Remake the World'* (pp. 161–89). Toronto: Between the Lines.

Bartholomew, A. & Breakspear, J. (2004). 'Human Rights as Swords of Empire'. In L. Panitch & C. Leys (Eds.) *Socialist Register 2004: The New Imperial Challenge* (pp. 124–145). New York: Monthly Review Press.

Brown, W. (2002a). 'Suffering the Paradoxes of Rights'. In W. Brown & J. Halley (Eds.) *Left Legalism/Left Critique* (pp. 420–34). Durham: Duke University Press.

Ceric, I. (2009). 'The Rule of Law: Transition, Intervention, Imperialism'. Paper presented at the 9th Annual Critical Race and Anti-Colonial Studies Conference (Montreal): Compassion, Complicity and Conciliation: The Politics, Cultures and Economies of 'Doing Good'. McGill University, Montreal, June 5–7, 2009.

Du Bois, W.E.B. (1945). *Color and Democracy: Colonies and Peace*. New York: Harcourt, Brace and Company.

Dunbar-Ortiz, R. & Grubacic, A. (2008). 'Roots of Resistance'. An interview with Roxanne Dunbar-Ortiz. *Z Magazine*, July. Available from: http://www.zmag.org/zmag/viewArticle/18054.

Goldsworthy, V. (1998) 'Inventing Ruritania: The Imperialism of the Imagination'. New Haven, London; Yale University Press.

Guilhot, N. (2005). *The Democracy Makers: Human Rights and the Politics of Global Order*. New York: Columbia University Press.

Harvey, D. (2003). *The New Imperialism*. Oxford: Oxford University Press.

Horvat, S. & Stiks, I. (2012). 'Welcome to the Desert of Transition: Post-Socialism, the European Left, and a New Left in the Balkans'. *Monthly Review*, 63(10).

Available from: http://monthlyreview.org/2012/03/01/welcome-to-the-desert-of-transition.

Ignatieff, M. (2003). *Empire Lite: Nation-Building in Bosnia, Kosovo, and Afghanistan.* London: Vintage.

Kennedy, D. (2002a). 'The International Human Rights Movement: Part of the Problem?' *Harvard Human Rights Journal, 15,* 101–25.

Kennedy, D. (2002b). 'The Critique of Rights in Critical Legal Studies'. In W. Brown & J. Halley (Eds.) *Left Legalism/Left Critique.* (pp. 178–228). Durham: Duke University Press.

Kennedy, D. (2004). *The Dark Sides of Virtue: Reassessing International Humanitarianism.* Princeton: Princeton University Press.

Kurasawa, F. (2006). 'The Uses and Abuses of Humanitarian Intervention in the Wake of Empire'. In A. Bartholomew (Ed.) *Empire's Law: The American Imperial Project and the 'War to Remake the World* (pp. 297–312). Toronto: Between the Lines.

Mandel, R. (2002). 'Seeding Civil Society'. In. C.M. Hann (Ed.) *Postsocialism: Ideals, Ideologies and Practices.* London: Routledge.

Meister, A. (1964). *Socialisme et autogestion: l'expérience Yougoslave.* Paris: Seuil.

Pokret za Slobodu. (2011). *Deindustrijalizacija i Radnicki Otpor* (Deindustrialisation and Worker's Resistance). Belgrade: Pokret za Slobodu.

Popov, N. (2011). *Radno Mesto Pod Suncem: Radnicke borbe u Srbiji* (A Job Under the Sun: Worker's Struggles in Serbia). Belgrade: Sluzbeni Glasnik/Res publica.

Robinson, W.I. (1996). *Promoting Polyarchy: Globalization, US Intervention, and Hegemony.* New York: Cambridge University Press.

Roy, A. (2004). Help That Hinders. *Le Monde Diplomatique* (English Edition). Available from: http://mondediplo.com/2004/11/16roy.

Sampson, S. (2002). 'Beyond Transition: Rethinking Elite Configurations in the Balkans'. In C.M. Hann (Ed.) *Postsocialism: Ideals, Ideologies and Practices in Eurasia.* London: Routledge.

Shukaitis, S., Graeber, D. & Biddle, E. (2007). *Constituent Imagination: Militant Investigations/Collective Theorization.* Oakland: AK Press.

Todorova, M.N. (1997). *Imagining the Balkans.* New York: Oxford University Press.

Verdery, K. (2002). 'Whither Postsocialism?' In C.M. Hann (Ed.) *Postsocialism: Ideals, Ideologies and Practices in Eurasia.* London: Routledge.

Vetta, T. (2009). '"Democracy Building' in Serbia: The NGO Effect'. *Southeastern Europe, 33,* 26–47.

Woodward, S.L. (1995). *Socialist Unemployment: The Political Economy of Yugoslavia, 1945–1990.* Princeton: Princeton University Press.

8

Peace-building and Violence against Women: Tracking the Ruling Relations of Aid in a Women's Development NGO in Kyrgyzstan

Elena Kim and Marie Campbell

Introduction

This chapter focuses on a women's NGO that receives development aid to support a network of women's crisis centers in Kyrgyzstan and to work in other ways toward a reduction of domestic violence[1]. In the absence of adequate involvement of the criminal justice system in addressing violence against women, Kyrgyzstan's crisis centers offer crucial services, even if they are organizationally weak and constantly under threat. Feminist critiques of NGOization (Bagić, 2004; Lang, 1997) suggest that building organizational capacity routinely supplants an NGO's activist work that otherwise, as in this case, directly or indirectly focuses on alleviating violence against women. Our analysis shows another side of NGOization and efforts to address women's domestic problems. In 2010, an acute episode of inter-ethnic violence, arising within Kyrgyzstan's post-Soviet political instability, brought international humanitarian relief and associated post-conflict planning into the country. Our inquiry, an institutional ethnography, focuses on the emergency-related structuring of development aid to explore how it is affecting the work and working relations of the women's anti-violence NGO.

The institutional ethnography we conduct addresses questions arising from ethnographic data we collected in 2011 about organizational changes that frustrated the NGO's staff, and mystified us. Through our analysis, we discover 'violence' being treated as a concept newly attributed to a discourse on international security, conflict resolution and peace-building that is now being institutionalized as part of the post-conflict coordination of aid. We learn how, as the director of the anti-violence organization maneuvers skillfully within the new processes and the associated funding opportunities, the policy direction of the NGO seems to be shifting away from its goals of reducing violence against women. Our research tracks the institutional relations that account for how things happen as they do, allowing us to make visible and more understandable the nature of ruling relations that are being enacted in this setting. While this finding is important in itself, we draw more general conclusions, arguing that the analysis we conduct of one NGO provides insights into the administered nature of the exercise of contemporary global power.

Using institutional ethnography to explicate ruling relations

Institutional ethnography is a feminist-inspired research approach to social analysis that Dorothy E. Smith (1987, 2005) pioneered and that she calls an alternative sociology. Its claim is to 'extend people's ordinary good knowledge of how things are put together in their everyday lives' (Smith, 2005, p. 29). To do this, an inquiry begins in ethnography and reaches 'beyond the locally observable and discoverable into the trans-local social relations and organization that permeate and control the local' (Smith, 2006, p. 65). In our case, we wanted to extend what people, such as those in settings we examine in Kyrgyzstan, could know about their choices, actions and organizational commitments beyond their own experiential knowledge and beyond the claims of even the best technical, managerial and professional practices that structure development projects. In this manner, our research addresses what critical development scholars such as Gould (2004) understand is the challenge for ethnographies of aid: to attend systematically to the trans-local relations in which development work is situated. Use of institutional ethnography also side-steps the problems such as Mosse (2006) encountered when a researcher's analysis is a subjective interpretation of ethnographic data, however competent, insightful or empirically supported that interpretation might be.

Institutional ethnography's beginning was in the scholarship surrounding the women's movement of the 1970s in North America. At that time, women were insisting that their experience was different from how it was authoritatively explained and how it was reflected in academic theory, in social policy or in institutional practices. Feminist scholars recognized that new methods of analysis were needed to generate more scientifically adequate and socially acceptable accounts of women and their everyday lives, capacities and troubles. Smith (2004), along with social constructivists, argued that all social life is enacted. By building on Marx's epistemology, Smith (2004) went on to introduce analytic attention to the social relations that coordinate people's doings, across their various settings of action. In this approach, ethnographic data on people's experiences become a conduit for analysis of the trans-local coordination of a setting, opening up what is otherwise missing from people's ordinary understandings. Missing from ordinary work knowledge is what institutional ethnographers understand to be the ruling relations coordinating people's everyday actions. The institutional ethnographer makes an 'explication' of this more or less invisible, but materially present, substratum of everyday life.

Although an institutional ethnography begins from a problematic, a puzzle arising in the experiences of people in the research setting, it must extend beyond ethnographic accounts of the setting. People's experiences of their work are organized somehow and traces of that social organization are there to be discovered in it. Smith (2005) speaks of 'actualities' (p. 223) to be explicated. Ethnographic data draws attention to something actually happening in the everyday world that needs explication in order to understand how actual people's lives are organized outside of their own knowledge and control. The choice of a problematic reflects the institutional ethnographer's explicit positioning of the research, which Smith calls 'taking the standpoint of people' (Smith, 2005, p. 10–11). In any institutional ethnography, the question that arises for researchers is not 'does an informant's statement offer the correct interpretation of what is happening?' Rather, the truth that institutional ethnographers seek comes from the inquiry conducted to discover how things have been organized so that speakers have the experiences that they speak about as they do. We are convinced that only through such discovery can local experiential knowledge be extended, and otherwise-authoritative institutional knowledge or an individual's preferred interpretation, be countered objectively. As we proceed, we will demonstrate how issues of knowing authoritatively and knowing experientially are important to the operation of the NGO we analyze.

Kyrgyzstan and its contemporary setting for development

Kyrgyzstan (also called the Kyrgyz Republic) is a former Soviet state, independent since 1991. It is inhabited by about five and a half million people, 43 percent of whom live in poverty and as many as one million live and work abroad (Ibraimov, 2011). The ethnic composition of the country is very complex and includes major groups such as ethnic Kyrgyz (67 percent), ethnic Uzbeks (14 percent), ethnic Russians (10 percent) and more than 80 other ethnicities. With little local industry and only a few natural resources (including gold, hydropower, and cotton) Kyrgyzstan is economically vulnerable. Its fertile agricultural areas with access to water have become a source of competitiveness, especially in the southern overpopulated Fergana valley, predisposing this area to social unrest. The valley's linguistically and ethnically distinct populations share borders with Tajikistan and Uzbekistan and in 1989 and 1990 violent conflicts flared up in this area between different ethnic groups. Despite being poor, Kyrgyzstan is considered to have 'infrastructure and government institutions [which] are relatively well developed. Government agencies and institutions are operational, though inhibited in their functions by under-funding and corruption' (Human Rights Watch, 2006, p. 8). Citizens do not trust the government to act in their interests and frequently take direct action to make their demands known. A popular and almost bloodless revolution in March 2005 forced the country's first president after independence to resign and leave the country. His replacement, Kurmanbek Bakiev, was overthrown five years later in April 2010, in a more violent manner. Political instability following Bakiev's departure laid bare many social problems including the ethnic question which in the summer of 2010 took the most dramatic turn. In the conditions created by a fragile interim government, and lacking official control, severe ethnic-based violence broke out. Four hundred people were killed, 375 thousand displaced and more than one million people suffered loss of property, physical injuries, and sexual and psychological harm in several days of widespread and indiscriminate violence, mass killings, looting, and arson. Today, regardless of the absence of fierce fighting, inter-ethnic relations remain fragile and sensitive.

Kyrgyzstan's transition to democracy has required and attracted considerable international development assistance. Recognizing gender equality as indispensable to democratic development, international donor organizations have made funding available to support initiatives to empower Kyrgyzstani women. Feminist analysts have observed contradictory characteristics of donor-funded women's NGOs in Kyrgyzstan. For instance, Hoare (2009) believes that 'NGOs working on gender and women's rights issues constitute one of the most active and vibrant sectors within "civil society" in Kyrgyzstan, both in terms of the provision of services, and advocacy and lobbying [. . .] but they remain marginalized within wider "civil society" [. . .]; perhaps more so than any other area of development work in the Kyrgyz Republic, donor priorities have determined the activities of these organizations' (p. 9). Simpson (2006) sees these contradictions for women's NGOs somewhat differently; she insists that 'it is important to conceptualize "local" women *not* as a homogenous group, and the movements they comprise *not* as static, either on the national level or from an international or global perspective' (p. 27). Simpson's sense of the social organization of the 'local' making a difference to how women's efforts play out relates to our own research. Campbell and Teghtsoonian (2010), for instance, analyzed the work of women activists on Kyrgyzstan's state budgeting processes that would build in appropriate attention to women's needs; it was argued that their efforts were shaped and undermined as they took up the prevailing discourse of Aid Effectiveness that was required for the Joint Country Support Strategy's planning of the distribution of development assistance.

This chapter advances a focus on what Simpson (2006) calls the 'multifarious factors affecting relations among local women's organizing' (p. 26). We identify effects on the use of development aid following the national emergency in 2010. The emergency motivated Kyrgyzstan's appeal to the United Nations (UN) for international humanitarian relief. The UN Flash Appeal triggered a strategic planning process called the Consolidated Appeals Process (CAP) to facilitate the quick and coordinated response to global emergencies (UNOCHA, 2011, p. 1–3). Besides bringing immediate relief in Kyrgyzstan, the CAP generated a longer-term response promoting peace and political stability. It must not be overlooked that Kyrgyzstan's internal troubles are part of larger regional and even global issues. The Middle East conflict and the war in Afghanistan are responsible for the United States (US) military air base on its territory and increased drug trafficking into and through Kyrgyzstan is also a feature of the regional strife. Martha Brill Olcott (2010), Central Asia expert from the US-based Carnegie Endowment for International Peace, commented in November 2010 on how the international community sees Kyrgyzstan's troubles: 'Competing narratives [have] developed to describe what happened in Kyrgyzstan . . . but many of the narratives being used inside Kyrgyzstan could serve to exacerbate inter-ethnic tensions within the country, and these are legitimate source of [international] concern'. Olcott also recognizes that inter-ethnic tensions might expand across national borders exacerbating international concern about the potentially dangerous outcomes of NATO's military withdrawal from neighboring Afghanistan. However relevant to international security, making peace-building the immediate focus of development aid adds an unexamined element to efforts that women in Kyrgyzstan have been making to address their serious everyday concerns, including unacceptable levels of domestic violence.

The organizational setting of the research

The organization at the heart of our analysis is the Women's Anti-violence Network[2] (henceforth called the Network), registered in Kyrgyzstan since 2001. In 2008, the Network received its first organization-building funding from the Dutch international development agency, Hivos. It was then already an umbrella organization for Kyrgyzstani crisis centers. Today the organization works with a network of twelve independent crisis centers located throughout the country and is contractually accountable to international donors for using their funds on specified objectives. A letter from Hivos to the Network written prior to the signing of the first contract shows that all its objectives, except one, were chosen to reflect the Network's own understandings of how to work toward reducing the violence experienced by Kyrgyzstani women in their homes, families and interpersonal relationships (i.e., what we are calling 'domestic' violence). A fourth objective, the exception, was chosen by Hivos and commits the director of the Network to seek additional funding locally from the government. The latter is how Hivos saw the Network becoming self-sustaining according to a Hivos program officer interviewed in 2008. As of this writing, however, international funding still covers all the expenses of the work the Network undertakes to reduce gender violence in the Kyrgyz Republic.

Our fieldwork in the organization has generated data on the Network office, the staff and the work associated with the Network's more recent Hivos-funded project entitled 'Reducing Gender Violence in Kyrgyzstan' that ran from October 2010 until December 2011. Besides this project, the Network now receives funding from the European Initiative for implementing a partner project with HelpAge International called 'Right to Life Without Violence in Old Age'. During the emergency, the Network participated with two UN agencies in a partnership project for the 'Coordination of emergency measures to render support to the victims of domestic violence in Osh and Djalal-Abad oblasts'.

The Network office is situated in two rooms of the building of the National Centre of Medical Diagnostics, in the capital city, Bishkek. The director of the Network (whom we call Sophia) is a physician who works in her own office one floor above the Network office, and from which she also provides medical consultation in the National Centre of Medical Diagnostics. Next door to her office is a crisis center called Chance, which is a member organization of the Network. Sophia founded it, and along with her other work, she continues to lead this crisis center. Sophia coordinates the Network and its projects with help from general office and project-specific staff: an accountant, an office manager, a secretary and at least one project assistant for each funded project. The full-time accountant (whom we call Shakira) manages the project budgets and writes financial statements to the funders and local tax authorities. The office-manager (Beka), besides managing the work of the secretary, corresponds with the crisis centers, donors and partner organizations, manages logistics for Network events, shops for office supplies, cleans and tidies the office and library, and helps the accountant with her work. As their position title suggests, the project assistants work on a project's programme. For example, Karina, the project assistant for the Reducing Gender Violence project prepares training, researches and writes training manuals, organizes training events, and produces detailed reports of them. The office shelves are filled with such reports.

Proper accountability for both the funding provided and the action taken on agreed objectives is an explicit conditionality for payment of funds by donors according to the contract between the Network and Hivos. According to the schedule, the organization is to submit to Hivos two annual reports, two financial audited statements and five progress reports over the thirteen months of this particular project's duration.[3] In this, as in any organization that manages and accounts for funding from external sources, accounting work intersects, and sometimes conflicts, with the substantive work, and in the Network we notice the tensions between the workers that this division of labor creates. We see this in the training-related work done by project assistant, Karina; it takes concentration and long hours and she rarely leaves her desk as she writes, and then revises, the program documents after Sophia has reviewed and commented on them. If the office is noisy, she may go to the kitchen and work there in silence. The office may be busy and loud owing to the pressured production of periodic financial reports, which is the major responsibility of the accountant. To do her financial accounting work, Shakira must compile reports coming in from all areas of the Network. She receives many phone calls from the crisis centers and elsewhere, and she feels free to talk loudly on the phone in the general office. Our observations suggest that the accountant has a particularly high status in the office and that she is confident and knowledgeable about all of aspects of the Network. She routinely consults with Sophia, and after spending about an hour or so every day in Sophia's office, she returns with instructions for the office-manager and initiates informal conversations with the other employees about the work. But Shakira's insistence on the primacy of her financial accountability work can be a source of tensions between her and other staff. In one such instance, Shakira openly rebuked Eugenia, a psychologist from an associated crisis center, for failing to get her reports submitted on time. This was particularly upsetting to Eugenia because it took place after she had spent most of the previous night attending to the needs of a woman who had called on the crisis center for help in escaping an acutely violent family episode. Eugenia's professional concerns included not just managing the woman's safety at the time, but also considering how the Network might use this experience to address the all-too-familiar indifference of the police on such occasions. Regardless of Eugenia's involvement in such pressing substantive issues, Shakira spoke sharply to her, insisting that she submit her reports immediately so that they could be added to the consolidated financial accounting that Shakira was finalizing.

In contrast to the office-bound and text-oriented work of her staff, Sophia, as Director, spends considerable amounts of her workday outside of her office. When she is in her office she is usually multi-tasking, as illustrated in the field note below in which the ethnographer captures some of the complexity of Sophia's office routine:

> Sophia sits in front of her computer with the '16-Days of Activism Against Gender Violence' campaign matrix on the screen that identifies the money each crisis center needs for the campaign. She is also reading a memo on gender issues in the emergency situation. Beside her computer are two office telephones, one of which is hers and the second of which is a parallel line of the Chance crisis center. The psychologist of Chance would regularly be away on the trips related to other work and Sophia would often take over the hotline operation. Sophia also has a mobile phone that keeps ringing. Besides those interruptions, patients of the National Center for Medical Diagnostics knock and come in asking her to give them their diagnosis and interpretations of their cardiograms, which she does on the spot, along with whatever else she is doing. For instance, we saw her talking on her office phone with a government official while writing an interpretation on a new cardiogram with a ruler in her one hand and a pen in her other hand (field observation, September 2011).

Outside her office, Sophia is busy representing the Network in various committees, giving reports at parliamentary hearings, attending public events, giving media interviews and responding to invitations by different organizations to provide her expert opinion. Besides all this, she participates in the regular project work of the Network, where she frequently contributes to training in the crisis centers.

A puzzle emerges from ethnographic data

Our ethnography provides a picture of how the Network's anti-violence efforts proceed on the basis of Sophia's management of the staff, the program and the funding. As we shall see, her management requires significant attention to accessing future funding as well. Nothing remains static within the Network and potentially troublesome elements appear in the data. We find particularly puzzling the stories that Sophia tells about responding to new demands on her very scarce time. A September 2011 field note records one such instance. Sophia tells Elena that a government official 'invited' her to her office for a private conversation and presented her with a new document called 'Standard Operational Procedures of Multi-sectoral/inter-agency Cooperation on Prevention and Response to Gender Violence' (henceforth, SOP). The official asked Sophia to 'read, see and explain clearly and understandably' what the document was about and encouraged her to comment and recommend changes. This request, in a sense, treats Sophia as an unpaid policy assistant. Yet Sophia agrees to perform the task and subsequently meets with the official several times, and also discusses the document at meetings in the ministry. She says that she is motivated by the desire to understand the SOP so that she won't feel lost in 'so much bureaucracy, all kinds of papers, reports and forms [while finding that] the work itself is not there!' She maximizes her privileged position as an invited expert to improve, to her own liking, the organizational basis for further (funded) involvement of the Network and its crisis centers, saying:

> I wanted this document to be workable and not just for the table. This document is about everything and nothing. So I tried to tell them how to improve it, i.e., write clearly about the responsibilities and roles, describe the work and [what supports it], describe types of support, i.e., legal, social, psychological, financial, etc. If I don't understand that, I cannot work further. . . .

She declares that 'we [the Network] are ready to work' as long as the funding and opportunity are provided. At this point, the organization of the new anti-violence undertaking that the Network might work on is still unclear to us, but Sophia's account of this consultation offers a focus for our inquiry and our tracking of the operation of ruling relations that Sophia is entering.

At the same time, a puzzle begins to form around new features of the Network's ongoing work within crisis centers. Various participants identify changes in the work and working relations that seem to 'just happen'. One vivid instance is Eugenia's angry outburst to Sophia about losing her skills for working with women who need support to contend with violence in personal relationships. Although that is her expertise and activist background, Eugenia finds herself working with elders in a crisis center for women. She feels tricked and unhappy at the turn of events whereby new funding is altering the target population.

Some comments from Karina also communicate an undercurrent of her mystification about Network decisions that detract, she thinks, from doing good work. She says:

> I was sent to conduct a training in Dzalal-Abad [in the south of Kyrgyzstan]. I was simply not ready. You know how we work at the Network: you do what you are supposed to do, office work, writing, reporting, etc., and one day you are told: 'Go somewhere and do a training'. Because of the routine work in the office, I physically did not have time to think about this training. And the topic was new to me. So, I arrived to Dzalal-Abad empty-headed and had to come up quickly with something.

Beyond the possible conflict between the objectives of accountability and (preparation for) training of crisis center staff that this comment suggests, Karina is noting that the way that her work is organized undermines the substance and quality of the anti-violence training she gives. She is unhappy about her inadequate preparation affecting her performance, and she also acknowledges that participants in the session evaluated the event as 'lacking depth' and being 'in need of improvement' too. But we note other aspects of the training that also worry Karina. As a project assistant she is familiar with the crisis center workers, knows the level of training they have had, and that they frequently lack any preparation for the job except that given by the Network. In light of their training needs, Karina makes a point that strikes us as particularly relevant. She questions the appropriateness of some of the topics being selected for upgrading workers' skills and knowledge. She was particularly critical about the topic 'mediation' that she had recently taught, assessing it as inappropriate for front-line crisis center workers at their particular level of practice. Speaking about this training, she says: 'All of this is so fake, this mediation seminar and other things. . . . They [seminar participants] do not even know and they did not learn the difference between mediation and psychological counseling. They do not use [mediation] and will not use it. They are busy with other things. . . .' We are struck by her use of the word 'fake' to describe the training on mediation; and we wonder 'what might be a fake reason for a choice made to teach mediation?'

On the basis of our analytic framework, we recognize that the changing features of the work that we discuss above are socially organized and that they are constituted by people acting within the social relations of the real world in which the Network is situated. We have seen that Sophia, as Director, acting within the institutional boundaries that define her responsibilities, opportunities and obligations, undertakes work that she recognizes will be beneficial to the Network. Her directorial responsibilities include decisions about funding and training that unsettle her experienced workers' sense of how best to do the work. With these Network actualities in mind as problematic, our inquiry moves to tracking the relations that rule the settings. What can we discover about the social organization to account for what happens?

Ruling relations and Sophia's direction of the Network

Sophia is eager to engage in public and private consultations with government officials, just as she readily accepts invitations to attend community meetings, conferences, and other working groups. She believes that her success and the success of the Network are directly linked to her public role on the Network's behalf. She explains:

> We must always be there where issues of violence are even minimally touched upon. In which role we appear there does not matter, but we must be there. We receive relevant experience; we learn all about it and how it is all put together. This must not pass us by. I always try hard to be there physically when the issue of violence is raised. . . . It is important to be 'in the know', be known and recognizable and have a reputation. If you fall out of this, you will get forgotten and very fast someone will catch it up and continue doing your work.

As institutional ethnographers, we are interested in Sophia's expression of being 'in the know' and its importance to her own work. We understand that her original funding objectives committed her to seek new funding, and she is clearly on the look-out for how to keep the Network afloat, financially. She explains how she moves into the physical spaces where she keeps up-to-date, learning the current discourses, and updating her expertise with reference to these concepts. Mediation, which frustrated her staff and puzzled us, is one of the concepts that has arisen for Sophia in her attempts to update herself about the new trends. She explains how it happened: '[Mediation] is very popular and heard about and I thought, if everyone is doing it, it means that I must also see if this can be of any use for the Network. Mediation is what is modern today and we must accept this'. She learns about the proposed initiative on building a national anti-violence network (NNGV) through her response to the government official who asked for her help understanding the Standard Operating Procedures (SOP) document of the NNGV. Sophia saw the invitation as an opportunity. 'My goal was to learn about it [NNGV] for myself and learn where we [the Network] can "*prilepitsya*" [translated as stick on, or adhere to it]', she says.

Prilepitsya informs her attempts to attune the activities of the Network with what is modern and popular, and we see in it an instance of ruling relations entering the work. After Sophia learns about mediation as something about which she needs to be 'in the know', she removes from the Network's program a block of anti-violence activities aimed at working with the male perpetrators, as was originally planned and approved by the funder. She substitutes a new program devoted to mediation and mobilizes her staff to prepare and deliver new training to teach conflict mediation principles and techniques, for which a manual on conflict mediation had to be produced. Sophia tells us that opportunities exist for the Network to offer training to other agencies, if the Network is recognized as already having expertise and experience with mediation. Sophia's plan accounts for the mediation entering the training work that we heard about from Karina earlier and from others, too. It accounts for the office staff and eventually the crisis centers' staff, spending their valuable time on conflict mediation, even when, as Karina predicts, '[our crisis center staff] won't use it'.

As we hear about mediation being programmed into the work of the Network and its crisis centers, we begin to track the linkages of this concept to the discourse on international security, peace-building and conflict prevention/resolution. We find traces of the discourse and its institutional connections in Sophia's comment that 'everyone is a mediator in the peace-building project', and in the training manual for crisis centers that she and her staff have published. There they describe mediation as an instrument for 'peaceful conflict resolution' and 'an approach to building civil society' which was 'introduced in Kyrgyzstan in response to the inter-ethnic conflicts in the country'. The ideas that we see being naturalized here in the Network circulate widely, attributed to multilateral organizations that have established conflict mediation and resolution as ways to advance democracy and peace (Bachelet, 2011). The UN is at the forefront of this policy development. In June 2011, the UN General Assembly adopted a resolution entitled 'Strengthening the role of mediation in the peaceful settlement of disputes, conflict prevention and resolution' which stresses 'the importance of mediation activities in peace-building and recovery processes, in particular in preventing post-conflict countries from relapsing into conflict' (UN General Assembly, 2011). Subsequently, the President of the General Assembly organized a meeting devoted to 'United Nations Mediation: Experiences and Reflections from the Field' to 'promote mediation as a promising tool of peaceful resolution of disputes with the Member States and other relevant representatives; and distil and collect UN-wide experiences on mediation from the prevention, peacemaking and peacekeeping perspectives' (UN General Assembly, 2011).

For our purposes, it is also important to note that besides promoting mediation as a mechanism for peaceful conflict resolution, these high-level decision-makers see women as especially appropriate mediators. As early as October 2000, women's role in peace-building and international security was being emphasized at the UN, where Resolution 1325 was adopted by the UN Security Council. The resolution recognizes 'the importance of the full and effective participation of women at all levels, at all stages and in all aspects of the peaceful settlement of disputes, conflict prevention and resolution, as well as the provision of adequate gender expertise for all mediators and their teams . . .' (UN Security Council, 2000). More recently, funding and organizational opportunities have been made available to support women's participation. The UN Peace-building Fund (UNPBF) expands the agenda of Resolution 1325 and 'aims to contribute to gender equality by increasing the participation of women in political processes, strengthen their voices in post-conflict planning processes and address their specific post-conflict needs' (UNPBF, 2011). By 2011, the Fund had disbursed ten million US dollars to support stability and peace-building projects in Kyrgyzstan (UNPBF, 2011). Three million dollars were allocated to fund a program called 'Empowering youth, women and vulnerable communities to contribute to peace-building and reconciliation in Kyrgyzstan' and, subsequently, seven million dollars funded peace-building projects, one of which was focused on 'Women Building Peace, Trust and Reconciliation in Kyrgyzstan' (Immediate Response Facility (IRF) of the Peace-Building Fund (PBF) 2nd UN Proposal May 30, 2011). Both of the latter explicitly emphasize the importance of enhancing 'the capacities of [women] for mediation, reconciliation and peace-building', and are implemented at the national level, involving as partners, collaborators or 'counterparts', many Kyrgyzstani women's NGOs. It is at meetings involving these women that Sophia hears about mediation and peace-building, about which she says 'everyone is doing mediation nowadays'.

The ideas that the collaborators learn to use are supplied in definite ways that we identify. Traces of the ruling relations that Sophia takes up in her new collaborative work appear in the texts reporting the humanitarian relief that the emergency in Kyrgyzstan had attracted (UNOCHA, 2010). Those reports identified the Consolidated Appeals Process (CAP) as the conceptual apparatus organizing both the immediate relief, and longer-term efforts in the areas affected by inter-ethnic violence. Analytically, we see the CAP as a text-based technology for emergency response, generated in or for the UN Office for Coordination of Humanitarian Affairs (UNOCHA), and available to be applied in any conflict area. As such, it provides a kind of template for quick strategic assessment of the emergency and for the planning and coordination of actions to be taken both immediately and later. The longer-term strategy turns donors and aid agencies into a coordinated team with national governments to address systematically the problems identified in the CAP (UNOCHA, 2010, p. 22–6). The identified targets and solutions express the peace-building discourse. This has the effect of coordinating aid toward CAP-specified topics, the funding for which is being made available, as noted. International development and donor organizations, policy-makers and practitioners are progressively recognizing peace-building as 'integral to effective development assistance' (Mihalik & van der Leest, 2009). The UN underpins and elaborates this direction. 'Peace and stability towards sustainable development' has been announced as the overarching goal of the UN strategic plan to inform the UN's work in 2012–2016 (UN Country Team, 2011).

Our analysis shows how in 2011, in Kyrgyzstan, the peace-building discourse was already being activated. The concepts of CAP's strategic apparatus (such as its categories of need, identified in clusters and sub-clusters) have become naturalized, their use as descriptors of what should be done simply taken for granted in the ongoing work of the women's groups in which Sophia was involved. For instance, the 'Protection Cluster' contained a sub-cluster on gender-based violence that was to address the issues of conflict and post-conflict protection of the most vulnerable groups, including women. In Bishkek, the UN Population Fund leading the sub-cluster on gender-based violence continued the post-conflict intervention in Kyrgyzstan, extending the work begun under funding from the Flash Appeal and its goals. We noted earlier that Sophia was invited to join this group, now renamed the National Network against Gender-based Violence (NNGV). The NNGV is the inter-agency collaboration of national government, UN agencies, donor NGOs and local NGOs that the CAP technology for conflict relief mandates. It is too soon yet to know exactly what projects are being carried out under its aegis; but our observations suggest that the funding being made available does not include action to reduce everyday violence against women. The internal document framing NNGV activities – the 'Standard Operational Procedures of Multi-sectoral/ inter-agency Cooperation on Prevention and Response to Gender Violence' – names its target groups as the 'various layers of population who suffered during the humanitarian crisis situation in the south of Kyrgyzstan in June 2010'. Its gender-oriented activities focus on 'sustainable strategic planning of responding and preventing gender-based violence and monitoring of national legislation and international liabilities of the Kyrgyz Republic including [specified] UN Resolutions 1325 [On Women, Peace and Security] and 1820 [the follow-up on the UN Resolution 1325 which confronts sexual violence in conflict and post-conflict situations] and CEDAW [Convention on the Elimination of All Forms of Discrimination Against Women]'.

A peculiar distortion results from the discursive amalgamation that the CAP coordination facilitates, in which the abstract concept 'violence' of the relief-planning document appears to express any experience of violence. For instance, it confounds inter-ethnic and domestic violence. This distortion reaches into our local research setting, where Sophia, one actor among many involved, is enacting the discourse. As used there, the 'violence' of the multilateral peace-building policy becomes synonymous with the violence women experience in their homes and on the city and village streets throughout Kyrgyzstan. This conceptual coordination affects the actions being taken in the Network. New decisions are being made that are apparently inappropriate for the Network, such as conflict mediation being adopted in its programs. Originally aimed at efforts to intervene to protect women in domestic settings, this addition gains its rationality from being tied to the ruling discourse. It seems to make sense to teach women conflict resolution instead of working with male perpetrators or the police. The discourse also rationalizes the Network's acceptance of project funding from peace-building sources that inserts work with elderly citizens into women's crisis centers. It justifies Sophia's writing of new proposals for funding from a number of agencies that support peace-building activities. For instance, the Network has recently written two project proposals to the Democratic Commission entitled 'Peacebuilding through Intergenerational Linkages' and is in the process of writing another proposal to the UN Women Trust Fund to End Violence against Women which currently has a major objective focusing on 'women building peace'. In these ways, the CAP plays out in Kyrgyzstan by advancing and promoting what we are calling institutional knowledge and interests over those arising from 'the field' where local experiential knowledge would otherwise be understood as authoritative. All this results in the Network staff being increasingly unsatisfied with their jobs, as their practical and professional expertise is diverted away from women who are victims or possible victims of domestic violence towards whatever work can be conceptualized within the new discourse.

Development NGOs and the ruling practices of peace-building

Our research adds an analysis of ruling relations and practices to other critical findings and characterizations of NGOization. We have demonstrated that development NGOs play a pivotal role in the new use of development aid for peace-building. Contemporary analysts of peace-building in development have identified its links with the neoliberal principles of the 'market economy, good governance and liberal democracy' (Frewen, 2011, p. 4); as advancing capitalism (Pugh, 2005); or expressing a 'particular model of development that generates poverty and inequality' (Guttal, 2005, p. 49). Our contribution is made by studying how this works in practice. We have seen how the CAP, as a United Nations administrative technology, coordinates post-conflict development aid as well as administering humanitarian relief. It supplies the language and institutional discourse for advancing a ruling development agenda and we show how the women's NGO we study is caught up in these processes. Participating in them as an NGO manager and anti-violence expert, our informant, Sophia, learns that because 'all the donor funding goes to peace-building today', to better position herself as an anti-violence expert and the Network as a resource on anti-violence work, she must adopt the discourse and make use of its 'modern' ideas. What she does with the new ideas helps generalize them non-critically in the local setting: their realization 'on the ground' is expected to address seamlessly the local expression of needs. But our research identifies a disjuncture in knowing, demonstrating that the new processes are not what they seem; not, that is, just good practices of administration. At issue is the conceptual coordination that these ruling practices accomplish in local settings. Conflict mediation is the example we use to demonstrate how 'violence' as it appears in the peace-building discourse coordinates and blurs different experiences (and distorts what subsequently can and will happen). Mediation as a solution for managing violence, when accepted into the Network's regular work, interferes with what the crisis centers typically do. Up until now, crisis center staff answer phone calls and talk to the women who need help, deciding in the conversation between them how best to help. The workers interrupt, when they can, instances of acute aggression or they provide a safe haven for women who turn up alone, in fear of facing the person who has been violent to them. The time and funds needed for such hands-on interpersonal work by the Network to keep women safe is compromised as Network staff and the crisis center staff study and teach mediation, and discover as our informant said 'it will not be used'. Moreover, local experiential knowledge and expertise generated by working with women in crisis centers is being eclipsed, ruled out of the new decision processes.

Our study of this women's NGO in Kyrgyzstan shows non-governmental organizations as essential participants in the rolling out of the UN's peace-building policy. Reliance on development aid makes such NGOs willing and non-critical partners. What Frewen (2011) calls 'neo-imperial' in the operation of peace-building policy, we explicate as the contradictory outcomes of discursive coordination of ruling relations. The ruling relations we track bring into view what Cornwall and Brock (2006) have called the 'interplay between "money changing hands" and "ideas changing minds" that is international development' (p. 50). The interplay is discursively organized to administer people and focus their efforts on the implementation of ready-made solutions. To distribute humanitarian relief, discursive and textual technologies make local settings and local people solution-ready through conceptualizing and identifying people and events as instances of the associated categories. For people in ruling institutions, ongoing violence in Kyrgyzstan adds to the current and future dangers arising in a region in which a variety of solutions, including military ones, are already at hand. Peace-building is the solution that 'promises' to stabilize the situation as it is authoritatively defined by supporting the people involved and reducing their propensity to resort to violence. While we are not arguing against humanitarian or development aid and its effective administration, it is widely accepted that the importation of even expertly designed, resourced and executed development initiatives consistently fail to deliver on promises; and they always carry costly and unexpected burdens for the populations involved (Li, 2007).

Our empirically based analysis suggests one such dangerous cost. By tracking the ruling relations, we begin to see the processes whereby ruling institutions routinely lose sight of actual people. We have found NGO staff in local sites engaged in very difficult struggles to reduce everyday violence against women. As these workers get caught up in the ruling definitions of violence, and the associated funded solutions, one effect is the re-writing and subordinating of local experiences that differ from the ruling version. This is how the actualities and people's experiential knowledge of them get lost and outcomes get misread. Neo-imperialism is one way of describing what happens when the aid-administered world is made over in the language, categories, numbers and images that conform to ruling ideas and interests. Development NGOs are key players in this discursively organized work.

Here we have seen that they are increasingly integral to and integrated into (the UN's) consolidated humanitarian relief strategies that frame development aid after an acute crisis ends. All this further complicates NGOs' attempts to work with and on behalf of local recipients of development aid.

Notes

1 This analysis is part of a larger research project exploring gender and international funding for empowerment of women in Kyrgyzstan (Campbell, forthcoming; Campbell & Kim, 2009; Campbell & Teghtsoonian, 2010). Funding from the Social Sciences and Humanities Research Council of Canada's International Opportunities Fund (Grant No. 861-2007-0019) is gratefully acknowledged.

2 The Network and the names of its participants quoted in the chapter have been changed.

3 Accountability to international funders, carried out in development agencies in Kyrgyzstan and elsewhere, is specialized work (Campbell & Kim 2009). For instance, Aid Effectiveness requirements for results-based management and reporting are part of the Network's accounting for funds from Hivos. The 'costs' to local development agencies of doing this specialized accountability work are not well understood.

References

Bachelet, M. (2011). 'Engaging Women in Mediation and Conflict Prevention to Advance Peace and Democracy'. Speech delivered at the Security Council Open Debate on Women and Peace and Security, 28 October 2011. Retrieved from: http://www.unwomen.org/2011/10/engaging-women-in-mediation-and-conflict-prevention-to-advance-peace-and-democracy/.

Bagić, A. (2004). 'Women's Organizing in Post-Yugoslav Countries: Talking about Donors'. In J. Gould & H. Secher Marcussen (Eds.) *Ethnographies of Aid, Occasional Paper Series*, International Development Studies, Roskilde University. Retrieved from: http://www.map.hr/dokumenti/AidaBagicTalkingAboutDonors.pdf.

Campbell, M. (forthcoming). 'Learning Global Governance: OECD's Aid Effectiveness and "Results" Management in a Kyrgyzstani Development Project'. In D.E. Smith & A. Griffith (Eds.) [tentatively titled] *Governance and the Front Line*. Toronto: University of Toronto Press.

Campbell, M. & Kim, E. (2009). 'Achieving "Results" from Internationally Funded NGOs in Kyrgyzstan: Aid-Effectiveness as Discursive Coordination of Global Ruling Relations?' Paper presented in Post-colonialism, Globalization and Development stream of the Critical Management Conference, University of Warwick, UK, July 13–15, 2009.

Campbell, M. & Teghtsoonian, K. (2010). 'Aid Effectiveness and Women's Empowerment: Practices of Governance in the Funding of International Development'. *Signs: Journal of Women in Culture and Society*, 36(1), 177–201.

Cornwall, A. & Brock, K. (2006). 'The New Buzzwords'. In P. Utting (Ed.) *Reclaiming Development Agenda: Knowledge, Power and International Policy Making* (pp.43–72). Basingstoke: Palgrave Macmillan.

Frewen, J. (2011). 'Neoliberal "Peace-building" and the UN, Part 1 and Part 2.' *Irish Left Review*. Published on-line, May 5th, 2011. Retrieved from: http://www.irishleftreview.org/2011/05/11/neoliberal-peacebuilding-part-1/.

Gould, J. (2004). 'Introducing Aidnography'. In *Thinking Outside Development: Epistemological Explorations 1994–2008* (pp. 12–18). Published on-line, June 17, 2008. Retrieved from http://blogs.helsinki.fi/gould/files/2008/06/thinking-outside-96-dpi-17v08.pdf.

Guttal, S. (2005, January). 'Reconstruction: A Glimpse into an Emerging Paradigm'. *Silent War. Focus on the Global South*, 39–53. Retrieved from: http://www.focusweb.org/pdf/Iraq_Dossier.pdf.

Hoare, J. (2009). *Development and Gender in Kyrgyzstan*. Research Report. Social Research Center. September, 2009. Bishkek.

Human Rights Watch. (2006). *Reconciled to Violence: State Failure to Stop Domestic Abuse and Abduction of Women in Kyrgyzstan*. Retrieved from: http://www.crin.org/violence/search/closeup.asp?infoID=10389.

Ibraimov, B. (2011). 'Continuing Ethnic Tension Speeds Exodus from Kyrgyzstan'. *Jetigen Weekly*. Retrieved from: http://jetigenweekly.blogspot.com/2011/06/continuing-ethnic-tension-speeds-exodus.html.

Lang, S. (1997). 'The NGOization of Feminism'. In C. Kaplan, S. Keates, & J.W. Wallach (Eds.) *Transitions, Environments, Translations: Feminisms in International Politics* (pp. 101–120). London and New York: Routledge.

Li, T.M. (2007). *The Will to Improve. Governmentality, Development, and the Practice of Politics*. Duke University Press: Durham & London.

Mihalik, J. & van der Leest, K. (2009). 'Does Peacebuilding Matter in Development Aid?' Retrieved from: http://www.initiativeforpeacebuilding.eu/pdf/Does_Peacebuilding_Matterin_Development_Aid.pdf.

Mosse, D. (2006). 'Anti-social Anthropology? Objectivity, Objection, and the Ethnography of Public Policy and Professional Communities'. *Journal of the Royal Anthropological Institute, 12*(4), (pp. 935–956).

Olcott, M.B. (2010). *Kyrgyzstan: Perspectives and Implications for the Region*. OSCE Seminar, 20/20 OSCE and Central Asia, October 12, 2010. Retrieved from: http://carnegieendowment.org/2010/10/12/kyrgyzstan-perspectives-and-implications-for-region/2u2.

Pugh, M. (2005). 'The political economy of peacebuilding: A critical theory perspective'. *International Journal of Peace Studies, 10*(2), 23–42.

Simpson, M. (2006). 'Local Strategies in Globalizing Gender Politics: Women's Organizing in Kyrgyzstan and Tajikistan'. *Journal of Muslim Minority Affairs 26* (1), 9–31.

Smith, D.E. (1987). *The Everyday World as Problematic: A Feminist Sociology*. Toronto: University of Toronto Press.

Smith, D.E. (2004). 'Ideology, Science and Social Relations: A Reinterpretation of Marx's Epistemology'. *European Journal of Social Theory, 7*(4), 445–462.

Smith, D.E. (2005). *Institutional Ethnography: A Sociology for People*. Lanham, MD: AltaMira Press/Rowman and Littlefield.

Smith, D.E. (2006). *Institutional Ethnography as Practice*. Lanham, MD: Rowman & Littlefield.

United Nations Country Team. (2011). *United Nations Development Assistance Framework (UNDAF) for the Kyrgyz Republic 2012–2016*. Bishkek, March. Retrieved from: http://planipolis.iiep.unesco.org/upload/Kyrgyzstan/Kyrgyzstan_UNDAF_2012_2016_eng.pdf.

United Nations Office for the Coordination of Humanitarian Affairs (UNOCHA). (2010). *Extended and Revised Flash Appeal for Kyrgyzstan 2010*. Retrieved from: http://www.unocha.org/cap/appeals/extended-and-revised-flash-appeal-kyrgyzstan-2010.

United Nations Office for the Coordination of Humanitarian Affairs (UNOCHA). (2011). *Consolidated Appeals Guidelines 2012*. Retrieved from: http://reliefweb.int/node/444055.

United Nations Peace-building Fund (UNPBF). (2011). *Kyrgyzstan Overview*. Retrieved from: http://www.unpbf.org/countries/kyrgyzstan/.

United Nations General Assembly. (2011). Strengthening the role of mediation in the peaceful settlement of disputes, conflict prevention and resolution: resolution adopted by the General Assembly, 28 July 2011, A/RES/65/283. Retrieved from: http://www.unhcr.org/refworld/docid/4e71a20f2.html.

United Nations Security Council. (2000). Resolution 1325. Adopted by the Security Council, 31 October 2000, S/RES/1325 (2000). Retrieved from: http://www.un.org/events/res_1325e.pdf.

9

Alignment and Autonomy: Food Systems in Canada

Brewster Kneen

It may be presumptuous to describe what is referred to as the food movement in a stable affluent country such as Canada as a social movement, but there is certainly a growing mass of people throughout North America expecting, demanding, and organizing for a very different food regime, not only for themselves, but for everyone. The corporations that have enjoyed a controlling interest in the food economy of North America since colonization are well aware that they can no longer consider the public to be a passive body of consumers, eager to eat up whatever they serve up, wherever it comes from and whatever the quality. Concessions, such as the presence of organic foods in the produce sections, free-range eggs, and organic milk in the dairy sections of large supermarkets, however, merely mask increasing corporate domination of the food system.

At the farm end of the system, 'commercial' agriculture is dominated by commodity trade associations composed primarily not of farmers but of the corporate suppliers, buyers, processors and traders that handle the commodity in question. While the public is drawing away from the controllers and profiteers of the corporate industrial food system, industrial-scale commodity farmers are ever more dependent on good relations with their corporate 'partners'. Thus the general farm organization in the province of Alberta, Wild Rose Agricultural Producers, voted to open up membership to corporations to gain more members and increased financial 'stability' at its Annual General Meeting (AGM) in 2012.[1]

There is, then, an increasingly intimate relationship between transnational trading corporations, 'input' suppliers (fertilizer, agrotoxins and seeds), and 'farm businessmen' on the one hand, while on the other hand there is a splendid array of citizens' groups and local organizations, along with a multitude of idealistic individuals, escaping from the corporate tent and constructing alternative food systems. The temptations and pressures for the latter to pick up the practices and culture of the former, however, are omnipresent and powerful. This is readily apparent when one looks at the list of corporate sponsors of organic/alternative trade shows and educational programs. The sponsoring corporations may produce organic yogurt or bread, and be smaller and more 'local' than their mainline counterparts, but the pattern and dependency are similar. The replacement of fieldmen ('ag reps') employed by provincial governments with advisors and consultants (salesmen) employed by the corporate agricultural input suppliers is indicative of the changing alignments of governments and the corporate sector.

As this movement has grown over the past dozen years or so, it has outstripped the capacity of its volunteer base, or professionals such as community nutritionists working 'off the side of the desk', to perform all the work required. Increasingly, groups have found themselves needing to raise funds, not just for the out-of-pocket costs of conferences and similar efforts, but to pay staff to carry out organizing and educational activities (including fundraising). At the same time, more formal structures have emerged, such as municipal food policy councils, with paid staff, along with the long-standing ones such as food banks. Whether they ultimately rely on corporate sponsorships, public/government funding or grants, philanthropic foundations, or funds raised through educational services (seminars, conferences) or events, they increasingly stand in a fuzzy area between broad social movements and NGOs.

In this chapter I map out the range of organizations and 'movements' in the agricultural and food sector of the Canadian economy and evaluate their relationship to the state (meaning various levels of government, from municipal to federal), their relationship to the corporate sector, and their degree of autonomy from both. The detailing of structures, practices and self-understanding reveals the assumptions behind the organizations occupying the territory of the dominant food system in Canada that must be contested if a vital food movement is to develop the power to actually transform the state and corporate capitalist domination. A similar analysis would be applicable to the United States (US) and elsewhere.

I will also reflect on the relationship between the desire for a mass movement to transform a society and the desire and satisfaction of building small projects and organizations at the village or municipal level from my personal experience, first as a farmer-activist and then as an urban food activist. While running a sheep farm in Nova Scotia, we developed a lamb marketing co-op (which celebrated 30 years of operation in 2012) whose success was based on strong social relationships built slowly and carefully among the farmers. Later, back in Toronto, we participated in the development of the Toronto Food Policy Council, and when we moved to Mission, British Columbia and set out to establish a local farmers' market, we quickly learned all about the power structure of the community, which enabled us to create a local 'social movement' that made the market a reality.

The food movement

Throughout North America people are moving: from one style of eating to another; from one kind of shopping for food to another; from highly individualistic approaches to the acquisition, preparation and consumption of food to a range of collective approaches to all these activities. There is also significant movement from what is wrongly called 'conventional' agriculture to organic and ecological farming, from industrial commodity production to artisanal, small-scale agriculture and fishing, from the quest to 'improve' and control Mother Earth (nature and the environment) to learning how to live with her. The food movement is not inclined to view land as a 'resource' that must be forced to be more 'productive', but rather as the base for living responsibly in the natural world, though this might not be true for the small minority of extreme libertarians.

The food movement includes farmers, fishers, health workers and teachers, as well as people engaged in a wide variety of enterprises to provide food for those marginalized by the capitalist economy, including Indigenous Peoples intent on recovering their traditional food-ways. Food-conscious people favor organic foods and are very concerned about centralization and corporate control of the food system. They reject genetically engineered foods and agrotoxins and want to know where their food is coming from; who grew it, caught it, processed or baked it? Many who are not farmers grow at least some of their own food and save seeds from season to season, in both rural and urban settings. Farmers' markets are now a primary struc- tural feature of the food movement, and there is also a rapidly growing 'urban agriculture' which challenges, in a very material way, how land is held and owned in the city, including by the city itself, and how it is utilized, including for growing vegetables and even raising poultry.[2] Growing food in a schoolyard by and for the students is a very, very long way from commodity production for export.

Just as women are the seed keepers and farmers in the subsistence agriculture that feeds billions of people, women are the leaders in every aspect of the food movement worldwide, while in the industrial sector, from the farm to transnational agribusiness, men remain 'the boss'.

Politically, food activists range from right-wing libertarians to left- wing anarchists, from conscientious middle-class folk desiring good food to cancer patients, 'welfare moms', and marginal farmers strug- gling to survive. Some of these farmers aspire to be effective entrepreneurs and business operators, but they are likely to bear little resemblance to the farm businessmen and are unlikely to appear at meetings in suits.

Two essential statements about context

First, Canada has never had a food policy. It has always had an agri- cultural policy, even as a colony, to maximize commodity food production for export. This remains federal policy, now buttressed by the argument that this is agriculture's essential contribution to Cana- da's balance of trade. The implied food policy can be summed up as dependency on imports for much of the country's food (including fish, absurd as that may be). If an economy is defined as how the family and the community go about organizing their material welfare, such a policy is an expression of utter economic irrationality.

Second, any consideration of organizations and social movements must recognize their geographic and demographic character. Both Canada and the US are characterized by sparse populations scattered over an immense geography, at least as far as agriculture is concerned. Distances are great, east to west, south to north, and in the case of Canada, the population is stretched in a comparatively thin line from coast to coast, meaning that outside of the major cities there are no hubs in which to gather a mass of people. This militates against grass-roots organizing on anything more than a local or regional basis simply due to the cost of travel – which is partly where corporate sponsorship comes in.

In the years before the industrialization of agriculture and fishing in the mid-1900s, there were many grassroots efforts to organize farmers and fishers, but these efforts have been hampered, not only by geography, but also by North American individualism, which has always worked against social solidarity. Homesteading on a quarter section of land (160 acres) with no villages nurtured 'rugged individualism'. (The settlement pattern in Quebec, with houses near to each other along the road and the farmland stretching in strips behind, may be part of the reason for the social and organizational development differences between Quebec and the rest of Canada in this regard.)

Shaping by capital

Even cooperative forms of business organization, initiated for social as well as economic reasons, have almost universally been pushed and pulled into a capitalist business mentality, valuing profit maximization for the co-op as being more important than providing social benefits for their members and society at large. Although some of the largest food businesses in North America, and elsewhere, got their start as cooperatives, only a few remain, incorporated as cooperatives but now with a capitalist mentality. The great Canadian grain cooperatives have all disappeared, gobbled up by the most aggressive capitalist-minded of them, the Saskatchewan Wheat Pool, which was subsequently privatized and merged with Agricore United in 2007 and the resulting company rebranded as Viterra.[3]

Similarly, fifty years ago there were many small dairy cooperatives, particularly in eastern Canada, which served their farmer members by processing their milk and providing milk and cheese for the community. Gradually these small plants were either bought out (by Kraft, in eastern Canada) and/or consolidated, losing their significant community economic and social role along the way. At the same time, farms were becoming larger, fewer, and more business-minded. Consequently, the pressure to make a profit, rather than to make a living, has worked against farmer solidarity and against farm organizations based on a larger vision than that of simply running a profitable business. As farmers were being indoctrinated by agribusiness and governments to think of themselves as businessmen engaged in the business of farming and commodity producers, their organizations became commodity-based business organizations and lobbies.

Meanwhile, back in the city, in a parallel development, supermarkets were replacing the corner grocery stores, industrially processed food was replacing home canning, and fast food was individualizing the eating experience. The public was reclassified as 'consumers': passive, paying receptacles for the products of the industrialized food system which featured 'producers' at one end and 'consumers' at the other, with little communication or understanding between them.

Breaking away, or trying to

My first book, *From Land to Mouth, Understanding the Food System*, published in 1989, was an analysis of the structure and logic of the industrial food system. By 1993, when a second edition was called for, I had to add a chapter about the rather sudden rise of many small exceptions to this system.

The late 1980s and the 1990s saw an explosion of organic farming, ecological agriculture, and new forms of farm management and food distribution, all locally oriented. None of this was referred to as a social movement or even a food movement at the time, even though these activities were laying a potentially solid base for a powerful social movement. Most of the people involved were too busy creating what was referred to as 'alternative agriculture', including organic, or very local food projects, such as community gardens and cooperative food buying clubs, some of which tried to meet the needs of hungry neighbors. Concurrently, food banks, which were supposed to be short-term stop-gap measures, became functional components of the industrial system while the long-standing tradition of church soup kitchens remained an essential charity in far too many communities.

The 'radical' developments on the ground – including a rejection of recombinant Bovine Growth Hormone (rBGH) and genetically engineered seed – did not bring changes to the established superstructure of the agricultural industry. On the contrary, these established organizations and government agencies, and particularly the rapidly consolidating transnational seed, biotech and agrotoxin industries, rightly perceived all these new activities as threats, and responded accordingly. More or less politely, they marginalized upstarts as quaint and harmless, if not ill-informed and backward, all the while proclaiming the 'progress' being made with 'improved seeds' through genetic engineering.[4] It was these same interests that were beguiling the public, including conscientious food activists, with the diversity of the fruits and foods of globalization, which may be one reason they were not paying enough attention to the structures of the dominant industrial food machine and the consolidation and concentration of corporate interests that was putting control of the food system and effective food sovereignty into their hands.

As a consequence, the issue facing the food movement in North America may have less to do with NGOization and the traditional regard for the state as its friend and its role as advisor to the state on policy matters as farmers (in suits and ties) sit at the policy table with department heads than an unwitting accommodation to the needs of capital. This is not surprising, given, for example, the replacement of governmentally employed fieldmen ('ag reps') by advisors and consultants (salesmen and women) employed by the agricultural input suppliers. Certainly in Canada, this is being encouraged, if not forced, by the federal government, which is in effect abdicating its role in relation to the public and forcing citizen organizations (and universities) to align with the corporate sector. I have called this process 'corporatization' but it is perhaps more accurately described as 'NGOization by proxy'.

In this process, all civil society organizations (CSOs), NGOs, voluntary, non-profit, and charity organizations are being pushed into dependency either on individual (private) donors or corporate sponsors, the latter referred to as 'partnering' with the private sector, with emphasis on business models and accountability and evaluation (management by objectives, results-based management). In addition, the organizations, of whatever sort, that have been receiving federal government support (financial and policy) have, in recent years, been increasingly subject to punitive treatment if they have been in any way critical of the government or deviated from government policy, which is now hardly distinguishable from corporate policy and practice.[5] The dismantling of the Canadian Wheat Board in 2011 is the outstanding example of enforcement of government commitment to corporate welfare at the expense of public and farmer interests, and, some would contend, in violation of the law. The organizations that are favored by the government are those that are essentially delivery vehicles for welfare programs or government 'humanitarian aid'.

Beginnings of a movement

There is a significant ideological and material gulf between the recognized, 'formal' industrial farm and agricultural organizations and the people's activities and organizing on the ground, most of which are very local, but with a slowly increasing number of regional and national organizations.

A limited number of well-financed industry-defined organizations, such as the Canola Council of Canada and the Canadian Federation of Agriculture – 'business-interest NGOs' (or BINGOs) with close ties to government – sit on one side, and on the other side are the National Farmers' Union, regional bodies such as Union Paysanne (Quebec) and Ecological Farmers Association (Ontario) and an almost bewildering diversity of local and regional projects, organizations, networks, food distribution projects and businesses. These constituted the group that came together in 2006 to form Food Secure Canada explained in more detail later.

In between the corporate industrial sector and the ecological public sector sit the 'charitable' aid and development organizations, such as Save the Children, Oxfam and the Canadian Food Grains Bank, that present themselves as non-political (or at least non-aligned), even while expecting and drawing on government financial support and, by their silence, giving passive approval to certain policies and practices (such as refusing to take a position on the use of genetically engineered crops in food aid).

The Canadian Food Grains Bank (CFGB) stands out as a 'genuine' NGO in that it raises money for food aid from its institutional church members and from its on-the-ground activity in commodity food production, with corporate support, which is then matched by the federal government. The CFGB and its professional staff also deserve credit for being the driving force behind the Food Security Policy Group which brings together the food aid and development organizations and, through careful and persistent lobbying, caused the federal government to untie its 'tied' food aid program.[6]

Soup kitchens and food banks, while continuing to operate as charities, have become significant participants in the food movement and the Canadian Association of Food Banks, now Food Banks Canada, was a founding member of Food Secure Canada. An indication of the failure of the industrial food system is the fact that food banks try to meet the needs of ever greater numbers of people who are not integrated into the industrial food system as customers (851,000 per month were using the 450 food banks in Canada as of March 2011, and thousands more cannot access food banks). If to that number are added the thousands of people who support food banks financially and with their donated labor, the total would certainly come to over a million people in a national population of 34 million. A million people could become a substantial base of a social movement to overthrow the capitalist system that has no use for them. But this would require a public that rejects the notion that their welfare depends on corporate generosity and leadership that does not hold a masters degree in business administration, but which does have experience in local organizing and non-capitalist forms of business. For example, the growing field of food studies should have a focus on socialist business alternatives.

Getting organized

The first Canadian national hunger conference, held in Toronto in 1986, focused on food banks and poverty, and the demand that the state improve social welfare programmes and reduce poverty – with no mention of causes, either economic or structural. Toronto's Daily Bread food bank was itself operating out of a disused Loblaws (Canada's largest supermarket chain) warehouse with the blessing of the company, which benefited with an efficient means of moving stale dated and surplus stock while obtaining tax benefits for doing so. According to its website, Daily Bread 'was meant to be temporary as the founding group would continue to press for changes in public policy to alleviate the problem of hunger'.

Starting from a reaction to the obscenity of hunger in a society as affluent as Canada, the power of the food movement has grown from its ability to connect social inclusivity and social justice with the desire for healthy food. While the movement in Canada (and the US) is fragmented, decentralized, bio-diverse in every sense, and highly informal, there is a great deal of organizational activity, structural cooperation, and common ground in basic assumptions about the world we live in and how we should live in it and with it. Thus it was possible, after several national gatherings of food activists from across Canada, to create Food Secure Canada in October 2006 to bring together the diverse elements of the food movement and to form a national voice on food security issues. Food Secure Canada is based on a commitment to the goals of zero hunger, healthy and safe food, and a sustainable food system as inextricably interlinked.

In 2008, the assembly of Food Secure Canada in Ottawa agreed to support the People's Food Policy Project as a key activity for the coming two years. The People's Food Policy Project was non-governmental in every respect, carried out by people with a 'special interest' in food, health, ecology and justice, most of them leaders within Food Secure Canada. With limited funding from some private foundations, virtually all of its work was done on a voluntary basis. In the words of its final document, 'Resetting the Table':

> Over the course of two years, more than 3500 people participated in a grassroots process that included three hundred and fifty 'kitchen table talks', hundreds of policy submissions, dozens of teleconferences, ongoing online discussions, and three cross-Canada conferences to collaboratively articulate a vision for a healthy, ecological and just food system that will provide enough healthy, acceptable, and accessible food for all.[7]

The People's Food Policy is based on the principles of food sovereignty, which calls for a fundamental shift in focus from food as a commodity to food as a public good, with food, water, soil, and air viewed not as 'resources' but as sources of life itself – a radical alternative to the current industrial capital-and-energy intensive system. It has become the stated political/social goal of the global food movement, requiring that the people, or peoples, have control over their own food system, from what is grown and how it is grown and harvested to how it is distributed and, finally, eaten. This global standard definition of food sovereignty was the outcome of a major meeting of food activists from around the world in Nyéléni, Mali, in 2007:

Food sovereignty puts those who produce, distribute and need wholesome, local food at the heart of food, agricultural, livestock and fisheries systems and policies, rather than the demands of markets and corporations that reduce food to internationally tradable commodities and components.[8]

In the People's Food Policy, this perspective has been emphasized by the addition of a seventh pillar of food sovereignty, in response to the project's Indigenous Circle: 'Food is Sacred'. While the People's Food Policy does call for federal government implementation of its policy recommendations, this in no way means that the multifarious activities of the food movement are waiting on the government to take action. The movement will continue to innovate and grow as a social movement independent of government funding, government policy dictates, and corporate pressures, although its final form and scope remain to be seen.

People's sovereignty and state sovereignty are, of course, contradictory, particularly when, as is now the case, capitalist states assume that the corporate industrial sector is their 'public', not the people themselves, with the result that 'overseas' aid programs become business development programs for corporations. NGOs are now expected to 'partner' with the corporate sector, for example becoming on-the-ground delivery vehicles for state programs such as food aid, working closely with transnational agribusiness as suppliers. Some, such as World Vision and Plan Canada, go much further in taking government funding to dress up the activities of transnational mining conglomerates as 'socially responsible' (see Coumans, 2012). These large NGOs do not relate to Food Secure Canada, while other much smaller NGOs are strong members of Food Secure Canada and do have funding arrangements, however cautious, with the federal government.

Corporate-national policy

Meanwhile, farm organizations, the agricultural industry and both federal and provincial governments are calling for a national food policy, exposing the very real fear they all harbor, consciously or not, of the power of the growing food movements, particularly with their production and distribution alternatives.

The intimacy of state, corporations and farm groups is bluntly stated by the National Food Strategy (NFS) developed by the Canadian Federation of Agriculture (CFA), which talks about 'finding broader solutions for the value-chain, taking into account everything from promoting the Canadian brand and healthy lifestyles to sustaining economic growth and ecosystems'. It explains that 'the NFS was developed by the agriculture and agri-food industry to ensure a more holistic and strategic approach to food and agriculture', through meetings in mid-2011 of the CFA with federal, provincial and territorial agriculture ministers and 'all commodities and provinces, as well as input suppliers, processors and farm financial and accounting services'.[9] The outcome, not surprisingly, was strong support for the current emphasis on industrial commodity production for export.

Clearly, food sovereignty, as understood globally and by the social movements in Canada, is not on the agenda of the CFA and its partners as they situate themselves in agreement with Canada's export-oriented, corporate dominated food system. In contrast, Food Secure Canada and its member organizations and individuals, by and large, approach both state and corporate sectors from a position of autonomy rather than subservience, which of course deprives them of corporate and state support, but underscores their integrity.

To grasp the weight of the question of sovereignty, however, one has to consider the history of state-corporate power relationships. As Antony Anghie (2005) shows so well, state sovereignty is one thing, but economic sovereignty is another. Since the days of the great trading companies, operating under crown charters (the first of these, the British East India Company, was given a royal charter by the Queen in 1600), sovereigns and sovereign states required that the territories they chose to operate in recognize the 'right to trade'. This was one of the principles of what became international law, and it remains effective now as evidenced in various multilateral and bilateral trade agreements that circumscribe the sovereignty of the state or states entering into them. State sovereignty, at least in regards to industrial agriculture and other extractive industries, thus becomes limited by international law operating in the interest of transnational corporations.

Movements for food sovereignty ignore at their peril the limitations to the sovereignty of the state imposed by the economic policies and practices of transnational corporate capital, the international financial institutions, and the continuing pursuit of trade agreements that make explicit the legal responsibility of a state to serve corporate interests ahead of those of the people.

While there is certainly broad public concern about the extent of corporate concentration and control of the food system, there is too little understanding of how this system works, controls, and accumulates. Without such understanding, the food movement is left to operate, in a sense, in the shadow of the industrial food order, unable to develop its projects and practices into a real structural alternative to the industrial system. One example is the way in which the corporations are able to adopt and adapt 'natural' and organic language and practices and market organic and 'natural' – and even 'local' – products with a very substantial markup at every opportunity, under the guise of providing these wholesome alternatives to the mass market.

In other words, it is not the corporate-captured state but the state-endorsed corporate industrial food system that the food movement must directly and explicitly challenge. The pursuit of food sovereignty requires that the food movement recognize it is up against the immense power of a few transnational corporations that continue to shape and control the industrial food system around the world to suit their interests. Developing structures that relate primarily to the state, including financial dependency (and hence a tendency towards NGO-ization) is thus misleading at best and counter-productive at worst.

A closer look at the landscape and actors

In every sector the pattern is the same: domination of the market by three to six giant corporations, very often collaborating for mutual benefit, but careful to stop short of creating obvious monopolies. Oligopoly is the rule, particularly in farm 'inputs' (seeds, agrotoxins and fertilizer) and farm machinery, with four to ten corporations dominating each subsector. The 'informal' challenge to this capital-intensive industrial system, and set well apart from it, is a growing diversity of meeting points for food suppliers providing mostly local or regional foods, from meat to baked goods and vegetables. I use the term 'meeting points' because the venue might be a farmers' market in a shopping mall parking lot, a one-time trolley barn, or a formerly vacant city lot. Less visible would be the immense number of schemes and programs to meet the needs of marginalized populations, from food banks to 'good food' boxes delivered regularly, Community Shared Agriculture projects and businesses, community gardens, school food programs, and even efforts to get good food into hospitals, universities and other institutions. In all of these activities the social element, creating communities, is of prime importance. A great many of these initiatives devise creative relationships with school boards, municipal boards of health, and other very local governing bodies. Together they form the building blocks of a civil society food movement (and a large part of the membership of Food Secure Canada).

Above ground, operating under a very different paradigm, are the professional farm organizations that enjoy cozy relationships (personal, political and financial) with the state as well as the corporate sector. These organizations, which usually refer to themselves simply as industry organizations or commodity groups, often formally include input suppliers, commodity traders and the processing sector as well as growers and farmers. They align themselves with corporate and state emphasis on production for export and lobby the government to pursue 'market access' in international trade. (Market access is simply a euphemism for 'the right to trade'). They might well be referred to as parastatal organizations rather than NGOs.

An extreme example of a commodity association is the Canola Council of Canada. Of the 17 members of its board of directors, 13 represent major transnational corporations dealing with canola as input suppliers, processors and traders – such as Monsanto and Cargill – and only one of the 17 appears to be a woman.[10]

Another is the Canadian Cattlemen's Association (CCA), which simply claims to represent 'every phase of the production system' without mentioning the corporate interests and identity in the different sectors. As befitting its name, the CCA has an all-male 28-member board of directors. Its major issue is 'market access', meaning in this case, access to the US as well as the Japanese and Korean markets.[11]

A third example is Grain Farmers of Ontario, representing Ontario's 28,000 growers of corn, soybean and wheat. It has a 15-member all male board of directors, is export oriented, and takes a strong position in support of biodiesel and genetic engineering of grains and oilseeds.[12]

All of these organizations emphasize their work in 'government relations', referring to their advocacy for government policies favoring their interests, such as trade policy and genetic engineering of crops, in the belief that the government is, or should be, their friend and ally. The Canadian Soybean Council (CSC) is quite explicit in defining its attitude to the federal government: 'The role of the CSC has grown to include building relationships with the Canadian government to ensure advantageous policies for Canadian soybean and expanding domestic market opportunities including attracting new investment in Canada and new uses for soybeans'.[13]

What is clearly absent from the policies and programs of these industry/commodity organizations is any public interest/public good activity, thus excluding them from any place in the food movement and illustrating why a strong non-corporate non-government food movement is necessary.

Whole-farm organizations

There is another set of organizations that represent the interests of whole farms and diverse commodities, but this does not mean that their policies and philosophy necessarily differ from those of the commodity organizations cited above. The Union des Producteurs Agricoles (UPA) in Quebec, the Canadian Federation of Agriculture (CFA), and the National Farmers Union (NFU) are the best known, but their political positions are very diverse. The focus of the CFA is on federal government policy while its provincial organizations also deal with provincial and regional matters. The UPA is an actual partner with the Quebec provincial government in formulating policy and delivering programs. The NFU is an explicitly political organization composed of farmers and farm families with a community-oriented (and to some extent socialist) outlook. While the NFU does lobby both provincial and federal governments on specific issues, much of its work is conducted at the community and regional level, with a strong research and publication program on major issues of both farm and public interest such as trade, energy and sustainable agriculture. The NFU is, perhaps, more of a social movement than a commodity or industry organization, with family-based membership, dedicated leadership positions for women and youth, and associate membership for non-farmers. The NFU also stands out as a founding member of the global peasant farmer network, La Via Campesina.

In addition, as mentioned earlier, there are regional organizations with a strong social orientation, such as Ecological Farmers of Ontario, which has been committed to ecological and organic farming since 1979: 'We are run by farmers, for farmers. We're non-competitive. We focus on helping each other make a better living growing real food while improving our soils, crops, livestock and the environment'.[14]

The situation of farmers in Quebec is unique in Canada. Quebec farmers have been required to be members of the UPA since it was accredited as the only official farmers' union in Quebec in 1972. The UPA is structured on the basis of democratically organized commodity groups and its programs are commodity and community based. In 2007, the UPA endorsed the concept of 'food sovereignty' as the basis for a new social contract between farmers, the people and governments ('*contrat social entre les agriculteurs, la population et les gouvernements*'). Their interpretation of food sovereignty emphasizes provincial ('national') food sovereignty, not people's food sovereignty.[15]

Union Paysanne, on the other hand, is a small voluntary Quebec organization of organic and ecological farmers and farm supporters and, as expressed in its name, it represents the peasant culture of small diverse farms in Quebec in contrast to the position of the UPA which is dominated by very large farms using industrial methods. Union Paysanne participates actively in the food movement and its organizations. Despite well-meaning efforts – for example, Food Secure Canada held its fully bilingual 2010 Assembly in Montreal – the language barrier continues to effectively divide the food movement in Quebec from the rest of Canada.

There are other important elements that will likely shape the food movement in this process. Among them is the Canadian Association of Food Studies, founded in 2005 by academics and professionals from governmental and community organizations interested in promoting interdisciplinary scholarship in the broad area of food systems.[16]

A less recognized element of the food movement is the growing number of small, and not so small, health food, whole food, organic and natural food stores in towns and cities across the country, as well as butchers, bakers, and of course restaurants and cafes, attracting a clientele interested in local, organic, healthy food. There are also several significant cooperatives operating as processors and distributors of organic foods and dairy products, and a couple of very large suppliers – Whole Foods Market and SunOpta Foods – representing the corporatization of the natural/organic retail food sector. Whole Foods Market is a high-end retailer of natural and organic foods. SunOpta Foods has grown since 1999 by buying out a large number of smaller, regional organic and natural foods processors and distributors. Whole Foods Market and SunOpta have, between them, swallowed up many of the Canadian pioneers in organic foods processing and distribution that also expressed a significant social consciousness.

There are many local and regional food projects that relate in one way or another to a government, often municipal, as mentioned earlier. The Toronto Food Policy Council (TFPC), for example, was established in 1991 as an agency reporting to the City Council through the Board of Health. This was a deliberate placing of food as a health issue. The council continues to be funded by the city, and with paid staff and a strong government relationship, the TFPC would qualify as an NGO. However in its broad community base and alliances with dissimilar organizations in the City of Toronto and well beyond, it is a model for other food policy councils and an important element of the food movement, both regionally and nationally.

Conclusion: The importance of context, or framing

We all need a framework for our thoughts and actions. We may simply assume or inherit a framework without really being even conscious of our choice, or our assumption. Or, we may choose one thoughtfully or even create an appropriate one that enhances our commitments and vision.

We might think of our framework as a picture frame. It might be a big frame for the Big Picture, or a very small frame for a very small picture. We place ourselves in that frame, its size and fit determining the scope of our vision and action and with whom we picture ourselves. But frames tend to come in predetermined standard sizes and materials, and if the frame does not fit the picture, we generally alter the picture, when what we need to do is alter the frame. So we actually have two options: manipulate or alter the picture to fit the frame, or make a new frame suitable for the picture. This poses a political question: are any of the frames on offer suitable for our picture – our vision or dream – or do we have to make a new one?

The structures, projects and organizations I have described as constituting the food movement in Canada can each be identified with a particular framework, with some of these frames appropriate to the objectives or vision of the project, and some definitely not. There are organizations and cooperatives for example, that operate within and are bound by identification with capitalist ideology, while other co-operatives identify more closely with a socialist outlook of service rather than profit. Some see themselves as forerunners of a very different order of political economy, while others desire to be successful capitalist businesses. Some are confused, picturing themselves as socially minded and important players in an alternative food move-ment even as they hire capitalist-minded managers. We can describe these as corporatized cooperatives.

Then there are the organizations that picture themselves in a govern-ment frame, identifying closely with government programs and counting on government financial support for their 'core funding' as well as project support, and even employment in a government agency. These are the vehicles of NGOization for both organizations and individuals.

On the personal, or individual, level, there are many projects and actions in the food movement that are highly individualistic just as there are many that are profoundly social in character. Community kitchens clearly require a social framework, while organic gardening and farming may be highly individualistic within a small frame, or collective enterprises within a large frame, of social transformation.

The challenge facing the food movement as a whole and all its bits and pieces – from farmers' markets to municipal food councils, from individual seed savers to hospital food programs – is to identify, consciously and articulately, the framework of social justice and economy that puts human need and respect for the environment ahead of capitalist profit. Paying more attention to the frame might well contribute to the sorting of political attitudes and presumptions, and make it easier to create or complete the frames that fit our pictures of holistic and healthy food movements.

Notes

1 See http://www.wrap.ab.ca/.

2 The global leader in urban agriculture is Cuba.

3 See a diagram of corporate evolution at http://en.wikipedia.org/wiki/Viterra.

4 For a number of years in the early life of biotechnology, Channapatna Prakash, of Tuskegee University, USA, was a major propagandist utilized by the biotech industry, such as Ag-West Biotech Inc. in Saskatoon, Canada. For example, Ag-West's August 2000 bulletin referred to Prakash as 'arguing there is no scientific evidence to support claims that GM foods are dangerous to humans or the environment'. Prakash is claiming that the anti-GM movement is 'a form of new imperialism, determined to exercise control over the production and distribution of foods in the Third World'. Prakash says he sees 'extremist groups opposed to biotechnology, using arguments about food safety and environmental impact to frighten Western consumers and to deprive the Third World of new technology that it desperately needs'. Of course, Prakash was reversing the true scenario in which it is the imperial army of genetically engineered and patented seeds developed and deployed by Monsanto that is colonizing global agriculture.

5 For example, in December 2009, the Conservative Government of Canada abruptly cut funding ($1,775,000 a year for four years) to KAIROS: Canadian Ecumenical Justice Initiatives, on the grounds that KAIROS was opposed to the government's strong pro-Israel policy. Up to that point, the Minister of International Cooperation had been telling KAIROS that funding was cut because its work did not fit current Canadian International Development Agency (CIDA) priorities of economic growth, food security and children and youth. In mid-December, however, a completely different reason was given in a speech by Jason Kenney, Minister of Immigration, who described his government's fights against anti-Semitism and, as an example of this fight, said the government had 'defunded organizations like KAIROS for taking a leadership role in the boycott, divestment and sanctions campaign' against Israel. KAIROS' reply was that Minister Kenney's charge against KAIROS was simply false: 'A Minister of the Crown says that his government decided, for what is a highly political reason, to cut funds for a proposal developed in consultation with and approved by CIDA . . . Two points must be made: criticism of Israel does not constitute anti-Semitism; and CIDA was developed to fund international aid and not to serve political agendas' (The website source of this quote is no longer available. See instead, for much fuller commentary on this issue, http://www.kairoscanada.org/get-involved/kairos-cida-funding/press-media/).

6 'Canadian Foodgrains Bank is a partnership of Canadian churches and church-based agencies working to end hunger in developing countries . . . On behalf of its fifteen member agencies, the Foodgrains Bank collects grain and cash donations, provides funds and expert advice for projects submitted by member agencies and their partners, manages the procurement and supply of food commodities, and engages in public policy and education activities related to hunger and food security. Canadian Foodgrains Bank is a registered charitable agency' (see http://foodgrainsbank.ca).

7 See http://peoplesfoodpolicy.org.
8 See http://www.nyeleni.org.
9 See http://www.cfa-fca.ca/programs-projects/national-food-strategy.
10 See http://www.canolacouncil.org.
11 See http://cca.org.
12 See http://gfo.ca.
13 See http://soybeancouncil.ca.
14 See http://efao.ca.
15 See http://upa.qc.ca.
16 See http://foodstudies.ca.

References

Anghie, A. (2005). *Imperialism, Sovereignty and the Making of International Law.* Massachusetts: Cambridge University Press.

Coumans, C. (2012). 'CIDA's Partnership with Mining Companies Fails to Acknowledge and Address the Role of Mining in the Creation of Development Deficits'. *Mining Watch Canada.* Retrieved from: http://www.miningwatch.ca/sites/www.miningwatch.ca/files/Mining_and_Development_FAAE_2012.pdf.

About the Contributors

Sonny Africa is the executive director of the IBON Foundation, an independent non-governmental organization providing research, information and education services to people's movements in the Philippines and abroad. He is also coordinator of the Institute of Political Economy (IPE), a fellow of the Center for People Empowerment in Governance (CenPEG), a member of the coordinating committee of 'Pagbabago! People's Movement for Change', and an editor of the online news magazine *Bulatlat*. He has previously worked as staff in the national economic planning agency, as an evaluator of NGOs, as a legislative officer in the Philippine parliament, and as a peasant organizer. He has been an active educator to community and membership-based organizations as well as a resource person for schools, NGOs, government and media since the 1990s. His writing on socioeconomic and political issues has been published by IBON and IPE as well as international NGOs.

Marie Campbell is professor emerita at the University of Victoria in Canada. Her research focuses on gender, human service organizations and institutional ethnography, and she has published analyses of the organization, management and conduct of many different kinds of front-line human service work. In 2005, she was appointed through the Open Society Institute as non-resident international scholar and social research mentor to junior faculty in the American University of Central Asia, Bishkek, Kyrgyzstan.

Sangeeta Kamat is associate professor in the School of Education at the University of Massachusetts – Amherst, USA, and is the author of the widely acclaimed *Development Hegemony: NGOs and the State in India* (2002). She has authored several articles pertaining to neoliberalism, education, civil society and development, which have appeared in various education and interdisciplinary journals, including *Discourse: Studies in the Cultural Politics of Education, Current Issues in Comparative Education,* and *Social Justice*.

Elena Kim is an assistant professor at the American University of Central Asia, Bishkek, Kyrgyzstan. She is concurrently undertaking her second PhD in the Department of Development Research at the University of Bonn, Germany.

Brewster Kneen is an economist, theologian, radio producer, farmer and author. He has been involved in almost every aspect of the food system as practitioner (farmer and eater), analyst (corporate control and public policy) and organizer (cooperative marketing, food policy council and opposition to biotechnology). He has published seven books relating to food system analysis. His most recent book is *The Tyranny of Rights*.

Luke Sinwell is a post-doctoral fellow under the South African Research Chair in Social Change at the University of Johannesburg. His research interests include the politics and conceptualization of participatory development and governance, social movements and housing struggles, non-violent and violent direct action as a method to transform power relations, ethnographic research methods, and action research. He is involved in a project called 'The Voices of the Poor in Urban Governance: Participation, Mobilization and Politics in South African Cities'. He is co-editor (with Marcelle Dawson) of *Contesting Transformation: Popular Resistance in Twenty-First Century South Africa* (2012).

Raja Swamy is a visiting assistant professor in the Department of Anthropology at the University of Arkansas, USA. His research focuses on the impact of neoliberal reforms in India, specifically the role of humanitarianism in shaping these processes as well as the growth of popular politics in response to ensuing challenges. He is presently investigating the production of memory in India's Coromandel Coast, as legacies of the past are brought to bear on contemporary strategies of spatial transformation, even as fisher responses simultaneously anchor current claims in deep and often unacknowledged histories.

Sharon H. Venne is an Indigenous Treaty person (Cree) and by marriage a member of the Blood Tribe within Treaty 7 with one son. She is currently the chair/rapporteur on the United Nations Seminar on Treaties. Sharon worked at the UN prior to the establishment of the UN Working Group on Indigenous Peoples in 1982. The background research to the many clauses on the UN Declaration on the Rights of Indigenous Peoples is included in her book, *Our Elders Understand Our Rights: Evolving International Law Regarding Indigenous Peoples* (1998). She has also written numerous articles and edited materials related to the rights of Indigenous Peoples, including works on laws of the Cree Peoples related to treaty-making published in *Aboriginal and Treaty Rights in Canada* (edited by Michael Asch, 1997) and *Natives and Settlers – Now and Then* (edited by Paul DePasquale, 2007).

Tamara Vukov is assistant professor in the Department of Communication, Université de Montréal, Canada, and was previously visiting researcher and postdoctoral scholar at the Center for Mobilities Research and Policy, at the Department of Culture and Communication, Drexel University, USA. She has published in such venues as the *International Journal of Cultural Studies*, *Social Semiotics*, the *Canadian Journal of Communication* and *Topia*. Engaged in social justice activism and alternative media for over fifteen years, she is in postproduction on *Tranzicija/Transition*, a feature-length documentary film following the experience of workers and refugees under the postsocialist economic transition in Serbia.

Index

Note: *t* following a page number denotes a table and *n* an endnote with appropriate number. Names of regional and national NGOs are found under the relevant country.

intellectual property rights, traditional
knowledge 27, 28–30
International Police Association 96

Jackson, M. 29
Jad, I. 10
Jara, Mazibuko 110
Jay, D.O. 10

Kamat, S. 4–5, 7, 9, 10
Kapoor, D. 11
Kurdistan, women's NGOs 10
Kyrgyzstan 185–206
ethnic composition 188
ethnic violence 185, 188–9, 190
geopolitical concerns 190
National Network against Gender-
based Violence (NNGV) 200
peace-building and conflict
mediation 198–201
UN humanitarian relief 189–90
women's NGOs 189
see also Women's Anti-violence
Network (Kyrgyzstan)

land rights 45–8
Langelle, Orin 35
League of Nations, and Indigenous
People 77–8
Long, D.A. 31
Luna, Alfredo 38

McNally, D. 6, 13
Makhoba, Bobo 113
Maoris, traditional knowledge 28–30,
39–40
Marais, H. 115n1
Mead, A.T.P. 27
Mexico
forestry 36–7
state and Indigenous Peoples
35–6
microcredit programs 153
militant particularisms x
military humanitarianism 165–7
Milosevic, Slobodan 172, 173, 174
mining industries
Conservation International 38–9

see also Orissa; Orissa NGO
activity
Mojab, S. 10
Mosse, D. 186
Mueller-Hirth, N. 104

nation-building 166–7
National Endowment for Democracy
169, 174
nationalism 163, 170–71
natural resources 45
neoliberalism
and grassroots power 113–15
and nationalism 163, 170–71
and NGO sector ix, xii, 4–5,
12–14
as post-Cold War neocolonialism
137–8
post-Yugoslav Balkans 165, 177–9
South Africa 104, 109, 115n1
see also capitalism
New Zealand, Maoris 28–30, 39–40
NGOization, definition 1, 3
NGOs
business-interest 214
compartmentalization 26
definition 82, 123
donor influence 172–6, 181
Government Controlled
(GONGOs) 82
hegemonic practices 19
professionalization 14–18
and social movements 5–9, 11
and the state xi, 6–7, 15, 52–3,
118
typologies 2–9
UN accreditation process 80,
94–7
UN consultation process 81,
90–92
Ngwane, T. 105, 112
Nieftagodien, Noor 110

Olcott, M. B. 190
Onorati, Antonio 39
Orissa
development-displaced persons 46
Indrāvati reservoir project 51